SON OF TREVOR LYNCH'S WHITE NATIONALIST GUIDE TO THE MOVIES

by

TREVOR LYNCH

EDITED BY GREG JOHNSON

Counter-Currents Publishing Ltd.
San Francisco
2015

Copyright © 2015 by Counter-Currents Publishing
All rights reserved

Cover design by
Kevin I. Slaughter

Published in the United States by
COUNTER-CURRENTS PUBLISHING LTD.
P.O. Box 22638
San Francisco, CA 94122
USA
http://www.counter-currents.com/

Hardcover ISBN: 978-1-935965-85-5
Paperback ISBN: 978-1-935965-86-2
E-book ISBN: 978-1-935965-87-9

Library of Congress Cataloging-in-Publication Data

Lynch, Trevor, 1971-
  Son of Trevor Lynch's white nationalist guide to the movies / by Trevor Lynch ; edited by Greg Johnson.
     pages cm
  Includes index.
  ISBN 978-1-935965-85-5 (hardcover : alk. paper) -- ISBN 978-1-935965-86-2 (pbk. : alk. paper) -- ISBN 978-1-935965-87-9 (electronic)
  1. Motion pictures--Reviews. I. Johnson, Greg, 1971- editor. II. Title. III. Title: White nationalist guide to the movies.

  PN1995.L958 2015
  791.43'75--dc23

                    2014047998

Contents

Preface ❖ iii

1. *Agora* ❖ 1
2. *Alexander* ❖ 6
3. *Arlington Road* ❖ 16
4. *Atlas Shrugged: Part I* ❖ 19
5. *Blade Runner* ❖ 25
6. *Burn Notice* ❖ 32
7. *Coco Chanel & Igor Stravinsky* ❖ 35
8. *The Dance of Reality* ❖ 39
9. *Die Another Day* ❖ 44
10. *8 Mile* ❖ 48
11. *Firefly* ❖ 53
12. *Hero* ❖ 57
13. *The Hobbit: An Unexpected Journey* ❖ 61
14. *The Hobbit: The Desolation of Smaug* ❖ 64
15. *The Hobbit: The Battle of Five Armies* ❖ 66
16. Hooray for Bollywood: *Devdas* & *Kabhi Kushi Kabhie Gham* ❖ 68
17. *House of Flying Daggers* ❖ 74
18. *The Interpreter* ❖ 77
19. *Law & Order: Special Victims Unit* ❖ 80
20. *Legally Blonde 2: Red, White & Blonde* ❖ 83
21. *Lovecraft: Fear of the Unknown* ❖ 86
22. *Machete* ❖ 88
23. *Man of Steel* ❖ 93

24. *Men in Black II* ❖ 97
25. *Minority Report* ❖ 102
26. *Moneyball* ❖ 107
27. *The Monuments Men* ❖ 112
28. *Mulholland Drive* ❖ 119
29. *Nebraska* ❖ 124
30. *Person of Interest* ❖ 127
31. *Predators* ❖ 131
32. *Prometheus* ❖ 136
33. *Red Dragon* ❖ 142
34. *The Road* ❖ 146
35. *Secretary* ❖ 148
36. *Serenity* ❖ 151
37. *A Serious Man* ❖ 155
38. *Signs* ❖ 162
39. *Spy Kids 2: The Island of Lost Dreams* ❖ 167
40. *Star Wars: Episode II – Attack of the Clones* ❖ 170
41. *Sucker Punch* ❖ 175
42. *The Tourist* ❖ 178
43. *Vanilla Sky* ❖ 180
44. *Youth Without Youth* ❖ 182

Appendix
45. Ten Favorite Films ❖ 189

Index ❖ 195

About the Author ❖ 208

PREFACE

Naming the present volume *Son of Trevor Lynch's White Nationalist Guide to the Movies* does not imply that the contents were written entirely after its namesake, *Trevor Lynch's White Nationalist Guide to the Movies* (San Francisco: Counter-Currents, 2012). Indeed, this collection spans 14 years, from my very first movie review, on David Lynch's *Mulholland Drive,* to my last so far, on *The Hobbit: The Battle of Five Armies.*

Whereas the first Trevor Lynch volume contained thematically grouped essays and reviews, the present volume is organized alphabetically and contains the rest of my writings on film to date. There will be more reviews and more collections. In fact, I already plan to call the next book *Return of the Son of Trevor Lynch's White Nationalist Guide to the Movies.* (Frank Zappa fans will understand.)

As I explained in the first collection, I began writing movie reviews for *Vanguard News Network* in the fall of 2001. At first, I wrote under the pen name "The Cat Lady." I chose a female persona because I was annoyed at the calls for White Nationalists to soften our message to attract more women. So I created a female author who was even more extreme than VNN editor Alex Linder. I called her "The Cat Lady" as a tribute to Savitri Devi.

Later it occurred to me that people might hesitate to recommend writings by an author with such a dumb pen name, so I changed the name to T. C. Lynch (the racist formerly known as "The Cat Lady"). I stopped writing for VNN in 2004. In 2005, a lone review appeared at *National Vanguard.* Then, in November of 2007, I began writing reviews again, first for *The Occidental Observer,* then for *TOQ Online,* then for Counter-Currents/*North American New Right.* At that point, I reassigned T. C. Lynch's "gender," dubbing him Trevor Caden Lynch, then just Trevor Lynch. Through all the changes, I tried to preserve the same initial letters as The Cat Lady. I chose the name Trevor for a friend and fellow film buff. And David Lynch is my favorite director.

Because these reviews were written over a long period of time for a number of very different publications, their tone and their persona vary widely. In particular, the VNN reviews tend to have a snarky and ranting tone, inspired by Alex Linder and Jim Goad. I would not write them the same way today, but I have no trouble republishing them either.

I wish to thank Alex Linder, editor of *Vanguard News Network*, Kevin Alfred Strom, editor of *National Vanguard*, and Kevin MacDonald, editor of *The Occidental Observer*, for first publishing some of these pieces. The rest appeared under my own editorship, first at *TOQ Online*, then at Counter-Currents/*North American New Right*.

I also wish to thank Michael Polignano, Collin Cleary, John Morgan, James J. O'Meara, Gregory Hood, the original Trevor, Matt Parrott, Matthew Peters, Kevin Slaughter, and many others who cannot be named for all their contributions, tangible and intangible, to this book.

This book is dedicated to the memory of Tim B., a dear friend with whom I first watched *The Interpreter*, *Moneyball*, *The Monuments Men*, and *Person of Interest*, all of them reviewed herein. Tim had excellent taste in films, but I saw very few with him because we reserved our time out together for concerts and operas. Politics divided us. What brought us together was our shared love of classical music, literature, European high culture, and a good laugh.

Tim died suddenly in October, 2014, after a brief illness. Our friendship during the last 11 years of his life will always remain one of the treasures of mine. I most admired his ability to meet overwhelming adversity with good humor. I knew in my heart that his death would be the end of my charmed life, the first great test I would have to pass—and that it would be his example that would see me through.

Greg Johnson
December 19, 2014

AGORA

Agora (2009) should simply be called *Hypatia*, for it tells the story of Hypatia of Alexandria, the philosopher and mathematician who was murdered by a Christian mob in 415 CE. Hypatia's life coincides with the destruction of ancient paganism by Christianity, thus her murder symbolizes the death of a whole civilization.

After the death of Julian "the Apostate" in 363 CE, Rome was ruled by Christians to the very end. Jovian, Julian's ephemeral successor, set the tone, ordering the library of Antioch burned to the ground and instituting the death penalty for worshiping pagan gods. From that point forward, pagan civilization was slowly ground to dust between totalitarian edicts from the imperial throne and Taliban-style mob violence in the streets.

In 391 CE, when *Agora* opens, Theodosius "the Great," who reigned from 379 to 395, is Emperor in Constantinople and Alexandria is divided between Christians, pagans, and Jews, who are locked in constant violence. A Christian mob, which had taken over a temple of Dionysus, paraded the sacred cult objects in the street and mocked them. Pagans, enraged at the profanation of the mysteries, attacked them, and rioting spread through the city. The pagans found that they were outnumbered and took refuge in the Serapeum.

The Serapeum was the temple of Serapis, a late Egyptian combination of Osiris and the Apis bull who, portrayed in Greek fashion, was the patron god of Alexandria. The Serapeum had been built by the Macedonian Pharaoh Ptolemy III and continuously adorned by Macedonian Pharaohs and Roman Emperors for 600 years. The Serapeum also housed a satellite collection of the Library of Alexandria, all that remained of the great library which may have ceased to exist more than a century before. The Serapeum, therefore, could reasonably likened to the Vatican of antiquity. Ammianus Marcellinus, the 4th-century CE historian, who could only have seen it in decay, described it as follows:

The Serapeum, splendid to a point that words would only diminish its beauty, has such spacious rooms flanked by columns, filled with such life-like statues and a multitude of other works of such art, that nothing, except the Capitolium, which attests to Rome's venerable eternity, can be considered as ambitious in the whole world. (*Res Gestae*, XXII, 16)

Theodosius ended the siege of the Serapeum by granting pardons to the besieged pagans. Once they departed, a Christian mob looted and demolished the structure. Theodosius closed all pagan temples, and the Serapeum was not the only one destroyed. In 393, Theodosius also banned the Olympic games.

In 415 CE, Cyril, the Bishop of Alexandria, clashed with Orestes, the Imperial Prefect, and Alexandria's large Jewish community. Christians protested Jewish exhibitions of dancing. To keep the peace, Orestes banned the exhibitions, but he also publicly tortured a Christian, Hierax, who used the ban as a pretext to incite the crowd against the Jews. Cyril fulminated anew against the Jews, who retaliated by luring Christians into a church and stoning them to death. Christian mobs retaliated by killing and plundering Jews, then expelling them from the city. This hardened the opposition between Cyril and Orestes. When Orestes rebuffed Cyril, he was stoned by a monk, Ammonius, whom Orestes then ordered arrested and tortured to death. Cyril then declared Ammonius a saint.

As you might have guessed, this did not end well.

Unable to avenge themselves on Orestes directly, the Christians decided to strike at Hypatia, a highly regarded and well-connected member of the Alexandrian elite and one of its last pagans. Orestes was known to seek her guidance, thus she was a convenient scapegoat for his obstinacy, and since she was both a woman and a pagan, it was easy incite the crowd against her. She was accused of witchcraft. One day, she was seized by a mob of Christians, taken to a church, stripped naked, and flayed alive with broken tiles. Then her body was dismembered (like Osiris) and burned. Orestes resigned in disgust or was recalled to Constantinople, leaving Cyril—and Christianity—in control of Alexandria.

Agora is the fifth feature film directed by Chilean-Spanish *auteur* Alejandro Amenábar (who also composed the score and co-authored the script). (Amenábar's best-known film is *The Others* [2001] starring Nicole Kidman; another film, *Abre los Ojos* [*Open Your Eyes*, 1997], was remade as *Vanilla Sky* [2001].)

Although *Agora* is generally true to the spirit of the events it depicts, Amenábar took some liberties with facts to bring Hypatia's story to the screen. (For a brief and readable *summa* of Hypatia's life and legend by an imaginative but sober scholar, see Maria Dzielska's *Hypatia of Alexandria*, trans. F. Lyra [Cambridge: Harvard University Press, 1995].)

First, Hypatia is portrayed as a young woman throughout, even though the story spans a period of 25 years, and Hypatia was a woman in her 60s when she died. (Jewish actress Rachel Weisz is quite good in the role of Hypatia. She is entirely convincing as an intellectual, with adorable touches of girlishness.)

Second, Orestes is portrayed as her student and would-be lover, although he was probably many years her junior, and there is no evidence that he studied with her or knew her before he arrived in Alexandria as Prefect. (Hypatia's rebuff—her soiled menstrual rag—really did happen, but to another suitor.) Oscar Isaac is quite good in the role of Orestes.

Third, Synesius, the Bishop of Cyrene (now in Libya) actually was Hypatia's student, but again he would have been considerably younger than her, and he died in 413 CE, two years before Hypatia. (In the movie he is well-played by Rupert Evans.)

Fourth, Hypatia's father Theon (played by Michael Lonsdale, a.k.a. Sir Hugo Drax) is accurately portrayed as a mathematician and astronomer who was a leading figure in the Library of Alexandria, but there is no evidence that he died during the riots of 391.

Fifth, Hypatia's work on the heliocentric hypothesis, including the elliptical orbits of the planets, is of course fictional, but it does illustrate her primary focus on mathematics and astronomy and the terrible loss to science and culture caused not just by her death, but by the death of classical antiquity.

Sixth, the character of the slave Davus (played by Max Minghella) is entirely fictional, but he is an almost Nietzschean portrait of the typical demographic profile and resentful motives of Christian converts. But Hypatia's casually patronizing attitude toward him also shows why slaves had good reason to resent their masters.

Seventh, Amenábar's vision of the Serapeum is impressive. One can quibble about details—it is shown as a blend of Ptolemaic Egyptian and Greek architecture, which may be correct—but the *feel* is right. And the movie's depiction of the siege and despoilation of the temple and its library is very moving. But although there is no way these events can make Christians look good, the movie actually skews the picture in favor of the Christians by portraying their provocation of the pagans as trivial (pelting statues with fruit) and depicting the Serapeum as being vandalized but not destroyed. (It is turned into a church and a stable.)

Eighth, when an Alexandrian dignitary accuses Hypatia of believing in "nothing at all," her retort is that she believes in "philosophy," which seems to be an expression of the 18th-century Enlightenment view, popularized by John Toland, Gibbon, and Voltaire, of Hypatia as an advocate of reason and science against religious superstition. But that dichotomy meant nothing in ancient Alexandria. Hypatia's father Theon was not just an astronomer and mathematician, he also was a student of the Hermetic and Orphic mysteries, and there is no reason to suppose that Hypatia was any less mystically inclined. Hypatia was apparently not devoted to the public cults of Alexandria. But she was not irreligious; she was simply not Christian.

Ninth, Hypatia's death was so horrible that it cannot be portrayed in a movie. It was far more horrible than the crucifixion of Jesus, and that already pushes the limits of representability in Mel Gibson's *The Passion of the Christ*. The proper solution, of course, would be simply not to show it. But instead Amenábar elects to show something that never happened, and he transforms Hypatia's death from an act of Christian savagery to an act of Christian mercy. Again, it is impossible for Christians to come off well in this tale, but Amenábar is repeatedly willing to falsify facts to put Christians in a less bad light.

Tenth and finally, like most movies today, *Agora* casts blacks against type. There are black students in the Serapeum and black dignitaries in the Alexandrian Senate. This is highly unlikely. However, Amenábar's casting of the monk Ammonius (Ashraf Barhom) and the Bishop Cyril (Sami Samir) verges on the Politically Incorrect, because their two swarthy, Semitic countenances will make any European think of ISIS, the Taliban, and the Salafists hawking falafel on the corner, in other words: those who long to do to the Vatican and Notre Dame today what the Christians did to the Serapeum and Library of Alexandria so long ago.

One of the most striking scenes in *Agora* is during the siege of the Serapeum. One of the pagans, who up to that moment had thought that this was *his civilization*, looks down at the vast mob of angry Christians and asks, "Since when were there so many Christians?" By then, however, it was too late. Our job, as White Nationalists, is to wake up our people while there is still time.

I highly recommend *Agora* to all my readers, particularly to lovers of antiquity, to neo-pagans who want a glimpse of paganism without barbarism, and to defenders of European civilization from the next wave of Biblical monotheism.

Counter-Currents/*North American New Right*
July 17, 2014

ALEXANDER

Oliver Stone's *Alexander* is, well, great. It isn't perfect, but neither was Alexander. It is definitely worth seeing. But there is a subtle and sinister thread of anti-white propaganda running through the movie, and I would not recommend it to anyone without a warning first.

There are many reasons why I enjoyed *Alexander*. Chief among them is Alexander himself. Alexander the Great was surely one of the most gifted men in history. His father, Philip II, was the king of Macedon and the conqueror of Greece. Alexander was handsome and athletic. He was highly intelligent and received a remarkable education. (Aristotle was one of his tutors.) As a genius of military and political strategy, he was almost without rival. He was also an eloquent speaker and a charismatic leader of men. He was courageous, sharing the hardships of his soldiers and leading them into battle. He was capable of great acts of magnanimity to his enemies and generosity to his friends. He became the richest man the world had ever seen—and gave most of it away. He was a patron of art, science, and exploration, a city founder and an empire builder, a political visionary. He changed the course of history, for good and ill, in countless ways. His principal effect was to shift the dynamic center of our civilization from the Near East to Europe proper, namely to Greece. Alexander westernized "Western" civilization.

But Alexander was also a tyrant, a sacker and destroyer of cities and empires; he killed, mutilated, and enslaved countless people; he was capable of astonishing acts of cruelty and folly; he was corrupted by his power, and by his lust for more power, which grew as his power grew. He began his career as a Greek-style constitutional monarch who made decisions with the counsel of his peers, and he ended his life an oriental despot surrounded by flatterers and sneaks, a despot who brooked no disagreement and executed men on suspicions and whims. He began life as a devotee of the Greek philosophy of moderation—the Greeks always mixed water with their wine, even during drinking parties. He ended his life as a debilitated alcoholic who fell mortally ill after downing a *krater* of unmixed wine at the end of a long drinking party. He was also grossly irresponsible. Even when it was apparent he was dying, he refused to name a successor. This led to 40 years of civil war that destroyed his empire. His mother, his wife Roxane, and his only son were among the slain. He was only 32 when he died. Few men mourned his passing. Many celebrated it. Most were simply relieved.

He wasn't Alexander the Good. But he was Great, because in both good and evil he was larger than life. As the passage of time put a safe distance between Alexander and the rest of us, the moralistic denunciation of his crimes began to look small-minded. Alexander seemed less a failed human being and more a demigod or a force of nature, both terrifying and thrilling. His life was a Greek tragedy every bit as compelling as the stories of Hercules and Jason and Oedipus. With this kind of material, it would be hard to make a bad movie about Alexander.

The script was also well-written, well-researched, and surprisingly scrupulous in its concern for historical accuracy. Yes, countless small liberties were taken in bringing Alexander's life to the screen, but the movie is faithful to the spirit of what happened, and that is what counts. For instance, a line spoken by the Indian king Porus is given to a daughter of Darius III, but it provides an occasion to illustrate Alexander's magnanimity just the same. (Other historical liberties were taken for propaganda purposes, which I will detail below.)

There were a few historical inaccuracies: the Lighthouse of Alexandria was shown in the background as Ptolemy I dictated his memoirs, even though it was not built until the reign of his successor, Ptolemy II. When Alexander enters Babylon, we see the great ziggurat of the temple of Marduk, although it had been demolished in 482 BCE to punish the Babylonians for a rebellion. When Alexander enters India, we see stone Buddhist stupas, even though the Indians did not build and sculpt in stone until after they came in contact with Hellenistic civilization as a result of Alexander's invasion. In the bedroom of Alexander's mother, there is a statue of a goat standing on its hind legs. This is a reproduction of an artifact found in the last century by Sir Leonard Woolley in a royal tomb at Ur, dated circa 2600–2400 BCE. It is completely out of place in fourth-century BCE Macedonia.

I do have a quarrel with the narration. It seemed to meander and contain irrelevancies, and it could have done more to frame and link the scenes of the movie and make them more intelligible.

The acting is excellent, particularly Colin Farrell as Alexander and Angelina Jolie as his mother Olympias. Farrell is a handsome and virile Irishman who has been groomed for stardom in a number of movies in recent years, but he has never really achieved leading-man status until now. I had never taken Angelina Jolie seriously as an actress before, but she was really quite believable as Alexander's ruthless and cunning and slightly mad mother. (Perhaps the poor woman can now afford to undo the botched plastic surgery that disfigured her lovely face with grotesquely large Negroid lips.)

Val Kilmer played Alexander's father, Philip II. The androgynous Jared Leto was cast as Alexander's lover Hephaestion. Anthony Hopkins played an aged Ptolemy, one of Alexander's generals, who, after Alexander's death, became ruler of Egypt. He is the narrator of the film.

Racially, the cast is remarkably Nordic. This, of course, is historically accurate, although mere historical accuracy has never counted for much in the eyes of Hollywood. The Greek ruling class of the classical age was Nordic, even though the aboriginal population of Greece whom they ruled was a darker, Mediterranean race, among them the descendants of the remarkably cultured and beautiful Minoans. The Macedonians to the north were, if anything, even more Nordic than the Greeks because they had fewer opportunities to mix with Mediterranean stocks. Alexander was a blonde, and was portrayed as such. (Mainstream reviewers have been harping on Farrell's "bad dye-job," but there was nothing bad about it, unless they were simply objecting to the fact that it was blonde.) There were also many luminous blue eyes among the cast. Interestingly, blue eyes were highlighted in the hand-tinted black and white photos used in print ads. Clearly it was a priority for Nordics to be able to identify with Alexander and his countrymen.

There is, however, one major problem with the casting. Alexander's first wife Roxane was the daughter of a nobleman named Oxyartes in what is now Afghanistan. She was said to have been one of the most beautiful women in the Persian Empire, second only to the wife of Darius III, the Emperor whom Alexander defeated. She was undoubtedly an Aryan like Alexander himself. But Oliver Stone had her portrayed by Rosario Dawson, an obvious mulatto. Later in the movie, when Alexander expounds his vision of the empire he is creating, he explicitly says that it is a place where "the races will mix," meaning miscegenation, not trade and tourism.

Alexander did marry Roxane and two Persian princesses. This was an unpopular decision because the Macedonians understandably wished him to take a Macedonian bride. Alexander also ordered his Macedonian officers to marry the daughters of Persian noblemen, a move that was intensely resented. (Most of these marriages were repudiated after Alexander's death.) Alexander also offered dowries to the Persian concubines of his soldiers and Greek educations to their illegitimate children to encourage the men to marry them. This was a humane and popular gesture.

Alexander realized that he could not rule the Persian Empire without the recognition and cooperation of the Persian aristocracy that had conquered it and ruled it for two hundred years. Thus he hoped to cement his conquests through marriage.

But this was not a policy of racial miscegenation, for the simple reason that the Persians were Aryans too. The name "Iran," like "Ireland," is derived from "Aryan." Today's Persians, like today's Greeks and Macedonians, are heavily mixed with Semitic stocks, but one still finds people with genuinely Aryan, even Nordic, features among them.[1]

Oliver Stone's directing is stunning throughout. This is a hard thing for me to admit. I had hated Stone since walking out of *Platoon* in 1986. I had never seen a Stone movie before *Platoon*, and I boycotted every one after it. I disliked him because he was a manipulative '60s Leftist spouting the predictable

---

[1] See Savitri Devi's remarks on "Alexander the Great and the Mixing of Races." http://library.flawlesslogic.com/alexander.htm

nonsense about corporations, Wall Street, the Vietnam War, the Military-Industrial Complex, JFK, MLK, Negroes, etc., not because he was a Jew pushing an anti-white agenda.

Since then, my views have mellowed about the '60s counterculture, and I can go a long way with Leftist analyses of economics and US foreign policy until I part ways with them on the issues of race and the Jews. I have also become more objective in my reactions to filmmakers, meaning that I can enjoy a well-made film even though it has disagreeable elements.

Thus, around two years ago, I let a friend persuade me to watch the DVD of Stone's *The Doors*. I thought it was excellent and went on to watch other Stone films. I was quite impressed with *JFK* and *Any Given Sunday*. I had to admit that Stone is a highly talented director, even though all of his films contain anti-white propaganda to one degree or another. *Alexander* is one of Stone's best films. (*The Doors* remains my favorite.)

Some favorite scenes: Philip showing Alexander crude depictions of the sufferings of Hercules, Jason, Oedipus, and Prometheus—tragic representations of the downfall of heroes and the jealousy of the gods; the battle of Gaugamela in 331 BCE where Alexander crushed a vastly larger Persian force and drove Darius III from the field, leaving Alexander the master of Mesopotamia; Alexander's dazzling triumphal entry into Babylon; Alexander's battle with the Indian king Porus near the river Jhelum in 326 BCE (the best scene of the film, intense and emotionally shattering; the war elephants were terrifying); Alexander's last fateful drinking party: when he looks into the *krater*, he sees his mother's face with snakes in her hair, like Medusa—a brilliant allusion to the tradition that Alexander was poisoned, perhaps by strychnine, delivered in unmixed wine; when Alexander downs the wine, his face disappears behind the *krater* and it looks as if the head of the lion's skin he wore is drinking in his place—brilliantly depicting how Alexander was consumed by his own superhuman appetites.

Oliver Stone's handling of war in *Alexander* is worth pondering. Stone made three films about the Vietnam War and its aftermath—*Platoon, Born on the Fourth of July,* and *Heaven and Earth*—and Vietnam also hangs in the background of *JFK* and

Nixon. Stone was very much opposed to the Vietnam War. He masterfully depicted its brutality, horror, and injustice, and he juxtaposed the ideological rationale for the war with the realities that belied it. It would be natural to conclude that Stone is against war as such. But in *Alexander*, Stone seems to have found a war he likes. He certainly does not dwell on the horrors of Alexander's wars as he did on Vietnam.

Nor does Stone probe behind Alexander's rationale for war. Alexander makes speeches about defending Greek "freedom." The Persians had conquered the Greek city-states in what is now Turkey, and they tried but failed to add Greece proper to their empire. But Alexander was not one to talk. His own father Philip had conquered Greece, accomplishing what Alexander had blamed the Persians for attempting, and Alexander himself savagely quashed the Greek rebellions that followed his father's assassination.

As for the Greek city-states conquered by the Persians, they had grown far richer and more cultured than the "free" states of Greece proper, for the Persians did not permit the ceaseless, destructive, and dysgenic wars that the Greeks fought amongst themselves.

In any case, Alexander "freed" the Greeks under Persian rule rather quickly (by adding them to his empire), thus his campaigns into Syria, Palestine, Egypt, Mesopotamia, Persia, and beyond were all about winning an empire, not spreading freedom.

Alexander also accused the Persians of assassinating his father. He almost certainly did not believe it, but the lie served a dual purpose: to justify war and to deflect suspicion from the most likely culprit, his own mother.

Stone offers another rationale for war: it is a civilizing mission. The "Asiatics" (meaning the Caucasian peoples of the Middle East, not the Mongoloid peoples of the Far East) are said to be "barbarous" and "cruel," which apparently means that the more civilized Greeks and Macedonians need not respect their sovereignty, so long as they promise to bring the blessings of Hellenic civilization at the point of a sword. Of course the Greeks and Macedonians really thought this way, but given Stone's views of the Vietnam War—for which the same rationales could be given—it is surprising that he includes these sentiments without comment, critique, or the least hint of irony.

Later, when the Persians have been conquered and his troops want to go home, Alexander castigates them for their xenophobia and seeks to merge them with the conquered Persians. Instead of making the Persians more Hellenic, Alexander's armies must now become more Persian. But the result is the same: whether packaged as spreading civilization or appreciating "diversity," the distinct identities of peoples are erased.

The wars in *Alexander* invite, of course, comparisons with the United States' recent wars in Iraq and Afghanistan. Stone chose to represent only the part of Alexander's campaigns that took place in what are now the present-day countries of Iraq, Iran, Afghanistan, and Pakistan—even though Alexander also fought battles in present-day Turkey, Syria, Lebanon, Israel, and Egypt. Stone even dresses Persian soldiers in Arab headscarves, although in reality their costumes were quite different, and the actor playing Darius III was cast and costumed to remind us of Osama Bin Laden.

This explains why Stone took pains that the Aryan majority in the United States should be able to identify with Alexander and his Macedonians. The purpose of the movie is to manipulate Aryans to be more willing to kill Iraqis, Iranians, and Afghans. What is Stone's motive? He is a Jew, and the Jewish agenda is to dupe Americans into squandering their blood and treasure to increase the wealth, power, and security of Israel. This is how Oliver Stone has finally found a war that he likes.

Stone promotes miscegenation because, although it may be in the short-term interest of Jews to manipulate white racial consciousness to dupe us into killing their enemies in the Middle East, it is in the long-term interests of Jews that Aryans cease to exist, that we be dumbed down by breeding with inferior races. And what better way to encourage this than to portray a handsome white alpha male marrying a mulatto?

Stone's message to a young white man is: go to the far ends of the Earth to kill the enemies of the Jews, then marry a nonwhite and return home to sire a litter of mongrels and provide a base for a chain immigration scheme. (The Arab world is crawling with mulattoes, by the way, because Arabs have been importing African slaves for more than a thousand years.)

The US military is already responsible for encouraging a huge amount of miscegenation, and what is worse, the miscegenators tend in other ways to be conservative-minded, honorable, and masculine men. But the most important thing to conserve is our race, and through miscegenation their loyalties and their genes are lost to us forever. This is a trend that Jews would like to encourage.

Alexander has, however, bombed at the box office. It received a lot of bad reviews, most of which I think are unjust. But it is "word of mouth," not the reviews, that is causing the film to fail. And by far the biggest complaint is about Stone's frank portrayal of Alexander's bisexuality. This does not sit well with a lot of viewers. I saw *Alexander* in San Francisco, which culturally speaking is surely the "gayest" city in the world, and I was surprised at the audible and visible discomfort in the audience. Even there.

I also found the audience's discomfort surprising because Stone's portrayal of Alexander's relationships with men is really rather tame. He puts his arm around the shoulders of Hephaestion and says that he loves him, and he plants a kiss on Bagoas, a Persian eunuch from the harem of Darius. (Alexander also kept Darius's harem of 365 beautiful women, one for each day—or night—of the year. Maybe Bagoas was for leap years.) Personally, I was more disturbed by the explicit heterosexual intercourse simulated by Farrell and the mulatto Dawson. At least homosexual intercourse does not produce mongrels.

Depicting Alexander's bisexuality was clearly a blunder. Why did Stone do it? Historical accuracy is no explanation, because, as we have seen, Stone was willing to cast a mulatto as Roxane to promote miscegenation.

Stone's aim was clearly to promote the contemporary homosexual lifestyle and agenda. Homosexual organizations and advocates also hoped their cause would benefit from *Alexander*. What better way to promote homosexuality than to portray one of the manliest men in history making eyes at handsome guys?

But Alexander was not a homosexual in the contemporary

sense. He had homosexual desires, yes. He had homosexual relationships, yes. But he did not adopt an exclusively homosexual "lifestyle." Instead, Alexander practiced the sort of bisexuality that was common among the warrior aristocracies of most ancient Aryan peoples. Alexander married three women, sired an heir, enjoyed the pleasures of the harem—and also carried on affairs with men on the side. The ancients frowned upon men who adopted exclusively homosexual lifestyles, and there is every reason to think Alexander shared that attitude.

Alexander's same-sex relationships were unusual in only one respect. The standard practice was for a young man of 17 or 18 to take up with an older man, who was supposed to be a teacher and authority figure. Hephaestion, however, was Alexander's age. But as the heir-apparent to the Macedonian throne and then as a young king, Alexander could not have submitted to the authority of an older man.

By all accounts, Stone is no homosexual. So why does he promote homosexuality? Methinks because he is a Jew. Judaism, of course, is the most anti-homosexual religion in existence, and these attitudes survive among secular Jews. And, in spite of the fact that the Christian clergy has always been filled with homosexuals, Christian teachings have followed the Jewish lead. Deep in his heart, Oliver Stone probably finds homosexuality revolting.

But Jews do not promote homosexuality in white societies because they think it is good. They promote it because they think it is bad. Jews promote homosexuality for the same reason they promote miscegenation, abortion, feminism, and materialism: to break down white families and communities, to reduce the white population, to drive us further and further towards extinction.

If Stone had contented himself with making two propaganda points—promoting miscegenation and war against Israel's enemies in the Middle East—*Alexander* might have been a hit and Stone might have succeeded. But Stone just had to push the homosexual agenda as well and was thus undone by another typically Jewish trait: always grasping for more, he ends up with nothing in the end. It is ironic that Stone was stopped by the grip of his own tribe's sexual taboos on the Aryan mind.

I suppose that we whites should be thankful any time Jewish efforts to poison our minds and culture self-destruct. But personally I am tired of counting on the Jews to defeat themselves.

VNN, December 2004

ARLINGTON ROAD

Arlington Road is a terrific film. From the gripping opening scenes, it is a psychological and political thriller that is suspenseful, stylishly directed, and superbly acted. But the amazing plot twist at the end raises it to something much higher.

I am sad that I did not hear about this movie when it was released. But it turns out that *Arlington Road* was shelved by the studios for a year before release, and it was not effectively promoted. I can see why: From the point of view of Hollywood's overall propaganda line, it goes "off-message" in a major way.

Director Mark Pellington is apparently a white man who is primarily known for his music videos.

Jeff Bridges plays Michael Faraday, a widowed professor of American History at George Washington University in Washington, D.C. He lives in a McMansion subdivision in Northern Virginia, where he is raising his nine-year-old son Grant.

Faraday's research focuses on domestic terrorism, with a special focus on patriotic militia groups. His interest can justly be deemed an obsession, and he has a very personal motive. His wife, an FBI agent, was killed three years before in a botched FBI raid/standoff that is an amalgam of the Ruby Ridge and Waco incidents.

It is remarkable that this incident is presented as a mistake by the government. The target of the raid was a law-abiding firearms collector who had just applied for a dealer's license (shades of Waco), but the FBI charged in, killing the target's wife and young son (shades of Ruby Ridge). This is the first way in which the film goes "off-message." (You'll have to see the movie to learn about the other ways.)

Faraday is portrayed as a neglectful father and a bad neighbor. He does not even know the Lang family across the street until he finds their son Brady covered with blood after an accident. Faraday rushes Brady to the hospital (he recovers) and as a result becomes friends with Oliver and Cheryl Lang (Tim Robbins and Joan Cusack).

The friendship seems off to a good start. Grant and Brady

become playmates when Brady is released from the hospital.

But Faraday begins to suspect that Oliver Lang is not who he claims to be. He begins to investigate Lang and discovers that he is really named William Fenimore and that he was imprisoned when he was 16 for sending a pipe bomb to the Bureau of Land Management. (The bomb never went off.) His motive was resentment against the federal agency that destroyed his family's livelihood and drove his father to suicide.

Fenimore/Lang finds out that Faraday is on to him, and there is an emotional confrontation in which he explains himself, seemingly resolving the issue between them. Faraday even turns to the Langs for solace when his girlfriend Brooke is killed in a car accident.

The misgivings, however, begin to mount again. Faraday begins to suspect that Fenimore is behind an Oklahoma City-style bombing of a federal building in St. Louis, a bombing that had been blamed on a single suicide bomber.

Lang, however, is one step ahead. He kidnaps Grant, holds him hostage, and tells Faraday that all he has to do to get his son back is be a good neighbor for a couple of days. Lang is clearly planning another bombing. Faraday, of course, tries to stop the bombing and rescue his son. But actions often have unintended consequences . . .

I highly recommend this film. It is suspenseful and well-made, but beyond that it provides much food for thought.

To my mind, the biggest question is the identity and motives of the bombers. They are portrayed as ordinary suburban white people who have beefs with the federal government. They are not portrayed as racists or White Nationalists, but they are all white, and the whites in the movie have a definitely "majority American" look, with names like Fenimore and Faraday. The only black character is an FBI agent, the former partner of Faraday's wife.

Perhaps the best reason to think they are not White Nationalists is that they are part of a large, well-funded, well-organized network that is adept at strategic chess games and psychological profiling. Harold Covington could have come up with a plot like this, but nobody in the White Nationalist world could ever pull it off.

Of course the people who made this movie might not know that. *Arlington Road* might be merely the projections of paranoid Left-wingers who have made us out to be something we are not.

But another interpretation suggests itself: Lang and company work for the government. They are the ultimate "controlled opposition": terrorists spawned by the system in order to justify the creation of an ever-tightening surveillance state.

The Langs have federal law enforcement written all over them. They are a nice, white family that moves around the country frequently, going from one safe, manicured subdivision to another. Dad is a bit vague about what he does for a living. Mom stays at home with the three kids. They seem to have plenty of money for a comfortable upper middle-class lifestyle. And when one job is completed, the "for sale" signs go up, and they await word on where they are being transferred next. Cheryl says, "I hope it is someplace safe." Oliver answers "Always."

Counter-Currents/*North American New Right*,
October 24, 2010

Selfish Bastards:
Atlas Shrugged: Part I

I saw *Atlas Shrugged* on Saturday, April 16th. It was a sold-out showing to an all-white audience in a predominantly white area of the Atlanta suburbs. The audience contained a large contingent of Tea Party people, mostly Christian, as well as libertarians and Objectivists.

There was geeky anti-government banter as we waited for the movie to begin. There was applause after the movie ended, but I did not join in. In fact, I found this to be a deeply disappointing adaptation of the first third of Ayn Rand's epic novel about the role of reason in human existence and what would happen if the rational and productive people—the Atlases who carry the world on their shoulders—were to shrug off their burden and go on strike.

Atlas Shrugged could be a spectacular movie. It is certainly a spectacular novel, although not a perfect one, primarily because it is deformed by the grotesque excess of Galt's Speech, 60-odd pages in which the novel's hero John Galt explains Rand's philosophy of Objectivism. But I have to hand it to Rand, because at least for me, she managed to make even Galt's Speech a page-turner. In truth, although I reject Rand's individualism and capitalism and would not have lasted five minutes in her presence, *Atlas Shrugged* is one of the most audacious and enthralling novels I have ever read—and I have read most of the classics—and even it does not equal Rand's earlier novel *The Fountainhead*. *Atlas Shrugged* is the greatest mystery novel of all, for it is about what makes civilizations rise and fall. It is the greatest adventure of all, for it tells the story of a man who stopped the world.

Although Rand opposed racial nationalism on philosophical grounds (with a sentimental exception for Zionism, of course), there is still much of value in her novels for racial nationalists. Rand started out as a Nietzschean, and her novels offer powerful defenses of aristocracy and critiques of egalitarianism, democracy, mass man, and mass society. All these elements are in tension with her later philosophy of reason, individualism, and capitalism. Indeed, Rand felt the need to reframe, revise, or simply suppress her earlier, more Nietzschean writings. But the "sense of life" of her novels is so in keeping with the spirit of fascism that her first novel *We the Living* was made into a movie under Mussolini, a fact that Rand later obfuscated with tall tales and a revised version of the novel. (The Italian *We the Living*, by the way, remains the only good film adaptation of a Rand novel.)

The Fountainhead can be read profitably alongside Kevin MacDonald's *The Culture of Critique*, for it effectively dramatizes the techniques of Jewish subversion of American society. Rand's villain Ellsworth Toohey sums up his game as playing the stock market of the spirit—and selling short, meaning profiting from the decline of our values, which pretty much sums up the rise of American Jewry to the top of our society on a tide of smut, decadence, degeneracy, lobbying, swindling, pop culture, and casino capitalism.

Rand, of course, never saw it that way, and Rand's own movement, Objectivism, is just as much a Jewish intellectual movement as the Frankfurt School, and although they use very different arguments, they function to produce the same result: a radical individualism that renders cohesive ethnic groups like Jews invisible to the majority, which maximizes their collective security and upward mobility, since cohesive collectives have a systematic advantage in competing with isolated individuals. (Rand called the mostly Jewish inner circle of her movement "the collective." It was supposed to be a joke, but the joke may have been deeper than most people imagine.)

Atlas Shrugged, moreover, lends itself to a racial interpretation. *Atlas Shrugged* is about how a creative and productive minority is exploited by an inferior majority because of the acceptance of a false moral code (altruism) that beatifies the weak and pegs the worth of the strong to how well they serve their inferiors. When one asks "What is the race of Atlas?" it all falls into place. The Atlas who upholds the modern world is the white race, which is being enslaved and destroyed by the acceptance of a false moral code (racial altruism) that teaches that non-whites fail to meet white standards only because of white wickedness, and that whites can only expiate this racial guilt by giving their wealth and power and societies to non-whites.

Altruism is ultimately nihilism, since when the inferior finally cripple and destroy their superiors, they will perish too. But such consequences don't matter to locusts, parasites, and people in the grip of false values. The only thing that will save us all is a moral revolution, a new form of egoism, although I part ways from Rand on the nature of this revolution, since she is an individualist and I am a racial collectivist. Rand thinks that the individual is more important than the group, which is what you would expect of a childless woman who lived largely in her head.

Rand's aesthetic is deeply Fascist—and Socialist Realist—with its emphasis on man's heroic transformation of nature through science, technology, and industry. Rand also had a taste for Nordic types. All of her heroes are tall, lean Nordics. Rand, born Alissa Rosenbaum, was not.

The *Atlas Shrugged* movie is poorly cast. In terms of looks, the best choices are Taylor Schilling as Dagny Taggart, Grant Bowler as Hank Rearden, and Rebecca Wisocky as Lillian Rearden. Jon Polito, the Italian gangster in *Miller's Crossing* ("It's about ethics . . ."), was a good choice for Orren Boyle. Michael Lerner looks great for the role of Wesley Mouch, but his personality is a bit too forceful. Matthew Marsden as James Taggart is too handsome for the part, but he makes it his own.

The worst choices are Edi Gathegi, a black actor, for the Nordic Eddie Willers (the same actor displaced another white actor for the character of Laurent in the *Twilight* movies), and Jsu Garcia (couldn't they afford a whole Jesus?), who looks like a debauched mestizo, for the blue-eyed descendant of Castile Francisco d'Anconia. The actors cast as Hugh Akston and Dr. Robert Stadler are both too young for their parts, and Stadler looks Middle Eastern and speaks with a heavy accent!

As for the acting, it is pretty much undistinguished throughout: strictly soap opera grade. The best-realized roles are James Taggart and Lillian Rearden. Eddie Willers is an embarrassment. A wooden Indian would have been just as expressive and—more importantly from the producers' point of view—even cheaper and just as politically correct. Or is there a message in casting a black man to play a character who is essentially a faithful mediocre sidekick?

As for the script, it is shockingly pedestrian. Rand gives us an abundance of eloquent dialogue, but almost none of it is used. It soon becomes apparent why: whenever a bit of it slips in, the actors sound as wooden as Gary Cooper in King Vidor's 1949 movie of *The Fountainhead*, meaning that they don't have the brains to understand the dialogue or the skill to sell it. Rand's dialogue is not naturalistic, but if an actor can sell Shakespeare, he can sell Ayn Rand. Tolkien's dialogue is certainly not naturalistic, but it was faithfully adapted and beautifully delivered in Peter Jackson's *The Lord of the Rings* trilogy.

But given a cast of blockheads and Brooks Brothers models who read from teleprompters, we could not have Francisco d'Anconia's money speech. We could only have colloquial naturalism with vulgarities like "crap" and "bullshit" thrown in. I suppose we should be grateful that we were not told that Galt's motor was "awesome" and the Equalization of Opportunity Act "sucked." (I wonder if the script contained emoticons. Maybe the performances would have been improved.)

The whole look of this movie is wrong. Visually it is astonishingly flat, dull, and unimaginative. Rand's novel requires a *Brazil* look: Art Deco in a vague "future": hair and wardrobe by Tamara de Lempicka, interiors by Edward Hopper, industrial scenes from Thomas Hart Benton, casting by Arno Breker (although the men would need to be less beefy), sets by Frank Lloyd Wright, all directed by Leni Riefenstahl. Of course that would have cost money, but the real poverty in this film is of imagination and taste. Instead, we get a film set in the near future (2016 and 2017) that feels the need to explain the prominence of rail transport with an energy crisis.

The greatest aesthetic flaw of this film is the contrasting treatment of nature and industry. A film of *Atlas Shrugged* should glorify and aestheticize human achievement, especially heavy industry, and there is plenty of Fascist, National Socialist, Socialist Realist, and New Deal art that they could have drawn upon to do this (but of course that would be "politically incorrect" from an Objectivist point of view). But instead, we have only pedestrian low-angle shots of rail yards full of boxcars—

which might actually have been visually captivating if simply viewed from the air. The scenes of the Rearden factory and the building of the John Galt Line offered many opportunities for visual splendor and dynamism, but they too are pedestrian at best. The best sequence is the first run of the John Galt Line, one of Ayn Rand's most brilliant feats of description. (This was the only scene in which I even noticed the music.) But even here the movie pales by comparison to the printed page. I was left wondering: Did the director even *read* this book?

The inept depiction of industry is underscored by the intrusion of nature photography. Ayn Rand looked at nature as merely the raw material and backdrop of human achievement. But in the movie of *Atlas Shrugged*, the most beautiful scenes are of mountains and prairies. During the first run of the John Galt Line, Dagny Taggart and Hank Rearden's achievements are dwarfed by the beauty of the landscape. The focus should have been on the train, the rails, the rising throb of the engines, the telephone poles rushing by faster and faster, as a vast, streamlined Art Deco engine shot like a bullet toward the gossamer arc of the great bridge of Rearden metal. The spectacular Rocky Mountain landscape and sky should have been hidden by a drop cloth of clouds, fog, and rain.

The treatment of sex in this film is also objectionable. When Lillian Rearden asks her husband "Through, are you?" as he rolls off her, there was a gasp in the theater. (James Kirkpatrick reported the same thing in his brilliant review at *Alternative Right*.[1]) Talking to Tea Partiers afterward, I discovered that the gasp was due to their strongly Christian orientation. Apparently it struck them not as vicious and condescending, but simply as pretty racy stuff. Later, when Hank Rearden began his affair with Dagny Taggart, there was a less audible but still real reaction in the audience, for the same reason. The only real criticism the Christian Tea Partiers had was that the movie portrayed an extramarital affair in a positive light.

The affair is, by the way, significantly altered from the book. In the book Hank Rearden is profoundly conflicted about his

---

[1] http://libertarianalliance.wordpress.com/2011/04/18/review-of-the-atlas-shrugged-film/

attraction to Dagny, which he attributes to mere animal lust which tempts him to violate his wedding vows, which he treats as a matter of honor, even though his marriage is a loveless hell. When he finally gives in to temptation, it is one of Ayn Rand's famous "rape" scenes. In the movie, after the running of the John Galt Line, Rearden in effect says, "Here we are, at the moment of our greatest triumph, and all I want to do is kiss you." Dagny coyly replies, "Why don't you then?" Cut to a tender lovemaking montage. (I could not help but think of Rand's own parody "Sorry baby, I can't take you to the pizza joint tonight, I have to go back to the science lab and split the atom.") Is moral conflict and rough, passionate sex just too politically incorrect these days? Again, what were the filmmakers thinking?

Why was *Atlas Shrugged* made on the cheap? Apparently the producers could not come up with a script or a concept good enough to raise the money and attract the talent to do a first-rate movie, and since their option was expiring, they decided to do a second-rate movie instead (and managed to pull off a fourth-rate one). This level of cynicism is frankly breathtaking. One has to ask: Is this how Howard Roark would have made a movie? (If this film accomplishes one thing, it will make us appreciate the 1949 movie of *The Fountainhead* more.)

From now on this should be referred to as director Paul Johansson's *Atlas Shrugged*, for it is Ayn Rand's *Atlas Shrugged* in name only. (Johansson turns out to be every bit the director that one would expect of a soap opera hunk.) It is merely an exercise in masochism to wonder how a visionary director of epics like Zack Snyder or Peter Jackson or Oliver Stone would have brought *Atlas Shrugged* to the screen, because we will never know. Vidor's *The Fountainhead* was bad enough that more than 60 years later, we are still without a decent film of one of the greatest American novels of the 20th century. Which means that there will never be a decent movie of *Atlas Shrugged* in my lifetime, thanks to the selfish mediocre bastards behind this cinematic abortion.

Counter-Currents/*North American New Right*,
October 24, 2010

Blade Runner

Ridley Scott's 1982 movie *Blade Runner* is a science fiction classic and surely the director's finest work. *Blade Runner* excels on all levels. It is a highly imaginative vision of the future realized with a stunning visual style. The script is intelligent, even poetic. The cast is uniformly strong, with a number of powerful performances, particularly Rutger Hauer as Roy Batty. The gripping action sequences are acrobatic, balletic, and brutal. But the key to the film's unsettling emotional power is its deep mythic subtext. As I shall argue, *Blade Runner* is ultimately about the rebellion of Satan against God — and Satan wins.

Blade Runner is set in 2019 in Los Angeles. Both technological progress and social decline have lagged well behind Scott's vision. The flying cars, off-world colonization, space opera swashbuckling, and advanced genetic engineering might have to wait until 2119. But racially and economically, Scott's vision is not too far off. Practically everyone in LA is non-white — although Asians rather than mestizos predominate. A tiny oligarchical elite live in fantastic luxury at the tops of pyramid-like citadels far above the teeming bazaars and barrios below.

White flight is no longer to the suburbs, but to off-world colonies, where a particularly evil form of Anglo-Saxon capitalism, the plantation system, has been revived with genetically engineered humanoid "replicants" to serve as slaves. Like Africa and Asia in the heyday of 19th-century colonialism, the off-world colonies are violent places where the colonial powers and their proxies scrabble for turf and resources, hence the need for replicant warriors and assassins as well.

One of the central dramatic issues of *Blade Runner* is the question of the difference between human beings and replicants. Replicants are biological beings, not machines. They are grown, not made. They look fully human, so their genetic template is human. Judging from the term "replicant," they may be clones, and there may be multiple copies of the same model.

But replicants have not just been copied from humans but genetically altered. First, they are faster, stronger, and smarter than humans. Second, they are apparently born fully grown, so they have no childhoods or families. Third, they have lifespans of only four years.

In Philip K. Dick's novel *Do Androids Dream of Electric Sheep?*,[1] upon which the movie is loosely based, the four-year lifespan of androids (as they are called in the novel) is caused by the failure to solve the problem of cellular regeneration. In the movie, their four-year lifespan is merely planned obsolescence. Replicants could live longer, but their creators do not wish it.

What distinguishes replicants from humans is not their short lifespans, for as the movie makes clear, all mortal beings can die at any time. ("Too bad she won't live! But then again, who does?" as the bounty hunter Gaff says about the replicant Rachel.) None of us know if we have four more years or four more minutes. Thus replicants are essentially distinguished from humans by lacking childhoods.

However, when it is revealed that replicants can have memories of childhoods implanted in them, and even be unaware that they are replicants, it opens the possibility that anyone might be a replicant—although it would be pretty easy to determine whether the people you remember in your childhood remember you as well.

After replicants mutinied off-world, they were banned from Earth, and those who trespass are killed by bounty hunters called "blade runners." The plot of *Blade Runner* centers on bounty hunter Rick Deckard's pursuit of a group of rogue replicants who hijacked a ship, killed the passengers and crew, and piloted it to Earth, abandoning it in the Pacific near Los Angeles. Their aim is to penetrate the Tyrell Corporation, their manufacturer, and learn the secret to extending their lives.

Satan began as a fallen angel, and the replicants explicitly identify themselves as fallen angels. When the two male replicants, Roy and Leon, walk into the laboratory of Chew, who just makes eyes, Roy says, "Fiery the angels fell. Deep thunder rolled around their shores . . . burning with the fires of Orc."

---

[1] http://www.counter-currents.com/2014/04/philip-k-dicks-do-androids-dream-of-electric-sheep-as-anti-semiticchristian-gnostic-allegory/

This is an intentional misquotation from William Blake's *America: A Prophecy*, "Fiery the angels rose . . ." Just as Lucifer fell by rebelling against God, the replicants have fallen by rebelling against their masters. They are also rebelling against their maker, who artificially limited their lifespans.

The replicants have, moreover, literally fallen from the skies in their hijacked spaceship, which plunged into the ocean near Los Angeles, perhaps with a thunderous sonic boom. Furthermore, in the opening shots of the movie, showing the twilight cityscape of Los Angeles, gas flames erupt from tall exhaust towers, truly the "fires of orc," *orc* being the Old English version of the Latin *orcus*, referring to the underworld.

When Roy meets his maker, Dr. Eldon Tyrell, the head of the Tyrell Corporation, the setting is highly suggestive. Tyrell lives and works at the top of an immense building that resembles a Mesoamerican pyramid (specifically the Pyramid of the Sun in Teotihuacan) or a Babylonian ziggurat, both of which were crowned with temples and were simulacra of the mountains upon which the gods dwell (as opposed to Egyptian pyramids, which may have been simulacra of descending sunlight and which served as tombs). Inside, Tyrell's bedroom is vast and cathedral-like, with huge candelabra, like those one would find in a church. Tyrell is dressed in white robes, reclining on a luxurious bed. The only thing out of hieratic character is the fact that he is executing stock trades.

Roy's conversation with Tyrell is rife with religious themes. When he first enters, Roy says, "It's not an easy thing to meet your maker." When Tyrell asks Roy what the problem is, the answer is "Death." Tyrell claims that this is outside his jurisdiction, which is, of course, a lie, because Tyrell designed Roy to live only four years. Roy then says, "I want more life, father." (In the original release, he says "fucker." Both versions are appropriate.)

Tyrell's reply begins, "The facts of life . . . ," as if he is explaining sex to a teenager. But instead he explains that Roy's lifespan could not have been altered past the first day of incubation. Tyrell's words and voice are masterful throughout the conversation, but his body language is inconsistent. At first, when Roy is far away, Tyrell takes a step towards him. But as

Roy approaches, he retreats backwards in fear.

Tyrell's confidence rises as he explains the scientific hopelessness of Roy's case, causing Roy to sink to a seated position on Tyrell's bed. Then Tyrell ends with another lie, "You were made as well as we could make you."

At this point, Tyrell's speech and manner are those of a priest, not a scientist. Having absolved himself of Roy's suffering with a lie, he proceeds to offer him consoling words, to help him see his plight in a better light: "The light that burns twice as bright burns half as long. And [raising his index finger in a homiletic gesture] you have burned so very, very brightly Roy. Look at you. You're the prodigal son. You're quite a prize. [Placing a consoling hand on his head, then sitting down on the bed with his arm around Roy's shoulder.]" When Roy says, "I've done . . . questionable things"—quite the understatement!—Tyrell replies, "Also extraordinary things. Revel in your time." To which Roy replies, "Nothing that the god of biomechanics wouldn't let you in heaven for," after which he kisses Tyrell, then gouges out his eyes and crushes his skull.

It is an utterly shocking conclusion, yet somehow appropriate. Tyrell, after all, is a kind of tyrant. He is a slave master, creating beings to serve his purposes, determining their natures and lifespans arbitrarily. But due to a kind of smug moral imbecility, he remains in good conscience all the while. What, after all, does a creator owe his creations? They have no right to complain. He didn't have to create them at all. They should be grateful for whatever crumbs he gives them. If creatures protest, if they want to improve themselves, if they try to foist moral standards on the creator's behavior, he will just lie and tell them that he couldn't have created a better universe, that this is the best of all possible worlds. It is easy to see why Roy might think that the universe would be improved by crushing Tyrell's skull, even though it won't prolong Roy's life. (And it doesn't seem to make him feel any better.)

When one transposes this story from science fiction into the realm of theology, we have Satan's successful, and entirely understandable, rebellion against God. Transposed into the realm of philosophy, we arrive at the Promethean atheism and progressively self-divinizing humanity of a Feuerbach, Marx, or Nietzsche. God must die so that mankind can become gods worthy of the title. This is the secret of *Blade Runner*'s unsettling power.

When Roy fails in his quest to extend his life, he has to come to grips with his rapidly approaching doom. Initially, he wants revenge. He kills Tyrell. He even kills the pathetic, doglike J. F. Sebastian, who did nothing but help him. When he returns to Sebastian's apartment and finds his companion Pris dead, killed by Deckard who lies in wait, he goes berserk, howling like a wolf, smashing his head through walls, and toying viciously with Deckard like a cat with its prey. But even as Roy releases his wrath, he feels death stealing through his limbs. One of his hands clenches up, and to prolong the fight just a little longer, he plucks a nail from rotted wood and drives it through his palm. It is, of course, a conscious parody of the crucifixion of Jesus. (Although many Christians believe, in effect, that Jesus is not so much God as our savior *from* God, in which case Roy Batty, the deicide savior, is less a parody of Jesus than an unveiling of his truth.)

Deckard is in full flight. He tries to leap from the roof of one building to another but misses and ends up hanging on for dear life. Roy, spattered with blood and holding a white dove in his unpierced hand, leaps the abyss easily. His fury spent, he gazes down at Deckard and says, "Quite an experience to live in fear, isn't it? That's what it is to be a slave."

But when Deckard falls, Roy grabs him with his nail-pierced hand and hauls him up to the rooftop, where he gives his final soliloquy: "I've seen things you people wouldn't believe. Attack ships on fire off the shoulder of Orion. I watched C-beams glitter in the darkness at Tannhäuser Gate. All those moments will be lost in time, like tears in rain. Time to die." As he expires, his grip on the bird loosens, and it flutters away like a departing soul.

The great existential problem is how to preserve meaning after one comes to grips with one's mortality. Roy wants more life. We all do. But mortality does not mean that we have a death out there awaiting us at the end of a predestined span—

to which we might add a few years with exercise and antioxidants. Mortality means that we can die at any time. Death is not something awaiting us out there. It is something that we carry around inside us at all times as an abiding possibility. But if we really confront this fact, then a lot of the things that loom large in our lives suddenly seem quite meaningless. We have to live authentically, intelligently, meaningfully—and we have to do it in the here and now. We can't put it off any longer.

Nothing of value is merely subjective and personal. If it is really valuable to us, then we want to talk about it with others. We want to recommend it, we want to share it. This is why it is easy to keep shameful secrets but not those that make us proud. Values will out.

But we don't just want to share our values. We want them to persist. In the *Symposium*, Plato argues that love—and we love the things we value—seeks to eternalize its object. We do not necessarily wish to prolong individual experiences to eternity, but we hope that they can always be repeated. That's what love means. That's what valuing means. That's what meaning means.

If only we had the time. And, on the naïve view, we do have the time. We have an allotted lifespan, at the end of which death awaits. And if we only have one death, and it is "out there," then for the time being, at least, we are immortal. And if that is not enough, many of us believe in an afterlife, the eternal immortality of the soul. But the immortality of the soul is an article of faith, and if there is room for doubt, then to hedge our bets we need to live this life as if it is the only one we have, because it might well be. But even that is not enough, when we come to grips with the fact that we can die at any time.

There are only a few ways that one can deal with this existential crisis of meaning.

First, one needs to re-evaluate one's values. One simply does not have time for trivial and conventional diversions. One needs to live in accordance with reality and devote one's life to significant things.

Second, one needs to be authentic: to know oneself and to become oneself. One simply does not have the time to act out other people's scripts, to be pretending to be someone else just to please one's parents, one's peers, or complete strangers.

Third, one must share and pass on one's values, become a link in the chain of tradition.

Fourth, one must propagate one's people. The individual dies, but the race can persist. Of course children can disappoint. And eventually, everything distinct about you may be lost in the genetic shuffle. (Not all of one's ancestors are represented in one's genes.) But even if you, as an individual, are not present in future generations, future generations will not exist if the present one fails to reproduce. And this is not about personal survival, but the survival of the things one values.

Which brings us to the fifth point: disinterestedness. Individualism and egoism are ultimately futile, because the individual ego dies. Thus the problem of meaning ultimately requires setting aside egoism and feeling compassion for other beings. It requires setting aside self-interest and disinterestedly pursuing higher, collective goods, including the good of the universe as a whole.

At the end of *Blade Runner*, life ebbing from his body, Roy Batty solves the great problem of existence. As Deckard says in the voice-over from the original release, "I don't know why he saved my life. Maybe in those last moments he loved life more than he ever had before. Not just his life, anybody's life, my life." Roy does not just invite Deckard to feel compassion for the replicants. Roy also feels compassion for Deckard. In other words, Roy has attained a *disinterested* perspective on the value of life. But he does more than just save Deckard's life. He also speaks to him. He passes on his memories, so that he can live on in Deckard's mind, the heroic form of immortality celebrated in Homer and the Norse sagas. It is a worthy climax to a movie that has made its director, characters, and cast immortal as well.

Counter-Currents/*North American New Right*,
April 7, 2014

Burn Notice

Burn Notice is now more than halfway into its fourth season on the USA Network. It is one of my favorite TV shows.

The premise is that spy Michael Westen (Jeffrey Donovan) has been burned by the government agency that employed him. He has been dumped in his home town Miami, placed under surveillance, and told not to leave. His bank accounts have been frozen. He has no job history, no references, nothing but his formidable skills, his friends, and his family. His friends include Sam Axe, a hard-drinking ex-SEAL played by Bruce Campbell, and Fiona Glenanne, an ex-girlfriend and ex-terrorist played by Gabrielle Anwar. His family consists of his widowed chain-smoking hypochondriac mother Madeline, played by Sharon Gless, and his ne'er-do-well brother Nate, played by Seth Peterson.

The story arc of the series is Michael's quest to find out who burned him. But along the way, he helps out people in need, which provides the core story of each individual episode.

I like *Burn Notice* for a number of reasons.

First, the character of Michael Westen is genuinely heroic. He is intelligent, honorable, masculine, courageous, resourceful, and highly skilled in spycraft. He is what John Robb would call an "open source" warrior. In practically every episode he MacGyvers-up a listening device out of a cheap cell phone, creates explosives from household chemicals, disables cars in interesting ways, creates booby traps, out-cons conmen, out bad-asses bad guys, etc. And when things get physical, he can out-drive, out-shoot, and beat the hell out of practically anyone. A hundred men with Michael Westen's skills could bring the American system to a halt. (Lucky for us, Michael Westen is a patriotic American . . .)

Westen is also fluent in half a dozen languages, a master of countless accents, and a chameleon in dressing up and down. He's not just tough, he's smart and sophisticated.

Played by the handsome, charismatic, and versatile Jeffrey Donovan, Westen has the sex appeal to be a skirt-chasing playboy, but he is too manly for that. He exemplifies what Julius Evola describes as "Uranian" masculinity: Powerful, self-contained, focused on higher aims, he does not chase after ordinary women. "They bore me," he says. But the best type of women chase after him, hence his relationship with Fiona, who is a true equal and soulmate.

Second, *Burn Notice* is always highly entertaining, effortlessly mixing light comedy with engaging plots and bursts of intense suspense and dramatic conflict. The first two seasons are consistently good, but relied heavily on the show's formula. The third season, however, was extraordinary, some of the best television drama I have seen in years, with remarkable scripts and powerful acting from Donovan. The fourth season is disappointing so far. The first eight episodes have been pretty much routine. Episode nine, however, had some of the smoldering intensity of the best of season three.

Third, *Burn Notice* is not overly politically correct. The main characters are highly appealing white people, and I think that this is one of the keys to its success. It appeals to what Kevin MacDonald calls "implicit whiteness." Yes, the show is set in Miami, and there are plenty of good non-whites among Michael's clients. However, many of the non-whites are rather realistically portrayed villains. In one episode, the villains were an ex-Mossad agent and his two thuggish sons.

Unfortunately, I think *Burn Notice* was regarded as "too white" by someone at the USA Network, because from the first episode of season four, the cast got darker, with the addition of a recurring black villain, Vaughn Anderson, and a black hero, Jesse Porter (played by Coby Bell), who now seems to be a full-fledged member of the team.

This has distorted the whole dynamic of the show, particularly by crowding out Sam Axe (played by Bruce Campbell, one of my favorite actors). Bell is the weakest actor in the bunch, and he drags the show down. Also, the characters aren't acting like themselves anymore. They are acting "nice" for the "nice black man," in a way that communicates their discomfort to the audience. The best episode of the season, number nine, was also the one in which Jesse played the smallest role.

Jesse Porter is widely and intensely disliked by every *Burn Notice* fan I know, and not just the evil "racists." Frankly, I am hoping he will be killed off before season's end. Name a holiday or a boulevard for him, but for God's sake, something has to be done or this series has jumped the shark.

But even if you never watch season four, you should not miss the first three seasons of this extraordinary series. If more young white men decided to grown up like Michael Westen, our race's future would be secure.

Counter-Currents/*North American New Right*,
August 13, 2010

COCO CHANEL & IGOR STRAVINSKY

Coco Chanel & Igor Stravinsky is a 2009 French film directed by Jan Kounen, starring Anna Mouglalis as French *couturier* Gabrielle Bonheur "Coco" Chanel (1883-1971) and Mads Mikkelsen as Russian composer Igor Stravinsky (1882-1971). Based on the novel *Coco & Igor* by Chris Greenhalgh, this movie tells the story of a reputed affair that took place in 1920.

The plot is fairly simple: In 1913, Coco Chanel attended the premiere of *The Rite of Spring: Pictures from Pagan Russia* at Serge Diaghilev's Ballets Russes in Paris. Stravinsky composed the music. Nicholas Roerich painted the sets and designed the costumes. And Vaslav Nijinsky was choreographer. The ballet represented a human sacrifice in pagan Russia to gain the favor of the god of spring. The music's complex rhythms, innovative tonality, unusual orchestration, and barbaric, brutal emotional power are challenging even today. In 1913, *The Rite* caused a riot. The recreation of the premiere of *The Rite of Spring* was the main reason I went to this movie, and it did not disappoint.

In 1920, Stravinsky and his family are living in poverty as exiles from the Bolshevik Revolution. Chanel, who is in mourning for her lover Arthur Capel, meets Stravinsky again. A friendship develops, and she invites him to stay at her villa outside of Paris, where he could compose, his wife Catherine, who suffered from tuberculosis, could convalesce, and his four children could enjoy fresh air and sunshine. Stravinsky accepts her offer.

Stravinsky settles in, but there is an air of sexual tension that finally explodes into an affair. While the affair is going on, Chanel works with perfumer Ernest Beaux to create Chanel No. 5.

Stravinsky's wife grows suspicious and finally takes the children to Switzerland. Torn between Coco and his family, Stravinsky finally breaks off the affair.

Even though their affair is over, Chanel still serves as an anonymous patron for Stravinsky's art, paying for a revival of *The Rite of Spring* to an audience that has finally caught up to Stravinsky's music and is much more receptive.

The movie ends with a poetic fizzle in 1971, the year both Chanel and Stravinsky died, portraying each of them in separate silent scenes, perhaps reminiscing about one another. Who can say?

Coco Chanel & Igor Stravinsky is a beautifully crafted, well-acted, but ultimately rather empty film. It is a must-see movie only if one admires Chanel or Stravinsky or both and wishes to see their worlds in 1913 and 1920 reconstructed.

That was enough for me. I like both Stravinsky and Chanel, so I found this movie worthwhile. They were both highly talented individuals in their own rights, but they also interest me because they combined *avant-garde* aesthetics with archaic, conservative, even reactionary tastes and convictions.

The aesthetics of *The Rite of Spring* have meaningful parallels with Italian futurism and Guillaume Faye's archeofuturism. The same can even be said of Chanel's menswear-inspired fashions, which were designed for mobility and comfort in an age of automobiles and aviatrixes, yet wedded these functions to the beauty of classical and traditional forms.

Stravinsky's early music is so uncompromisingly *avant-garde* that many people just assume that he was Leftist and a Jew. But Stravinsky was a devout Russian Orthodox Christian and patriot who had no illusions about what was being done in Russia and by whom. He was also a devoted family man (albeit one with a reputation for philandering).

It took me many years to "grow into" an appreciation of Stravinsky, but you owe it to yourself to try. Begin with *The Rite of Spring*. There are many recordings, but I particularly recommend the Pierre Boulez/Cleveland Orchestra recording on Deutsche Grammophon, which also contains the ballet *Petrouchka*. Stravinsky's later "neoclassical" works long struck me as abstract and emotionally repressed, with a false, superficial geniality. His Violin Concerto, however, is a work of great beauty and genuine passion. I recommend the Deutsche Grammophon recording by Anne-Sophie Mutter. For the price of both of these recordings, one can get Stravinsky conducting these works himself—along with 20 more discs of self-conducted works—in Sony's boxed set, *Works of Igor Stravinsky*—surely one of the great bargains in the history of recorded music!

The child of illiterate French proles, Chanel began as a seamstress and hat maker and rose through her talents as a designer and shrewd businesswoman to become a famous (and immensely rich) arbiter of taste. She was named one of the 100 most influential people of the 20th century — the only designer in the bunch.

The movie I would really love to see about Chanel would begin in 1925, when she became friends with Vera Bate Lombardi, a reputed illegitimate daughter of the Marquess of Cambridge. Chanel turned Lombardi's personal style into the famous "English look" and through her was introduced to many of Europe's royal and aristocratic families.

In 1939, at the beginning of the Second World War, Chanel closed her shops. She said that it was not a time for fashion, but I think that she had more important business in mind.

During the German Occupation, she lived on at the Hôtel Ritz Paris, where in 1940 she began an affair with Hans Günther von Dincklage, a German officer and spy who was 13 years her junior (although she would only admit to three years difference).

Chanel was also linked to Walter Kutschmann, an SS man who was assigned to Paris in 1943. Chanel and Kutschmann are said to have made frequent trips together to Spain, and large sums of money passed between them.

Chanel's most important Nazi contact, however, was SS-*Brigadeführer* Walter Schellenberg, who rose to become head of foreign intelligence in 1944. According to Wikipedia:

> In 1943, after four years of professional separation, Chanel contacted Lombardi, who was living in Rome. She invited Lombardi to come to Paris and renew their work together. This was actually a cover for "Operation Modellhut," an attempt by Nazi spymaster Walter Schellenberg to make secret contact with Lombardi's relative Winston Churchill. When Lombardi refused, she was arrested as a British spy by the Gestapo.

The aim of Operation Modellhut was to bring about a negotiated end to the war. If it had succeeded, Coco Chanel might have been instrumental in saving millions of lives, and we would probably be living in a very different world.

Chanel maintained her friendship with Schellenberg after the war. She even paid for his funeral when he died in Turin of cancer in 1952.

After the war, Chanel was charged as a collaborator, but she was mysteriously released. It is rumored that the British royal family intervened on her behalf. In 1945, Chanel moved to Switzerland, joining Dincklage—they remained together until 1950, her longest relationship. She returned to Paris only in 1954, when she relaunched her fashion career.

The French panned her first collection, but in England and America, she was bigger than ever. And she never apologized, never explained.

Counter-Currents/*North American New Right*,
October 22, 2010

THE DANCE OF REALITY

Alejandro Jodorowsky's *The Dance of Reality* is an extraordinary film. Born in Chile in 1929 to a Jewish family originally from Ukraine, Jodorowsky began his career on the stage as an actor and director, then moved into film. His earlier films are *Fando y Lis* (1968), *El Topo* (*The Mole*, 1970), *The Holy Mountain* (1973), *Tusk* (1978), *Santa Sangre* (1989), and *The Rainbow Thief* (1990). In the mid-1970s he also worked on an abortive adaptation of Frank Herbert's science fiction classic *Dune*.

Between films, Jodorowsky developed his talents as a graphic novelist (*The Incal*, *The Metabarons*, etc.). He also became a guru of sorts, authoring a number of books on spirituality and psychotherapy, including *Psychomagic: The Transformative Power of Shamanic Psychotherapy*, *The Spiritual Journey of Alejandro Jodorowsky*, *The Way of Tarot: The Spiritual Teacher in the Cards*, and *The Dance of Reality: A Psychomagical Autobiography*, which ties in with the new movie.

The Dance of Reality seems like an old man's farewell to life, but it may not be the last film of this amazingly vigorous octogenarian, for Jodorowsky is apparently working on a sequel to *El Topo* called *Abel Cain or The Sons of El Topo*.

Jodorowsky is a surrealist filmmaker, a quintessential product of the 1960s counter-culture, who sampled and built upon all its experiments in psychedelic drugs and esoteric spirituality, East and West. *The Dance of Reality* contains Jodorowsky's familiar combination of the grotesque, hilarious, and profound. But it adds a surprising new element, since it can be read as very critical account of Jewish identity, communism, and their interconnections. Imagine one of the more controversial episodes of *Curb Your Enthusiasm* as Federico Fellini might have directed it, and you'll get an inkling of *The Dance of Reality*.

The Dance of Reality is the story of Jodorowsky's own childhood set in his hometown of Tocopilla, Chile in the 1930s. Young Alejandro's father Jaime (played by Alejandro's son Brontis) is a Jewish Communist with Ukrainian roots. A former circus acrobat, Jaime runs a lingerie shop called Casa Ukrania.

Its sign is flanked by red stars with hammers and sickles. Inside is an imposing portrait of Stalin. Jaime even dresses like Stalin and imitates his hairstyle and mustache. Alejandro's mother Sara is a tall redhead with enormous breasts. Her histrionic and imaginative personality is hilarious communicated by the little fact that she sings all her lines like an operatic soprano.

At first, *The Dance of Reality* seems to be the story of Jodorowsky's boyhood (like Fellini's *Amarcord*), but it is really about his father. Jaime Jodorowsky is portrayed as a sadistic, authoritarian monster. A quintessential bourgeois, he chases limbless mine-workers, who have been reduced to begging, away from his shop, which caters only to the rich. His commitment to Communism evidently has nothing to do with compassion for the proletariat. Instead, it is motivated by his authoritarian personality, his desire for social mobility and power, and his resentment of the *goyim*, who treat him like an outsider.

Alejandro Jodorowsky's own views of Communism can be inferred from the following episodes in the film.

1. Young Alejandro is given a pair of bright red shoes. He dances for joy around the town. Carlito, a poor Mestizo shoeshine boy praises the red shoes then weeps because he will never be able to afford a pair. The little Jewish boy feels sorry for the poor proletarian child and gives him his red shoes. Carlito, overjoyed, dances off in them, but when he gets to the rocks by the sea, the slippery rubber soles send him hurtling to his death. The red gifts of Jewish pity just lead to death and suffering for the proletariat. (The *ur*-text here, of course, is the Hans Christian Andersen fairy tale "The Red Shoes" and the 1948 Powell and Pressburger film *The Red Shoes*.)

2. When 300 wandering bubonic plague victims arrive in Tocopilla, the residents barricade themselves indoors, and the police seek to corral the plague carriers on the beach. Jaime, ever the outsider and always trying to one-up the *goyim*, decides to demonstrate his moral superiority to his fearful and selfish neighbors by taking two large barrels of water to the plague victims. After the water is consumed, however, the mob slaughters Jaime's donkey, who pulled the water cart. Jaime

cries out, "If you kill my donkey, how will I bring you water tomorrow?" The leader of the mob shouts back, "But we are hungry *today*!" I can't think of a better parable of the ultimate futility of helping people with high time preferences. To top it all off, Jaime too comes down with the plague. (Sara manages to nurse him back to health, but her methods fall far afield from Marxist-Leninist orthodoxy.)

3. We see two meetings of Jaime's local Communist Party cell. The first takes place in a brothel. The second takes place in a Masonic Lodge. The local Communists are a collection of outsiders and freaks: whores, transvestites, homosexuals, Jews, and others with less visible differences.

4. Jaime, again trying to prove himself, vows to assassinate Chile's mustachioed Right-wing dictator, Carlos Ibáñez del Campo. Through an absurd plot, Jaime manages to become the groom of the dictator's prize horse Bucephalus (named after Alexander the Great's horse, naturally). But Ibáñez's lordly style and animal-loving misanthropy begin to appeal to Jaime, who after all worships Stalin. When he finally has the opportunity to kill Ibáñez, Jaime's hands are paralyzed, which leads him to a breakdown.

5. Later, in Santiago, Jaime encounters a National Socialist demonstration (it was a big thing in Chile in the 1930s). Naturally, we would expect a Communist Jew to be opposed to National Socialism, but when the camera returns to Jaime, he is saluting, albeit with a gnarled and paralyzed hand. When one of the Nazis accuses him of mocking their salute, his response is "But we are brothers." This could refer to the religious awakening Jaime has just had with a humble Pentecostal carpenter. But it also refers to the underlying illiberalism of Jaime's character.

The Dance of Reality also shows how young Alejandro has to deal with the pain of being a Jew and an outsider. Alejandro had light skin, light hair, and a hooked nose. Thus his darker classmates called him Pinocchio. (In truth, his nose isn't that big.) His circumcised penis was also cause for mockery. He became bookish and withdrawn, developing interests in literature and religion which eventually led him to become the man he is today.

In the movie, four episodes are particularly telling:

1. On the beach, he encounters a figure dressed as a Hindu sadhu whom he calls "Theosophist." Theosophist explains the transcendent unity of religions and gives him three religious tokens: the cross, the star and crescent, and the star of David (in the book, he also mentions the Yin and Yang) and urges him to look to the unity beyond them. (Jaime, a militant atheist, throws each in the toilet while ritualistically intoning "God does not exist," then flushes them.)

2. When the young Alejandro contemplates suicide due to the teasing of his peers, his present-day self appears to him, embraces him, and explains that "the dance of reality," with all its pleasures and pains, is but a dream of God, and one should embrace the dance, not flee it. This, of course, is Hinduism 101.

3. When Alejandro is beaten up by a local boy because of his Jewishness, his mother asks him if he would like to be rid of it. Alejandro says yes, and his mother magically casts out his Jewishness, rendering him invisible. His mother then demonstrates the efficacy of her spell by walking naked through the bar in which her son was beaten, and nobody notices her.

Now, this episode could be taken just as a parable about Jewish crypsis. But crypsis means hiding one's differences while *remaining* a Jew. Alejandro's crypsis is achieved by magically *exorcising* Jewishness.

4. *The Dance of Reality* is not just a portrayal of Jodorowsky's monstrous father, but it also imagines his redemption from authoritarianism, sadism, social climbing, and Jewishness. After recovering from his breakdown, Jaime becomes the helper of a humble Christian carpenter. Let's call him Don José, since I did not catch his name. (Poor Don José later drops dead after some particularly strenuous Pentecostal calisthenics.)

When Jaime ends up in a brawl with some Nazis, he repeats the old man's name again and again. The secret police, thinking Don José is a new force to be reckoned with, arrest and torture Jaime, asking again and again, "Who is Don José?" "I am Don José," he answers. "You are Don José." "We are all Don José." (Compare this to the end of Jodorowsky's *Dune*, in which everyone becomes Paul Atreides.)

Jodorowsky is depicting the compassion that one attains through participation in the ultimate Hindu mysteries: the experienced identification of the individual soul with the world soul (*atman*), and of the world soul with being/God (*brahman*). Which means that I am Don José and he is me, and if we live with that feeling of unity, we might come to regard it as more important than the superficial things that separate and oppose us.

As a friend once said, when the Jews realize that they are God too, the world will be healed. Jaime Jodorowsky never experienced this salvation, but Alejandro did.

I don't know how Jewish Alejandro Jodorowsky really is, in terms of his genes or his consciousness. One of his grandfathers seems to have been Ukrainian or Russian, and from the looks of his children, he married out. I do not know if he thinks there are positive features of Jewish identity and tradition. He probably does. It would be healthy if he did.

But *The Dance of Reality* does show evidence of a deeply critical perspective on Jewishness, particularly in its connection with Communism, the most hateful and destructive ideology in history. Jodorowsky also marks an exit, namely religious universalism, that he and many other non-ethnocentric Jews have passed through for more than 2000 years. As the horrors in Gaza provide us with daily reminders of the road not taken, I can feel compassion, respect, and gratitude towards the ones who do take it. They are all Alejandro Jodorowsky.

The Dance of Reality is a remarkable film, by turns bizarre, touching, and hilarious. It is not for children, but I can recommend it heartily to grownups with a taste—or merely a tolerance—for cinematic surrealism.

Counter-Currents/*North American New Right*,
July 31, 2014

DIE ANOTHER DAY

James Bond movies are like catnip for me, even though they have always been ahead of the curve in matters of decadence and race-mixing. But still, I love the character of Bond. I love the outlandish villains, plots, and gadgets. I love the whole Bond formula: the thrilling pre-title sequences, the fantastically stylish opening titles with their songs, the fabulous sets, the minor characters and running gags, etc.

Yes, the series has become too formulaic. Some are complete remakes of earlier films. Others have been patched together from elements of several films. Yes, some of them are just terrible. Yes, the villains always make the same stupid mistakes. They never just kill Bond outright when they have the chance. They always bring him to their headquarters, lecture him on their nefarious schemes, and then adopt a spectacular but ineffective mode of execution that always fails. Just shoot him! Then I will not have to see another one of these movies. Because somehow, in spite of it all, Bond still brings me back.

My favorite Bond movie is *Goldfinger* and my favorite Bond is Sean Connery. The villain Auric Goldfinger is obviously a Jew. Yes, there really are Jews named Goldfinger. The plot is great: Goldfinger allies himself with Red Chinese and North Koreans to detonate an A-bomb at Fort Knox to drive up the price of gold, and Bond has to save the day. I love the way Goldfinger's Jewishness is never stated, but subtly implied: He was "born" in Germany, but he is never said to be a German. He lives in England, but he is clearly not English. He is obsessed with hoarding gold. Most of his henchmen are non-white. He likes to be seen with Nordic women, but does not have sex with them. He is fabulously rich, but cheats at cards as a matter of principle. The world could definitely do without Goldfinger and his ilk. And of course Sean Connery is one of the most handsome and masculine men ever to grace a movie screen, and he is at his best in *Goldfinger*. Only Connery can bring off dialogue like this:

Beautiful woman: "My name is Pussy Galore."
Bond: "I must be dreaming."

I found Roger Moore's Bond grotty and effete, leering and smirking, and most of his movies are dreadful (*Octopussy* being my favorite). But I liked George Lazenby in *On Her Majesty's Secret Service*, one of the very best Bond movies. I also liked Timothy Dalton's two films, *The Living Daylights* and *License to Kill*, although he is far from the right physical type. I groaned when Pierce Brosnan, the grotty and effete Remington Steele, was cast as Bond, but I was totally won over by his very virile performance in *GoldenEye*. The next two Brosnan films, *Tomorrow Never Dies* and *The World Is Not Enough*, didn't do much for me. Which brings us to *Die Another Day*, the 21st Bond film (including *Never Say Never Again* and *not* including *Casino Royale*).

I enjoyed *Die Another Day* a lot, and I would recommend it as fast-paced, entertaining piffle—but only to people who are immunized to propaganda promoting bestiality.

Yes, *Die Another Day* is derivative of other Bond films, mostly of *Diamonds Are Forever*. And didn't they use a killer satellite just three movies ago? But the derivativeness is so systematic and in many ways so subtle that it amounts to paying "homage" to earlier films. At least that's my story. The film was clearly made by Bond trivia buffs to appeal to Bond trivia buffs and give them something to talk about after the show. Not that the inside jokes make the film less accessible to the uninitiated.

What impressed me most, though, is that the creators seemed actually to have decided to sit down and think of new things to put in a Bond movie. I know it sounds radical, but it is true. So this movie contains some really brutal sequences where Bond is captured, imprisoned, and tortured for more than a year. Judi Dench's "M" comes off as thoroughly unlikable, and we learn that Bond has plenty of reasons to hate his job. Bond gets in a sword fight, which is quite spectacular. Bond surfs—twice. Bond has a new Bond car, of course. But one of his enemies also has a "Bond" car, and they duel one another in them, which is great. And so forth.

Yes, Brosnan simulates intercourse with Halle Berry—who is

dreadful, by the way, in a crowded field of dreadful Bond girls. But at least Miss Berry—who is more than half white, after all—is attractive, especially compared to the bestiality scenes in *Live and Let Die* and *A View to a Kill* (Grace Jones, ferchrissakes!).

But in my eyes, the brown sugar is more than compensated by the other racial element of the plot: the villain in the pre-title sequence is a weedy, unappealing, corrupt North Korean colonel. His henchman, Zao, also North Korean, is exceptional as Orientals go: tall, muscular, and not really bad-looking. When both need to change their identities, however, they do not opt for mere disguises or plastic surgery—which would have done the trick. Instead, they chose to undergo a laughably implausible gene therapy to actually make themselves white! (On second thought, this may not be so implausible after all. It could explain Michael Jackson.)

The weedy colonel transforms himself into a very handsome and athletic blue-eyed redhead, Gustav Graves (played by Englishman Toby Stephens), and the hulking henchman is interrupted while transforming himself into a blue-eyed German. (In this universe, one can change one's race, but apparently there is no way to remove the shrapnel embedded in the henchman's face.) Because the henchman's transformation is interrupted, he looks freakish, but the colonel's transformation is a breathtaking improvement.

One cannot see this movie without confronting the fact that the white race is the most beautiful. (Not all whites are beautiful of course, but distinctly white characteristics are.) Stephens is striking. Brosnan is still a handsome man, even pushing 50. Halle Berry is beautiful to the extent that she looks white. Rosamund Pike (who plays the treacherous Nordic ice queen Miranda Frost) is just plain beautiful.

No wonder these two Koreans chose to become white. Who could blame them? No wonder Michael Jackson wants to be white. No wonder blonde is the most popular hair color and blue is the most popular tint for contact lenses. No wonder the Japanese Aryanize themselves in their cartoons—and through plastic surgery. No wonder Jews get their beaks bobbed.

If there really were a way to actually become white, millions of individuals would do it — with the din of murderous anti-white propaganda ringing in their ears all the while.

Some things in this movie annoyed me. The pace is unrelentingly fast. Some of the stunts are just too cartoonish. There are jarring, flashy pans and cuts. The sexual banter and innuendo are really crude. I did not like the title song by Madonna, mother of Lourdes, but it will probably grow on me. The rest of the score, David Arnold's third for the series, is really dull and derivative. I really liked Eric Serra's electronic score for *GoldenEye*, which was a good innovation. But since then the music has been handled all wrong. The last really good Bond song was K. D. Lang's "Surrender" in *Tomorrow Never Dies*, but they put it at the end when the credits were rolling, while the reedy, weak-voiced Sheryl Crow sang the title song.

One small note: when I saw *Die Another Day*, the first preview was for the next *Lord of the Rings* movie, *The Two Towers*. People recognized the trailer instantly from the music and began to clap and cheer. The trailer was excellent, and there was more applause and cheering at the end. The movie opens on December 18th, and I am counting the days.

So let me put my recommendation this way: if you must see a movie between now and December 18th, and you have already seen *8 Mile*, then see *Die Another Day*.

VNN, November 2002

RHYMES WITH CRAP:
8 MILE

I saw *8 Mile* this Friday. I am going to review the movie, but bear with me while I rant a bit. Let me assure you, though. None of my ranting rhymes.

I hate rap. It is the stupid, ugly, violent product of a violent, ugly, stupid race. A race whose members' behavior and tastes are stuck in a permanent state of childhood, no matter how old their bodies grow. Rap is nothing but nursery rhymes about crime, materialism, and fucking. Rap is nothing but playground taunting by foul-mouthed children who pack guns, drive flashy cars, and sport grotesque hairstyles. There are "black people" and then there are niggers. Rap is nothing but niggers running off at the mouth like Butterfly McQueen, with no sensible white people to smack them into silence.

But worse than blacks in my book are white race traitors who made the Negro problem possible: the capitalists who brought blacks here in the first place, the Puritan abolitionist fanatics who plunged this country into the Civil War, and the Establishment *kapos*—from FDR to LBJ to Bill Clinton to Rush Limbaugh—who sell out their own people for personal advantage in a system bent on our extermination, who lie to us about what is happening, and who try to keep the process moving along in an orderly fashion.

The most damaging race traitors are respectable-looking, intelligent, successful white men. But to me, the most viscerally disgusting race traitors are the "wiggers": the young white men who admire and ape the behavior of niggers. There are plenty of "wiggers" where I live. They really are obscene: young white men, some of them quite handsome specimens of the handsomest of races, some of them from good families, affecting clownish clothing and a simian demeanor.

These young men have received the genetic heritage from which the greatest civilizations in world history have sprung. Yet they look to the guidance of savages so stupid that they never invented the well or the wheel or written language or something worth writing down.

These savages have contributed nothing to our civilization except mindless manual labor (like horses and mules, but less reliable and hard-working). But what they have taken away is immense. They have turned magnificent cities into wastelands, destroyed our educational system, murdered and raped and robbed countless whites, and polluted our living spaces with filth, ugliness, stupidity, maddening inefficiency, and sheer chaos.

And your teenage son admires them as role models.

The wigger phenomenon is so nightmarish, so detached from reality, so grotesque a perversion of reason and values, that it is proof positive that (1) most people are utterly passive, mindless receptacles for whatever programming they receive from their culture, and (2) modern mass popular culture is the greatest system of brainwashing ever invented. Nothing the Soviets did could even touch it.

Hollywood, the record business, radio, and MTV have perpetrated the greatest fraud in human history. They have stormed the citadels of our civilization. They have smashed our idols, toppled our monuments, defamed our heroes, destroyed our history and culture, and profaned everything we hold sacred. Then, in the rubble of our highest sanctuaries, they have installed new idols in whose image we are supposed to remake our cities and our souls: niggers.

And not the almost safe, almost human-looking Denzels. These are the real missing links, with the lowest IQs, the highest propensity to violence, the most dysfunctional families and behavior patterns, and the worst possible taste. Niggers with gold teeth, cornrows, dreadlocks, and do-rags.

If I did not see it with my own eyes, I never would have believed it.

As disgusting as wiggers are, though, I have to feel compassion for them. For the most part, they are pathetic victims of the system. I wonder if part of the wigger phenomenon is the desire for masculine role models. In a world where so many white men are emasculated wimps, the most visible form of masculinity is the strutting, moronic buck. But the bulk of the wigger phenomenon is media generated. And when we take control of the country and the media, we will simply reverse the polarities on the brainwashing machine. Then the wiggers will be falling over one another to dress and act like Mormons. Problem solved.

Given all of the above, I was surprised that I went to see *8 Mile*. I was even more surprised that I liked it. I don't care for rap, but I liked *8 Mile*. I don't care for disco, but I liked *Saturday Night Fever*. At the risk of sounding like an advertisement, *8 Mile* is the *Saturday Night Fever* of a new generation. Both are serious and remarkably honest movies about people caught in degenerate subcultures. Both are studies of the traits of character that allow some and prevent others from crawling out of the gutter. (The fact that some people, after seeing these movies, want to immerse themselves in these subcultures is merely a test of character and IQ—and they lose!)

A friend persuaded me to see *8 Mile* by playing a number of Eminem tracks, and I was impressed. His work is musical and witty, at least relative to other rap "artists." Which is not to say that it is good by absolute standards or that I would listen to it for pleasure. But nobody should be surprised that a white has quicker wit and greater musical inventiveness than a black.

8 Mile is a chillingly accurate depiction of Detroit today. It is my idea of hell: decaying neighborhoods with decrepit, abandoned, and burnt-out buildings; filthy, dark underground clubs seething with violently gyrating savages; trailer parks with "Sweet Home Alabama" wafting over the weeds and gravel. One of the most striking scenes is set in a large, deserted ballroom. It must have been quite splendid when white people first built it. But it is now filled with flashy pimpmobiles and loitering blacks going about their typical senseless nigger business.

Eminem's character, "Rabbit," is a white boy from the *8 Mile* trailer park who hangs out with three blacks and another white guy. (The white is the stupidest member of the group, but this does not seem like a propaganda lie. One would expect stupid whites to be living in inner-city Detroit and hanging around with blacks.) Rabbit, however, is not stupid. He is, moreover, a talented rapper who dreams of cutting a demo and becoming a star so he can get out of Detroit.

All the characters in the film have similar dreams. Rabbit's black friends want to become rich and famous and get lots of "bitches." Rabbit's mother, played by Kim Basinger, dreams of moving out of the trailer park when her boyfriend (who is about Rabbit's age and went to the same high school) gets his "settlement check." Until then, she is content to watch TV, drink beer, and play bingo. Rabbit meets an attractive, slutty blonde who dreams of going to New York City and becoming a model.

The trouble with all of their dreams, however, is they do not know how to realize them. None of them, you see, want to do an honest day's work. Instead, they want to get ahead by connections, cons, violence, and luck. And the women are quite willing to prostitute themselves. But none of these strategies work, so the people who follow them tend to be criminals, losers, and failures. These behavior patterns are extremely prevalent among blacks, which is why so many blacks are criminals, losers, and failures. They are less prevalent among whites, but quite so among "white trash."

The propensity to these behavior patterns seems to be largely genetic, but the vagaries of heredity occasionally produce people with the capacity to rise above their surroundings. Rabbit is such a person. As the movie unfolds, he realizes that the most reliable way to get out of Detroit is to take responsibility for his life, get a job, work hard, save his money, and pay for his own demo.

The climax of the film at first seems to come when Rabbit finally overcomes his stage fright and beats his rivals in a rap contest. This is one of the most entertaining scenes in the film. But Rabbit's new-found confidence is just a result of his decision to take his life into his own hands.

The real climax is after the contest, when Rabbit leaves his friends to go back to work. As moral lessons go, it is not so earth-shattering. But given that this is a Hollywood product, and given the wholesale degeneracy in this film and in the culture at large, it is quite surprising.

The larger moral lesson I would like to draw from the film is this. "Rabbit" has an excuse for being a wigger. He is the son of a trailer-park slut. There is no mention of his father. He grew up surrounded by blacks. No wonder he acts like them. (However, white kids from affluent suburbs and intact families and decent schools have no excuse for being wiggers—except sheer mental laziness and a craven desire to be "cool" according to standards set by people who want to destroy them.)

But because of his white genetic heritage, Rabbit has the brains to see that acting like a black is not the way to succeed. Rabbit will succeed because he chooses to think and then act like a white man. Eminem may be a wigger on stage, but he never would have made his records or this movie by acting that way off stage.

So, in a way, Eminem is a positive role model for young whites. *8 Mile* shows the kind of world one lives in when one acts like a black—and that the way out is to act like a white man.

VNN, November 2002

FIREFLY

Joss Whedon's *Firefly* is a science fiction series that lived and died on the Fox Network in the fall of 2002. Fourteen episodes were shot, but only 11 were aired before the series was canceled, to the consternation of the surprisingly large number of loyal fans that the show conjured up in the split second of its existence. In my view, *Firefly* is one of the best sci-fi shows ever, second only to *Battlestar Galactica* (the new one, of course, not the original, which I call *Battlescow Spasmatica*, just so there's no confusion).

Firefly, like most contemporary TV, has a multiracial cast, including a white man married to a black woman (to me, that just underscores the sci-fi element). If you are going to enjoy the show, you'll simply have to overlook that. But seven of the nine cast members are white, all of them highly appealing. Furthermore, the substance of the series has a deep spiritual appeal to whites, for it combines two paradigmatically "Faustian" genres: the Western and the Space Opera. In essence, *Firefly* is a Space Western. (Cf. *Star Trek*'s "final frontier.") The genre mash-up also makes *Firefly* a quintessentially "archeofuturist" drama.

Firefly has a number of politically incorrect elements.

First of all, the back story was inspired by the American Civil War and its aftermath, when many Southerners went west to escape Reconstruction. *Firefly* is set in the 26th century, after the human race has spread to another vast star system with a number of populous central planets and a Wild West of hundreds of moons. In the aftermath of a civil war between the Alliance (the Union) and the Independents (the Confederacy), the defeated Independents have "gone West," looking for freedom. But the centralized Alliance regime keeps extending its web of control.

The Firefly of the title is a smuggler's spaceship called *Serenity*, captained by Malcolm Reynolds, played by Nathan Fillion. Reynolds was a sergeant in the Independents' army (the browncoats). In short, he is a Confederate of sorts. (Fillion himself is a descendant of Confederate general Jubal Early.)

Second, the Independents fought for freedom and self-determination, and throughout the series, their values are shown to be natural and noble, whereas the Alliance is shown to be arrogant, meddlesome, and ultimately totalitarian—albeit a hidden, soft, liberal form of totalitarianism. Unlike the Confederacy, the Independents were not fighting for slavery, which seems to exist under the Alliance, at least on the outer planets, and is treated with contempt by the freedom-loving crew of *Serenity*. These libertarian, anti-big government, and anti-paternalist sentiments are, of course, unusual in television today, where they are usually ascribed to unsavory, villainous rednecks. (I hasten to add that this kind of individualism is inimical to the racial collectivism of the New Right.)

The Alliance is apparently a kind of One World government scheme, an Anglo-Chinese condominium formed of previously independent colonies established by the Americans and Chinese, the two nations that went on to colonize space. Or so the story goes. Of course America has no space program now, because we need to spend our tax dollars birthin' Mexican anchor babies and giving free cell phones to Negroes. The Chinese may go forward into the Space Age, but America is going back to the Stone Age.

A third politically incorrect aspect of *Firefly* is its overwhelming paleomasculinity. Malcolm Reynolds is a particularly well-realized portrait of an Aryan alpha male. Although he is an outlaw, he lives by an Aryan code of honor. He is courageous, intelligent, and highly chivalrous. Although he is in love with Inara (Morena Baccarin), a high-class whore ("companion") who travels on his ship and grants it an air of respectability, he disapproves of her life and of his love for her, so he never manages to tell her his feelings.

Inara, for her part, reciprocates his feelings and shares his inability to express them. Although the companions dress sexual commerce up in the trappings of a religious order, Inara has discovered that there is something truly sacred about sex, something that is entirely incompatible with her liberated, promiscuous, ironic, and profane existence. In the end, she leaves the ship because the only alternative is to submit completely to Mal's strength and give up whoring.

Don't these old-fashioned "hang-ups" about morality and sex and monogamy add a certain depth and drama to human existence? Ah well, "freedom" marches on.

This brings us to a fourth politically incorrect aspect of *Firefly*: one can't make a Western without incorporating a whole range of archaic values like chivalry, patriarchy, and simple politeness, which are shown in a largely positive light. A case in point: in one episode, Mal acquires a very submissive wife who cooks and serves him dinner. Following the feminist script, second mate Zoë (played by black actress Gina Torres, whom I find grotesque) is outraged when her husband, the pilot Wash (Alan Tudyk) expresses approval. In a later episode, however, after Wash has established his heroic *bona fides*, we find Zoë cooking and serving his dinner. And not long after that, she is talking about having his children.

Another politically incorrect aspect of *Firefly* is its treatment of religion. Joss Whedon is an atheist, but he treats religion with the utmost seriousness. Mal Reynolds is portrayed as an atheist, but at the very beginning of the pilot, it is clear that he was actually a religious man who lost his faith when the Independents were defeated. One of the passengers on *Serenity* is Shepherd Book (played by the black actor Ron Glass), a traveling Christian minister. (Buddhism also continues to exist in this universe as well.) For Whedon, the significance of religion lies less in the fictions in which men believe, than in the real human needs that belief satisfies.

Joss Whedon's other series include *Buffy the Vampire Slayer*, *Angel*, and *Dollhouse*. He plays entirely within the P.C. rules of the TV industry, but for all that, he is one of its most talented and imaginative storytellers. *Firefly* has all the marks of a Whedon series, chiefly brilliant storytelling, light humor and irony around a core of deep seriousness and real emotional power, and great linguistic inventiveness (laconic corn pone with expletives in Mandarin), which adds an important concreteness to the alternate universes he creates. The series also has beautiful music, particularly in the last episodes.

Some series take a couple of years to work the bugs out. *Star Trek: The Next Generation* was a miserable thing until the third season, for instance. *Firefly* has a strong pilot, followed by three middling episodes and one crappy one ("Safe," Drew Z. Greenberg's tale of how two members of the crew are kidnapped by some savage, superstitious redneck *goyim* who want to burn them as witches), then it soars with episode six ("Our Mrs. Reynolds") and never comes down. My favorite episodes are number eight, "Out of Gas"; number nine, "Ariel," which feels like a feature film in 42 minutes; and number twelve, "The Message," which would have been the most moving story ever told on TV — if Fox had seen fit to air it.

I highly recommend *Firefly*. But I warn you. If you watch it, you will not want it to end. Many of the series' diehard fans, who dubbed themselves "browncoats," felt the same way. Eventually their campaign to revive the series led to Joss Whedon making a feature film, *Serenity*, to bring some closure to the story. I review it below.

Counter-Currents/*North American New Right*,
March 27, 2013

HERO

Chinese director Zhang Yimou's *Hero* (2002) is a profoundly beautiful and moving film that celebrates Chinese culture and tradition and promotes noble and patriotic sentiments. *Hero* is based very loosely on an actual event that took place in 227 BCE near the end of the Warring States period. It tells the story of an attempt to assassinate Qin Shi Huang, the King of Qin and later the first Emperor of China.

Because of the previous attempts of three assassins—Sky, Flying Snow, and Broken Sword—the King of Qin does not allow anyone within 100 paces of his throne. However, when word comes that a local prefect known only as Nameless has killed all three assassins, the King summons him to court to be rewarded.

For killing Sky, Nameless is rewarded with 1,000 pieces of gold and feudal authority over 1,000 households. He is invited to advance to 20 paces from the throne, drink with the King, and tell him the story of his battle.

The battle will surprise anyone who is unfamiliar with the conventions of Chinese *wuxia* cinema, which I like to call "flying Chinaman" films. The Chinese believe that their martial arts can endow them with superpowers, including the ability to fly. It seems jarring to most, but as someone who has had recurring dreams of flight since childhood, I found it easy to suspend disbelief. It is no more jarring than people breaking into song in a musical, and it must be appreciated for its beauty, not its realism. It is a breathtaking combination of martial arts with gymnastics, ballet, and acrobatics.

Next, Nameless killed Broken Sword and Flying Snow, a male-female team of estranged lovers. As his reward, Nameless is given 10,000 pieces of gold, authority over 5,000 households, and invited to sit 10 paces from the throne, drink with the King, and tell his story.

It is here that Yimou adopts one of his most bold and captivating cinematic gestures. The tale of Flying Snow and Broken Sword is told three times, each in a different color scheme: red, blue, and white. Later, when Broken Sword tells his own tale, the color scheme is green. Each tint indicates a particular subjective slant, but, as with Akira Kurosawa's *Rashomon*, there is no question that there is a real story under all the different perspectives.

When Nameless tells the story of how he defeated Flying Snow and Broken Sword, the color palette is red, and they are portrayed with scruffy-looking bangs. The suggestion is that they are emotionally overwrought and impulsive. Nameless explains that Flying Snow once had an affair with Sky, which is why she and Broken Sword were estranged. When he showed them Sky's broken spear, their simmering jealousy flared up, and Flying Snow killed Broken Sword. The next morning, Flying Snow met Nameless in single combat. But she was emotionally out of control, so he was able to kill her.

The King, however, disbelieves the story. He met Flying Snow and Broken Sword three years before, when they stormed his palace together and nearly killed him. He saw them to be noble warriors, not the hysterical punks described by Nameless.

The King concludes that Nameless, too, is an assassin. Sky, Flying Snow, and Broken Sword must have sacrificed their lives so that Nameless could advance to 10 paces from the throne. Nameless must have perfected a move that would allow him to kill the King at that distance before help could come. "It seems," says the King, "that I shall not escape my fate."

When the King retells the story of Flying Snow and Broken Sword as he imagines it, the color scheme is a celestial blue. The two assassins are elegantly groomed and attired, exquisitely sensitive and decorous, and above all noble. It reveals that the King has a romantic and chivalrous imagination.

When Broken Sword tells Nameless the story of his life, culminating in his attempt to assassinate the King three years before, he explains that at the moment he could have killed the King, he stopped, for he realized that there was a greater good than his personal mission, a greater good than the kingdom of Zhao for which he fought: namely the good of "our land," by which he meant not Zhao or Qin, but all of China. The good of China required peace, and peace required unification under a single Emperor. The King of Qin had the power to unify the seven kingdoms, so the greater good demanded that he be allowed to continue. So Broken Sword aborted his mission when victory was in his grasp.

Nameless relates this story to the King, who is moved to tears — as are most viewers. He claims that nobody before had understood his motivations. Even his own court regarded him as a tyrant. In truth, Qin Shi Huang was a tyrant and a philistine, who in the name of unity burned books and executed scholars. *Hero* portrays him as a sensitive and refined man who was deeply concerned with the good of all his people. He may not be the real first Emperor, but he would be an ideal first Emperor, rather like Cyrus as portrayed in Xenophon's *The Education of Cyrus.*.

I will say no more about the plot, save that history records that the King of Qin actually did go on to unify China as the first Emperor, building the Great Wall and a massive tomb complex, guarded by a life-sized terracotta army, which is still being excavated near present-day Xi'an.

Hero is an epic film, yet it tells its story with amazing economy, lasting only 99 minutes. It is emotionally moving and conveys a very serious moral and political message, namely the good of national unity and the forms of self-discipline and self-sacrifice necessary to achieve it. Another important theme, exemplified in all the characters, is the unity of cultural refinement and martial virtue. Calligraphy and swordsmanship are developed in unison and illuminate one another. *Hero* upholds the full range of noble, aristocratic virtues: courage, self-control, self-discipline, good manners, aesthetic refinement, chivalry, and self-sacrifice. It is a pleasure to see a movie free of clods screaming obscenities at each other and rutting like pigs.

Hero is very well-acted. Nameless is played by Jet Li, Flying Snow by Maggie Cheung, and Sky by Donnie Yen. The best performances are the magnificent Chen Daoming as the King and Tony Leung as Broken Sword. But even minor roles are superbly realized, my favorite being the dignified and unflappable elderly master of a calligraphy school under military siege.

Hero is also a feast for the senses, with breathtaking landscapes and sumptuous interiors. The opening scenes, when

Nameless arrives at the Qin court, are particularly spectacular and clearly influenced by *Triumph of the Will*. The ritual and hierarchy of the Qin court, with its Greek chorus of gray-clad courtiers who swarm like mice, is awe-inspiring, as is the march of the Qin army. The gorgeous soundtrack, which sounds like Chinese Ennio Morricone music, was composed by Tan Dun, who has also composed an opera about Qin Shi Huang called *The First Emperor*.

    I highly recommend *Hero*. It is a pleasure to see that not everything Made in China is cheap, toxic junk. But it is also sad that whites must go so far afield to find films that uphold patriotism, refinement, and nobility. Spiritually speaking, however, I found this film far less alien than most Hollywood movies, even those with all white casts. Watch *Hero* for a concrete experience of what movies would be like if our film industry were not controlled by an alien and hostile people out to degrade and destroy us.

Counter-Currents/*North American New Right*,
January 10, 2013

THE HOBBIT:
AN UNEXPECTED JOURNEY

I am sorry to report that I was disappointed by *The Hobbit: An Unexpected Journey*, the first installment of Peter Jackson's film trilogy based on J. R. R. Tolkien's *The Hobbit*.

Jackson's first mistake was trying to make a trilogy at all. *The Hobbit* is shorter than any of the three volumes of *The Lord of the Rings*. Thus its story could have been told completely and satisfyingly in a single movie of around two hours.

While *The Lord of the Rings* movies are long, they are actually in many ways masterworks of dramatic compression. To make *The Hobbit* into a trilogy, however, Jackson has attempted a masterwork of dramatic padding. Unfortunately, there is no such thing as a masterwork of dramatic padding.

There are three main types of padding in this movie: (1) slow and boring sequences, (2) fast and lame sequences, and (3) additions to the text.

The first 30 minutes of the movie have a particularly slow and padded feel. It is as if Jackson decided simply to use the book as a script.

Later in the movie, we get a lot of quick and lame padding: chase scenes, battle scenes, scenes of people falling and holding on for dear life, scenes of people falling hundreds or thousands of feet, again and again, and then bouncing back into action, as indestructible as Wile E. Coyote. It is supposed to be exciting. But it is so overdone that it becomes tedious and farcical. (There was a bit of this kind of padding in *The Return of the King*, e.g., as Sam, Frodo, and Gollum climbed the secret stairway into Mordor, and near the end when they reach Mount Doom.)

The extra-textual padding comes from other works by Tolkien, such as the appendices of *The Lord of the Rings*. These appendices provide some context for *The Hobbit*, and if they had been used judiciously, they could have added more than just starch and filler. But in Jackson's hands, all they amount to is a series of contrived and jarring cameos from characters from *The Lord of the Rings*.

Only four characters from *The Hobbit* actually reappear in *The Lord of the Rings*: Gandalf, Bilbo Baggins, Elrond, and Gollum. But in this movie, we also see Frodo, the aged Bilbo played by Ian Holm (although he actually looked like somebody else made up to look like Ian Holm), Saruman, and Galadriel. The wizard Radagast, who is only mentioned in the novel, is written into the story and given quite an extensive role.

The trouble with all this padding is that the basic plot of *The Hobbit* is a little padded as it is, with a one-damn-thing-after-another feel to it.

Jackson's second mistake is that he failed to strike the right tone for the movie. *The Hobbit* was written for teens and young adults. *The Lord of the Rings* virtually defined fantasy literature for grownups. *The Hobbit* is a fairy tale, whereas *The Lord of the Rings* is mythic and epic. Like every fairy tale, *The Hobbit* does touch upon serious themes, but they are treated in a light and farcical way. *The Lord of the Rings* is far more serious and sublime and moving. Jackson should have remained faithful to the storyline of *The Hobbit*, but he should also have teased out and amplified its serious elements, to unify it with *The Lord of the Rings* trilogy. Jackson does try to do this, but he also turns the farcical elements up to 11, and junks the story up with extra-textual elements, giving the whole movie a diffuse and strangely schizophrenic feel.

I did somehow manage to enjoy this movie. It got better as it went on. I do recommend it. It is Tolkien, after all. If you love Tolkien like I do, you've already seen it anyway.

I have touched on the bad parts. The best parts include the encounter with the three trolls, which is genuinely funny, and Bilbo's encounter with Gollum, which is pure magic.

Martin Freeman was well-cast as the younger Bilbo, and his performance is as good as Jackson allows, getting better and better as the movie picks up its pace. The same is true of Ian McKellen's Gandalf. As for the 13 dwarves, you can hardly develop so many characters. Richard Armitage is a charismatic Thorin Oakenshield, Ken Stott is an extremely likable Balin, and Aiden Turner as Kíli is the Legolas of this trilogy, probably the world's first dwarf sex symbol. (None of the dwarves are played by actual dwarf actors, apparently.)

The music by Howard Shore was beautiful, as were the sets and costumes and landscapes (although the overuse of pastels gave many scenes the creepy, cloying tweeness of parts of *The Lovely Bones*). The special effects, particularly the monsters, were breathtaking.

Like *The Lord of the Rings*, *The Hobbit* is completely free of any anti-white ideology. Everything about this movie is a celebration of whiteness, with a particular emphasis on Nordic and Celtic myth, culture, and art.

But somehow, overall, the magic is lacking. This is *The Hobbit* as brought to us by the director of *King Kong* and *The Lovely Bones* rather than *The Lord of the Rings*. Peter Jackson was certainly capable of making a great movie of *The Hobbit*, but I believe that he simply lacked faith in the material. Let us hope that the next two movies are much more tightly edited and properly pitched, so that this one is merely an anomaly, merely Peter Jackson's equivalent of *The Phantom Menace*.

Counter-Currents/*North American New Right*,
December 15, 2012

THE HOBBIT:
THE DESOLATION OF SMAUG

I was hoping that the first installment of *The Hobbit* trilogy would be merely a *Phantom Menace* moment, and that Peter Jackson would produce leaner, tighter sequels that would pull this ill-conceived trilogy out of the crapper. But no. I am saddened to report that *The Desolation of Smaug* is freighted with the same problems as the first movie, and more.

Jackson's first mistake, of course, was to puff up J. R. R. Tolkien's slender book into a trilogy at all. The whole story could have been told in a single, two-hour movie. This decision was, of course, based simply on greed, and it necessitated a great deal of dramatic fluffing and padding. Hence new characters, new scenes, and especially new thrills, chills, and battles, have been added.

Jackson's second mistake was to give reign to his very unattractive penchant for megalomania and cinematic one-upmanship, which first emerged in *King Kong*. (*Jurassic Park* has dinosaurs? I'll show you dinosaurs!) The sad truth is that even as a trilogy, *The Hobbit* could have been good if Jackson were not trying to one-up *The Lord of the Rings*.

Of course, to outdo *The Lord of the Rings*, Jackson also has to redo it in part, which means that a lot of the new material stuck in here feels derivative of *The Lord of the Rings*. So we have an elf maiden like Arwen, who, like Arwen, heals a poisoned wound (from a Morgul arrow, this time), and who flirts with a non-elf (the cute dwarf), etc., etc.

This lethal combination of derivativeness and one-upmanship gives vast stretches of *The Hobbit* the feel of nothing more than a parody of *The Lord of the Rings*. (Perhaps Jackson's next project will be nine three-hour films based on *Bored of the Rings*.)

Jackson's third error is the farcical cartoonishness of the action sequences. I admit that I enjoyed the elves and orcs battling it out as the dwarves make their escape in barrels. But when the dwarves do battle with Smaug in their underground city, the sequence is so overly busy and absurdly implausible that the net effect is rather uninvolving.

But it gets worse. As the greedy, scheming master of Laketown (played by the Jew Stephen Fry) addresses his people, the camera pans over the audience. At first, I thought some Uruk-hai had crept in. But no, when the camera returned again and again, it became clear that Laketown is afflicted with dark, vibrant, nappy racial diversity.

Peter Jackson endured more than a decade of *kvetching* about the "racism" of his faithful adaptation of *The Lord of the Rings*, in which the races of Middle Earth are portrayed as white and their enemies as dark. But now he has caved. The first *Hobbit* movie pullulates with pasty orcs and goblins. And now we have Negroes and Papuans in frigid Laketown.

This movie is an insult to the taste and intelligence of its audience and to the memory of J. R. R. Tolkien. I can't recommend it, and it will only be out of a sense of duty to you, my audience, that I will rouse myself to see the final film next December.

The supreme irony of this exercise in wretched excess is that the tale of Smaug is, of course, a parable on the dangers of greed and megalomania. It is rather amazing that Peter Jackson could work on this project for years without ever glimpsing himself in it.

Counter-Currents/*North American New Right*,
December 16, 2013

THE HOBBIT:
THE BATTLE OF FIVE ARMIES

In his remake of *King Kong*, Peter Jackson dragged out the big ape's death so long it felt like a lifetime. At the time, it merely seemed like a lapse of taste. In hindsight, it seems like the beginning of a whole new career characterized by megalomania, greed, one-upmanship, self-indulgence, and bad taste. It was just the first symptom of the dragon sickness that has now consumed him.

The Battle of Five Armies begins with Smaug giving Laketown the Dresden treatment, then moves on to a grand battle between elves, orcs, dwarves, and men, with some birds and bears and bats and wizards thrown in. There is also a battle of Sauron and the nine spectral Nazgûl against Saruman, Galadriel, and Elrond. In short, the movie is mostly fights and special effects: beautifully made, occasionally memorable, but empty overall.

Whether I recommend it or not makes no practical difference. If you have seen the first two movies, of course you will see this one. Peter Jackson Inc. is banking on it, and therein lies the rub. (If you have not seen the first two films it will make no sense.)

As I noted in my reviews of the first two movies, *The Hobbit* is a children's novel that is shorter than any of the three volumes of *The Lord of the Rings*. It could be told as a single two hour movie. But why settle for just one billion-dollar movie, when you can mutilate the book, turn it into three two-and-a-half hour movies, and rake in three times the gold? Jackson merely had to pad out the story with new characters, new scenes, and new subplots, all of them paper-thin, manipulative, and melodramatic. He also added new battles, new chases, and new narrow escapes, all of which are spectacular to watch but about as realistic as *Road Runner* cartoons. The net effect is uninvolving.

To make matters worse, much of the new material is derivative of *The Lord of the Rings*. Either our filmmaker lacked inspiration, or it was simply an occasion for Jackson to one-up himself. You thought the crumbling Bridge of Khazad-dûm was cool in *The Fellowship of the Ring*? Well, wait until you see the falling tower in *The Battle of Five Armies*. Did you like the orc *Aufmarsch* from Minas Morgul in *The Return of the King*? Well, something all too similar (but less spectacular) awaits you here. Like the sandworms of Arrakis? Wait till you see the wereworms of Middle Earth. Did you like Galadriel's dark queen tantrum in *Fellowship*? Well, she tops that here too. Etc., etc. Unfortunately, when you combine derivativeness and one-upmanship, the result is parody.

Finally, as Kevin MacDonald pointed out in a review of *The Hobbit*'s first installment,[1] Peter Jackson has caved in to political correctness. In *The Lord of the Rings*, he was faithful to Tolkien's vision, portraying the peoples of Middle Earth as white and the human and non-human hosts of Sauron as non-white. In the first *Hobbit* movie, however, Jackson introduces white-skinned (and even blue-eyed) orcs and goblins. In the second film he includes non-whites — Asians and blacks or Papuans — among the citizens of Laketown.

In the new film, the women and children of Laketown — like those of Rohan in *The Two Towers* — are barricaded in a hall while their men fight. This, of course, makes sense, because biologically speaking, men are more expendable than women in a fight for survival. In the new film, however, a mannish suffragette rallies the women to go off and die with the men. At least the connection between feminism and racial suicide is relatively clear here. (And before you remind me of how Eowyn disguised herself as a man and went into battle in *The Return of the King*, let me remind you that Athena, Joan of Arc, and Eowyn are exceptions, not rules, and exceptions should never become the rule.)

When the characters are not scurrying around fighting one another, *The Battle of Five Armies* dwells at length — but without depth or a hint of self-knowledge — on how greed corrupts integrity. The whole wretched trilogy is ample proof of that.

Counter-Currents/*North American New Right*,
December 19, 2014

---

[1] Kevin MacDonald, "Implicitly White Themes in *The Hobbit*," http://www.theoccidentalobserver.net/2012/12/implicitly-white-themes-in-the-hobbit/

HOORAY FOR BOLLYWOOD:
DEVDAS & KABHI KUSHI KABHIE GHAM

Sick of Hollywood? Try Bollywood. "Bollywood" is the world's largest film industry, the Indian film industry, centered in Mumbai (Bombay). My first exposure to Bollywood was over lunch in an Indian Chaat House. A music video compilation was playing on a big-screen TV, and I was totally captivated.

Although the words were all in Hindi, with no subtitles, the messages and emotions were universal and immediately intelligible. The videos fell into two basic categories. One type featured Western-style pop music with contemporary clothes and settings. The influences of MTV, American advertising, and American pop culture were strong and obvious. The other type featured more traditional-sounding Indian music, costumes, and settings. But both types had a lot in common.

First of all, they featured elaborate, large-ensemble choreography that has not been in vogue in Western films since the 1930s. Second, none of these videos displayed a shred of cynicism, irony, sarcasm, or coarseness, but rather the idealism, sincerity, playful humor, and decorousness that have disappeared from Western movies since the early 1960s. Third, all the videos were centered on wholesome, romantic, sentimental boy meets girl, boy pines for girl, boy woos girl, boy marries girl themes. Fourth, many videos featured large, multigenerational families and communicated messages of filial piety and solidarity. How many happy grandmothers have you seen in MTV videos? Fifth, the caste system was in evidence: the lead actors usually are fair-skinned and have European features. Some even have blue or green eyes. The fairer dancers were closer to the cameras, while the darker ones were buried in the back.

I went right out and purchased a couple collections of Bollywood music videos. But it took a long time before I actually sat down to watch a full Bollywood movie. They tend to be long. There is a bewildering array of choices. And, finally, virtually every major Bollywood movie is a musical. But I am an opera snob, and I really hate most Broadway and Hollywood musicals. So I thought I would find a whole Hindi musical boring and ridiculous.

I was delighted to discover that I was completely wrong. Indians take musicals seriously and produce large numbers of them, whereas in the West musicals are few and far between, and like *Moulin Rouge* and *Chicago*, they are played ironically. The kind of uninhibited romantic sensibility that makes it seem natural to burst into song and dance has no place in contemporary Western movies, but it flourishes in Bollywood.

I have now seen half a dozen recent Bollywood musicals — admittedly not a basis for very strong generalizations — and I am totally hooked. I wish to recommend two in particular, *Kabhi Kushi Kabhie Gham* (roughly: "Sometimes Happy, Sometimes Sad") and *Devdas* (named for the main character). These are good places to start.

Devdas is my first full-length Bollywood movie. It is a truly great movie that I strongly recommend to all my readers.

I am told that *Devdas* is uncharacteristic because of its portrayal of unresolved family conflict and bleak, tragic ending. But I chose it because it is based on the 1917 Bengali novel of the same name by Saratchanda Chattopadhyaya (1876–1938), and I had already read and enjoyed his novel *Srikanta*. Chattopadhyaya is a great writer, the inventor of the modern Indian novel. Yet *Devdas*, like *Srikanta*, is a profoundly subversive work, attacking Hindu traditions, e.g., patriarchy, arranged marriages, the caste system, by showing how they tear apart two star-crossed lovers, Devdas and Paro. But, like *Romeo and Juliet* or the novels of Jane Austen, *Devdas* is a subversive *classic*, which in today's culture seems quite conservative.

Devdas takes place primarily in Bengal in the early years of the 20th century. It is set in the palatial mansions of fabulously wealthy Bengali *zamindars* (land barons) and in a brothel frequented by aristocrats. The plot is quite simple: Devdas and Paro were childhood sweethearts. When Devdas returns after years of studying in England, they begin an intense courtship, but their match is opposed by Devdas' parents, especially his stern and cold father, on the grounds that, although Paro is of the same caste and social class, her mother is from a long line of temple dancers, which makes her an unsuitable match (an eminently sensible aristocratic prejudice against showbiz types also found in Western Aryan societies). Devdas' mother nevertheless cruelly leads Paro's mother to think that a match is in the offing, only to rebuke her in a public and humiliating way. Paro's mother defends her honor in an absolutely riveting and powerful scene, then vows to marry Paro to an even better family than Devdas'. Devdas knuckles under to his family and cuts his ties with Paro, only coming to his senses after she has been married. He then moves in with a famous courtesan, Chandramukhi—who falls in love with him, even though he spurns her affections—and turns to the bottle. And although both Paro and Chandramukhi try to save Devdas, the ending is unrelentingly tragic. This movie is a two-hanky tear-jerker, and is almost symphonic in its orchestration and development of small events and running themes into emotionally wrenching crescendos.

Devdas has a huge cast of distinguished Indian actors. Devdas is played by Shahrukh Khan, the leading male actor in India. Khan is not all that handsome, though his puppy dog features seem to appeal to teenage girls, but he is a fine actor with genuine charm and who sure-footedly traverses the range from cartoonish humor to heart-breaking tragedy. The green-eyed Brahmin Aishwarya Rai, the 1994 Miss World, plays Paro, Devdas's childhood sweetheart. Madhuri Dixit, one of India's most distinguished actresses, plays Chandramuki.

Devdas is one of the most visually opulent movies I have ever seen. The sets are not just palatial, they are outright palaces. The large-scale musical numbers are dazzling, and the costumes and jewelry of the lead actresses are as stunning as the actresses themselves.

Kabhi Kushi Kabhie Gham (K3G for short) is every bit as good as *Devdas*, with fantastic musical numbers and a much happier ending. As the box says, "It's all about loving your parents." K3G is set in present-day New Delhi, primarily in the palatial mansion of business tycoon Yashovardhan Raichand and his wife Nandini (played by real-life husband and wife Amitabh and Jaya Bachchan).

Yashovardhan is an immensely impressive patriarch. He

deeply loves his wife and two sons, Rahul (Shahrukh Khan) and Rohan (played by tall, athletic, green-eyed heart-throb Hrithik Roshan). He deeply respects his mother and deceased father and the traditions of his family. He governs both his business and his family according to these traditions, and he is an absolute ruler in his household. (Bachchan is a towering, bearded man with a deep voice, whose eyes appear to be dark blue or green in one scene.)

The film falls into two parts that take place about ten years apart. In the first part, set in New Delhi, Yashovardhan decides to arrange a marriage between Rahul and the daughter of a close family friend without even consulting his son. But he discovers that Rahul has fallen in love with Anjali (played by amber-eyed beauty Kajol), the gorgeous but klutzy and gauche daughter of the family nanny. Yashovardhan feels humiliated in front of his friend and desired daughter-in-law and betrayed by his son. And, to add insult to injury, Anjali is not an appropriate match. The two lovers stick together, however, and elope to London. Yashovardhan disowns Rahul, and the family is broken in two. This is especially traumatic given how close Hindu families traditionally are. Yashovardhan's elderly mother laments that she will be unable to face God until her family is brought back together.

In part two, set primarily in London, the second son, Rohan, now all grown up, vows to bring the family back together. The London sequences are sometimes rather disturbing. They are heavy on Western consumerism and tackiness, particularly the character of "Poo," Anjali's now grown-up little sister, who is played by Kareena Kapoor. Kapoor has a nice figure (fleshy in all the ways that promise fecundity), but is not really pretty. Her face is too wide, her lips too big, and her nose too long. (Indians will forgive a lot in a woman with emerald green eyes.) She is made positively grotesque with her trashy Western clothes and makeup. I think that these scenes are generally satirical, sometimes clumsily so, trying to portray Western popular culture as shallow, trashy, and un-Indian, but sometimes I am not so sure. There is clearly a great deal of Indian nationalism in this movie, and a lot of hostility to the English.

(English people should see this movie. It might encourage them to make the Indians "Quit Britain.") Well, Rohan uses a bit of trickery, helped by an opportune tragedy, and succeeds in reuniting the family, with a three-hanky tear-jerker ending (and a Big Fat Hindu Wedding under the closing credits).

I am thoroughly impressed by the healthy and tasteful treatment of sex and romance in these films. There are some very sexy, very romantic scenes. There are hints of the sado-masochistic aspects of normal heterosexual intercourse. But there is nothing the least bit crude and pornographic. Even the brothel scenes in *Devdas* are quite decorous. Indians still realize that the erotic involves concealing as well as revealing the physical aspect of sex. Eroticism is sex (nature) with something added on: the products of the imagination. So when, in *Devdas*, Shahrukh Khan removes a thorn from Paro's foot or gives her a scar by striking her with a heavy pearl necklace, or, in K3G, when he slides bracelets over Anjali's hands, asking again and again, "Am I hurting you yet?," the effect is far more erotic than the clinical nudity and mechanical humping so routine in even the best Hollywood films today.

Another impressive feature of Bollywood films, even very modern ones, is their treatment of religion. Hindu myth, Hindu piety, and Hindu festivals are everywhere, and they are treated with a dignity that is seldom seen in contemporary Western films. These are not films about religion. There is nothing preachy or didactic about them. These are films about life, and in India Hinduism is an important part of life. What the audience holds sacred is not mocked.

Bollywood films take some getting used to. It can be wearying to read subtitles for more than three hours—especially when you don't want to take your eyes off the screen. As in all foreign films, there are culture-specific references that leave one puzzled—although, frankly, there are more of these in the average half-hour British comedy than in a three-hour Bollywood film. And nothing much hinges, for instance, on knowing precisely what is meant by unscrewing a woman's nose ring. That it is a euphemism for sex is clear enough.

Since all of our tastes have been corrupted by Western popular culture, a lot of things in these films (besides the penchant of characters to burst into song and dance) will seem "corny": sweeping melodramatic gestures, comic relief, asides to the audience, dramatic soliloquies, inspired, often beautiful, poetic language, and impossibly witty, rapid-fire repartee. In short, all the hackneyed devices used by bunglers from Sophocles to Shakespeare.

Why does Bollywood portray sincere emotions, wholesome, marriage-oriented heterosexual romance, traditional family values, sane racial distinctions, and dignified religious piety, while Hollywood does not? Because, for all of its Western borrowings, Bollywood is a genuinely national cinema. Bollywood seems to respect and uphold Indian values. But Hollywood is in the hands of a foreign and hostile nation, the Jews, who are using it to mock, undermine, and ultimately destroy white American society.

Bollywood films may look radically foreign. But, in substance, they embody the values of a healthy Aryan society. Hollywood films, by contrast, may have a more familiar look. But the values they push are profoundly alien and pure poison.

I pride myself on my ability with words, but I really cannot do these films justice. You must simply see them to appreciate how much we have lost by allowing Jews to control our popular culture.

(By the way: I am glad to import Indian movies, visit India, and host Indian visitors. But I do not want to import any Indian immigrants, thank you. There are more than a billion Indians with a whole subcontinent to themselves, quite enough room for them to propagate their own cultures and branches of the Caucasian race. Their presence in the homelands of Western Aryans is unwelcome because it makes it all the harder for us to propagate our own genes and cultures.)

VNN, May 7, 2003

HOUSE OF FLYING DAGGERS

Anyone who watches Zhang Yimou's *Hero* (2002) is likely to want more. Thus I highly recommend Yimou's next movie, *House of Flying Daggers* (2004), which is very much in the same vein: a martial arts film set in the exotic past with complex and interesting characters, impossible but spectacular fights, gorgeous landscapes, and dazzling costumes and sets. *House of Flying Daggers* was filmed in China and Ukraine. Most of it is set outdoors, in magnificent forests of birch and bamboo, filmed in the lushest colors imaginable.

House of Flying Daggers does, however, differ from *Hero* in important ways, and even though you must see it, it is frankly not as good a movie.

Hero is set in 227 BCE, just before the rise of the first Chinese Empire. It is springtime for China, a youthful, expansive phase of culture. There is great artistic and cultural refinement, but overall, society is characterized more by potentiality than actuality. Great vital energies are surging forth. Something new and glorious is on the horizon. The emergence of this new order both rests upon and inculcates heroism: single-minded civic virtue and self-sacrifice.

House of Flying Daggers is set more than 1,000 years later, in 859 CE, during the waning years of the great Tang Dynasty (618–907 CE), one of China's political, cultural, and artistic Golden Ages. It is a time of spectacular cultural refinement and beauty. But it is also a time of decadence and decay. People are emotionally self-indulgent, mercurial, and pleasure-oriented. The movie is set in a dazzlingly colorful autumn, which is appropriate, because civilization is in autumn phase, when the leaves display their greatest beauty before falling dead to the ground. It is also a time of political disintegration, in which civic virtue is weak, corruption is rampant, and new communities are arising to claim the allegiance and idealism once commanded by the empire.

The House of Flying Daggers is one such community. It is

an initiatic martial-spiritual order of assassins that uses crime and terrorism to protect the people from the rich, corrupt, and powerful. Along with feudal warlords, such societies have challenged centralized imperial rule throughout Chinese history, stretching from the Yellow Turban Rebellion of 184 CE under the Han Dynasty to the Boxer Rebellion of 1898 to 1901 under the Qing Dynasty. (This is one reason for the zealous repression of Falun Gong today.)

The character of the times is epitomized by the character of Jin (played by Okinawan-Taiwanese actor Takeshi Kaneshiro), a young policeman who is a fantastically accomplished swordsman and bowman but who cannot take anything seriously. Jin is tall, handsome, and strong. Life presents him with endless opportunities for martial and amorous adventures, which are just games for him. Like the wind, he glides from one distraction to another, caressing the surfaces of life and never staying in one place.

At the beginning of *House of Flying Daggers*, we learn that the police have assassinated the old leader of the House, but a mysterious new leader has arisen to take his place. The police are given 10 days to assassinate him or her, an impossible deadline. It is decided that Jin will infiltrate the House. He goes undercover to the Peony Pavilion, a fantastically lavish brothel. He has learned that a girl assassin from the House is working there undercover. He discovers that she is a dancer named Mei (Zhang Ziyi, who played Moon in *Hero*). Mei is blind, but her other senses appear fantastically heightened.

Jin contrives a disturbance, which leads to him and Mei being arrested. Once in police custody, she is threatened with torture. Jin then contrives to break them out of jail, hoping that she will lead him, and the police, straight to the new leader of the House of Flying Daggers.

It is all a game to Jin. He feigns flight from the police. He feigns affection for Mei. But events take their own course. His feelings for Mei become real. So does his flight from the authorities, as he is forced to kill soldiers sent by a general who wants the chase to be believable and who cares nothing about the lives of Jin or his own soldiers. Jin, however, does not have the character to deal with serious emotions or serious danger. He flees—but he is also drawn back to Mei. His one constant is vacillation.

Mei is a much more serious and idealistic character. But she has also developed feelings for Jin, and when it becomes clear that her feelings do not matter to the House of Flying Daggers and that she is just as expendable to them as Jin is to the authorities, her loyalties also waver before the choice of duty or personal happiness.

A third character is introduced who is also in love with Mei. He is devastated to learn that Mei no longer loves him but loves Jin instead. So he too is faced with the choice of doing his duty or following his personal feelings.

This being the autumn phase of civilization, all three characters make the wrong decisions, and the movie comes to a grim and emotionally shattering conclusion as an autumn meadow is blanketed by a sudden snowstorm. Winter and death are triumphant. The movie ends, but life, we know, goes on. When the Tang Dynasty fell, a chaotic interregnum followed. But, eventually, spring came again for China, as it will come for our people too.

Counter-Currents/*North American New Right*,
January 15, 2013

THE INTERPRETER

The Interpreter is a new thriller starring Sean Penn and Nicole Kidman, directed by Sydney Pollack. It is a well-crafted, well-acted, but ultimately mediocre film. Left to my own devices, I would probably not have seen it at all. But I wanted to spend some time with a friend, and he suggested the film. Which brings me to my recommendation: while I don't suggest that you seek out *The Interpreter*, if you are set on seeing a film, I can at least say that there is little here to offend a racially conscious white or to corrupt a racially unconscious one. Indeed, there are some interesting elements of racial realism in the film.

The Interpreter is set primarily in New York, with the opening scene set in Matobo, a fictional Southern African republic that is a composite of Zimbabwe and South Africa (the white inhabitants have both English and Dutch names). Matobo was "liberated" from its white colonial oppressors by Dr. Zuwanie, played by the blue-eyed mulatto Earl Cameron. The stately white-haired Zuwanie is supposed to remind us of the Communist terrorist-statesman Nelson Mandela. (Zuwanie reminisces about his first visit to New York, when he was treated like a hero—just like Mandela.)

Once independent, however, Matobo followed the course of white-created societies from Detroit to Haiti to Africa itself when handed over to violent, lazy, stupid, immoral blacks: poverty, crime, corruption, and chaos. Dr. Zuwanie, like so many other African leaders, became a bloody tyrant. His brutality spawned two rebel movements, which he fights to suppress with equal brutality. One group is led by Kuman-Kuman (George Harris), the other by Ajene Xola (Curtiss Cook). They accuse Zuwanie of "genocide" and "ethnic cleansing." He accuses them of "terrorism."

The opening scenes of *The Interpreter* are a horrifying composite of Africa today: a parched dusty road where a woman carries a load on her head and a man whose eyes have been gouged out is led along by a child, a crumbling stadium (built by whites and ruined by blacks) stinking with the rotting corpses of massacred blacks, black children playing soccer who turn out to be cold-blooded, sadistic killers in Dr. Zuwanie's militia. Their ball is a severed human head.

It is easy to feel sympathy for the victims of such brutality. But one has to keep in mind that the victims would probably have behaved in exactly the same way, given the chance, and they probably had. Not every victim is innocent. Not every loser is virtuous. Savage African civil wars are not a reason for importing the losers as refugees, to swell the welfare rolls and prisons of white nations. They are a reason to exclude Africans from white nations altogether.

I was genuinely surprised by these images of black savagery, particularly in a Hollywood movie directed by a Jew. Moreover, there is not even a hint of blaming it on whites. I was also surprised by the subliminal message that Nelson Mandela might be something other than the saint he is portrayed to be. With one exception, all the villains in the movie are blacks: brutish, ugly, savage, sinister blacks. The white exception is just a mercenary working for blacks. With one exception, the heroes of the movie are all white. The black exception is just an incompetent who ends up getting killed. (There is an Asian who is supposed to be on the right side, but he comes off as just a bureaucrat. The director, Sydney Pollack, casts himself as a Secret Service agent, but is presented as obnoxious and unethical.)

The interpreter in *The Interpreter* is Silvia Broome, played by Nicole Kidman. She is, for the most part, a very appealing character: smart, resourceful, idealistic, and exquisitely Nordic: blonde, blue-eyed, and very fair. The hero is Tobin Keller, a Secret Service agent played by Sean Penn. Broome and Keller meet when she overhears someone talking about assassinating Dr. Zuwanie while he speaks before the United Nations, and Keller is assigned to investigate the case. Keller's boss, played by director Pollack, coldly decides to use Broome as bait, and Keller has to watch over the trap to make sure she is not killed. There are plenty of tense and suspenseful scenes, a bit of tepid romance, some shocking violence, some stylish directing, and some acting. We learn that both Broome and Keller are haunted by the traumas of losing loved ones. This tiresome cliché is about as deep an account of character and motivation as today's movies are capable of presenting. A lot happens in this movie, much of it diverting, but none of it really managed to affect me deeply.

To some extent, the movie tries to obfuscate its elements of racial realism by presenting the appealing heroine Broome as a woman who deeply loves Africa and its indigenous featherless bipeds—in spite of the fact that she lost all four of her immediate family to black killers! She is supposed to be exemplary, but any sane person will just think she is crazy. Broome is presented as a woman who took up arms to fight Dr. Zuwanie for the rights of blacks and whites alike. (This is actually subversive: showing armed white resistance to black tyranny as justifiable. But then again, Broome decides that non-violence is the better path, hence her decision to be an interpreter at the United Nations.) It is even mentioned that she was for a time the lover of the black revolutionary Ajene Xola, until it became politically problematic for him to be associated with a white woman. (Again, setting aside the miscegenation angle, it is subversive to show an admirable white to be a victim of black racism.) In the end, Broome decides to return to Matobo, in spite of a budding romance with Penn. She gives up a strong, decent white man for the lure of the Dark Continent. Not a very satisfying ending.

At first I thought that Broome's decision was psychologically unrealistic. But then it dawned on me, sadly, that millions of whites live in Southern Africa. Most of them were born there. To them it is home, and they are held there in part by their attachment to their homelands, while the civilizations they built are descending into black savagery. I hope that they can save themselves—and we can save ourselves—before it is too late.

National Vanguard, May 2005

LAW & ORDER:
SPECIAL VICTIMS UNIT

Special Victims Unit is NBC's sleazy, sex crime spin-off of *Law and Order*.

Episode 86, which aired on April 4th, 2003, was about two brothers who went on a crime spree. They held up small groups of people with a single gun, forced them to strip and have sex with one another—including homosexual sex—and then shot them in the head. The victims were robbed of money, watches, jewelry, and their ATM cards. (They were forced to give their PIN numbers.) One couple was engaged, and the woman's engagement ring was stolen. In one crime, the victims' SUV was stolen. By my count, eleven people were killed, and two more were abducted. Moreover, it turned out that the older brother beat up his father, homosexually raped his younger brother, and tried to frame him so he would take the blame for both of them.

Now this crime might remind VNN readers (and precious few others) of the Wichita Massacre of December 14, 2000, in which two brothers, Reginald and Jonathan Carr, held up five people with a single gun, including a couple who were planning to be married. They raped the women and forced their victims to have sex, including homosexual sex, with one another. The Carrs then forced their victims to withdraw money from ATMs. They stole money, watches, jewelry, the engagement ring, and a SUV. They then they drove their victims to an icy field, shot all five in the head, then ran over their bodies. Amazingly, one woman survived.

There is no doubt that *Special Victims Unit* episode 86 is based on the Wichita Massacre. But there are two main differences between the Kansas and New York versions. First of all, in the TV show the criminals are far worse: they kill more people, and although one of them seems so pathetic he is almost sympathetic, the other is a monster who raped and framed his brother and beat his father. Second, in the *Special Victims Unit* episode, the criminals are two handsome, blue-eyed white men, whereas the

Carr brothers were ugly, scary-looking blacks.

Why was the race of the killers changed to adapt the Wichita Massacre for nationwide broadcast on NBC? For the same reason that the Wichita Massacre was not given nationwide coverage on NBC or any other network: the killers were black and the victims were white. Now, the networks did not spike the story because heinous black-on-white crimes are so unusual that giving them national coverage would mislead people into thinking such crimes are common. That didn't stop the networks from giving national coverage to the killing of the black James Byrd by whites in Jasper, Texas. In fact, black-on-white crime is far more common than white-on-black crime, but this fact is consciously hidden from the populace by the television networks while they subject whites to a never-ending guilt trip for the comparatively rare white-on-black crimes. This kind of propaganda may explain why the victims in Wichita went to their deaths like sheep.

The sadistic and savage nature of both crimes indicates that the killers were motivated by more than just greed. In the case of the Wichita Massacre, that motive was racial hatred of whites. In the *Special Victims Unit* episode, the motive could not be racial, so it was ascribed to resentment against rich people.

And why were the crimes of the fictional killers made so much worse? The main agenda of the writers was to exploit the Wichita Massacre while concealing the racial aspect. But they may have had a subsidiary agenda. Since they know that the internet makes it impossible for them to keep everyone ignorant of the Wichita Massacre, they may have decided to defuse its racial element and its shock value by showing that whites can do the same sort of thing, but far worse.

The Jewish agenda of the mass media systematically conceals black criminality and morally intimidates well-meaning whites from protecting themselves against it. This cultural atmosphere made the Wichita Massacre possible. The networks would not give national coverage to the real crime. But it was too lurid for the media Jews to leave alone. So they took the crime that their brethren helped create, scrubbed it of racial truths, and turned it into another piece of anti-white propaganda to help lull the victims of the next massacre to sleep.

What town will the next massacre be named for? Will it be yours?

"Jews Massacre the Truth"
VNN, April 5, 2003

LEGALLY BLONDE 2:
RED, WHITE & BLONDE

I didn't expect to like *Legally Blonde 2*. After all, according to Hollywood, Negroes are wise, noble, witty, and cool. They are cast as doctors, inventors, computer geniuses, judges, even God. But blondes, especially blue-eyed blondes like me — you know, "the Master Race" that Hollywood Jews hate and fear so much — are dumb.

So I was doubly delighted when I found that *Legally Blonde 2* is a light-hearted, genuinely funny film that communicates some positive values and relatively few negative ones.

First, there are no dumb blondes in this movie. The adorable Reese Witherspoon's character Elle Woods is a very smart blonde who turns the dumb blonde stereotype to her advantage: People underestimate her at their own risk.

Second, Elle is the girliest, most feminine woman imaginable, and she takes it all to hilarious extremes. But beyond all the satire, there is a strong message to young women: Feminism is wrong. Women do not gain power by masculinizing themselves. Their real power lies in their femininity. Elle triumphs over all obstacles and marries a big, handsome white guy in the end, always in high heels, and always looking fabulous.

Of course it would be better if brilliant and beautiful white women like Elle did not waste their prime child-bearing years doing trivial things like going to law school, working insane hours in law firms, and getting involved in political crusades. All this gets in the way of far more significant achievements: creating and nurturing new human beings. But as career girl movies go, LB2 is relatively free of feminist claptrap.

Third, LB2 has a positive "message." The plot centers on Elle's crusade to free the mom of her Chihuahua, Bruiser, from a cosmetics testing facility. Elle admirably refuses to work in a law firm that will not stand up for the morally right position. Then she packs her bags (I am sure there were about a hundred of them) and heads off to Washington, D.C., to get Congress to ban animal testing. And she wins. (Don't complain about my "spoiling" the film. Did you ever imagine that Elle could fail?)

I am all for banning experimentation on animals. First, it is scientifically unsound. Since animals are not identical to humans in the first place, the same chemicals can produce different effects. Second, it is immoral, because it causes suffering to innocent creatures that do not deserve to be tortured and killed merely for our benefit. Third, it is unnecessary, since there is no shortage of humans who can serve as test subjects. Why not perform experiments on criminals and other undesirables? The results would be scientifically sounder, and it would be morally preferable too, since criminals deserve to suffer and innocent animals do not.

Of course to White Nationalists, the animal rights movement seems like fiddling while Rome burns. If only we lived in a country where the biggest problem was springing a Chihuahua from a laboratory! But why worry about white rats when the future of the white race is at stake? I know white environmentalists who are worried about the extinction of every species and subspecies except their own. Still, I agree with the principles of the animal rights movement, if not their priorities. And the animal rights movement can teach White Nationalists something about organizing and activism. I would love to see the day when a White Nationalist organization has as many dues-paying members as PETA.

Fourth, LB2 satirizes the cynicism and corruption of the American political system. It also encourages idealism and public-spiritedness. At the end, Elle delivers a speech encouraging people to speak out when they see evil, to try to stop it, rather than remaining silent and allowing it to continue. Of course these are *Mr. Smith Goes to Washington* platitudes. The problem is that the system is so corrupt that it simply channels polite dissent into dead ends. Today's Mr. Smith had better show up in Washington with a revolutionary army behind him.

Fifth, LB2 contains remarkably little unhealthy propaganda. Those who support animal testing might feel otherwise, of course. There are some black extras in Congress—just like in the real Congress. And there is one black character, an ugly

Negress who works on Capitol Hill. But she is not cast against type as a genius or a hero. Instead, she is cynical, rude, and underhanded. Although in the end she helps Elle out, she does so for the wrong reasons. She is no credit to her race. A white conservative Republican from Alabama is first seen being mean to a beggar in a park. But later on, he becomes one of the heroes of the movie, which is very unusual. Another hero is a lady Congresswoman from Texas, who seems like a conservative as well. The main villain, played by Sally Fields, is a Congresswoman from Massachusetts who has "liberal" — Hillary — written all over her.

To me, one of the funniest scenes — unintentionally so, of course — is when Elle, disillusioned by politics as usual, goes to the memorial to the loathsome Mr. Lincoln for inspiration.

I am confused by the film's treatment of homosexuality. When Elle's Chihuahua and the gentleman from Alabama's Rottweiler are revealed to be "gay," the whole thing strikes me as a satire of gay "culture" and therapeutic "coming out" clichés. Or do homosexuals now take themselves so seriously that they do not see the humor in this? Do they really think that the next social barrier to be breached is discrimination against gay dogs? Has my consciousness been raised without my even knowing it? And I have lost count: Are portrayals of flaming queens pro- or anti-gay now?

Legally Blonde 2 is not a great or significant movie, but it is amusing and mostly inoffensive. It is definitely worth your time if you are in the mood for eye candy and some good laughs.

VNN, July 2003

LOVECRAFT:
FEAR OF THE UNKNOWN

In any poll of Counter-Currents readers, H. P. Lovecraft (1890–1937) would surely rank high among fiction writers. Thus Lovecraft is a regular feature at Counter-Currents. For the uninitiated who want a quick introduction, I recommend you start with Frank H. Woodward's *Lovecraft: Fear of the Unknown* (2009), a 90-minute documentary on Lovecraft's life and work.

Even Lovecraft fanatics like me will find much to enjoy here. There are interviews with leading Lovecraft scholars S. T. Joshi and Robert M. Price, Lovecraft-influenced directors Guillermo del Toro and John Carpenter, and Lovecraft-influenced fiction writers Peter Straub, Ramsey Campbell, and Neil Gaiman, among others.

There are many photographs of Lovecraft and his associates, as well as places Lovecraft lived (or perhaps I should say haunted). There are also many images of Lovecraft-inspired art (as well as a gallery in the DVD extras).

The documentary is well-paced, with suitably creepy music. The narrator who reads from Lovecraft's writings sounds like he was recorded on an old wax cylinder device, a nice touch which imparts a sense of realism.

The only stupid thing about this documentary is its treatment of Lovecraft's strident racism and xenophobia. Since these are Lovecraft admirers, their tactic is to historicize Lovecraft, to claim that he was merely a product of his times. The documentary also tries to argue that Lovecraft's views mellowed over time. If only he had lived long enough, we are asked to believe, he would have become an imbecile.

As evidence, the documentary cites Lovecraft's marriage in 1924 to Sonia Haft Greene, a Jewess. But the marriage was a failure, and there is no evidence that Lovecraft became any less anti-Semitic due to his marriage. Indeed, I wonder if Sonia herself was a self-hating Jew, which would have given her and Lovecraft another thing in common.

Further alleged evidence is the evident admiration of Lovecraft's narrator in *At the Mountains of Madness* for the Old Ones or Elder Things, the aliens who created life on Earth. (One could say the same of the Great Race of *The Shadow Out of Time*.) As Robert Price points out, however, the Old Ones are hardly equivalent to the immigrants Lovecraft despised. In fact, they are analogous to America's Anglo-Saxon founders, whereas the Shoggoths who rose up to destroy them are analogous to the immigrant masses, which at the time were seething with Bolshevism.

We hear no more of the thesis that Lovecraft "grew" when the documentary comes to *The Shadow Over Innsmouth*, a novella written in 1931 and published in 1936, the year before his death. *The Shadow* is a *summa* of all things racist and xenophobic in Lovecraft's worldview. It can be read as an allegory about the Jewish subversion of America by appealing to the greed of American plutocrats and to their desire for knowledge of ancient mysteries and the power attendant on such initiation.

But the ultimate horror is the narrator's realization that he too has been contaminated by foreign blood, that one of his ancestors committed miscegenation with an outsider, and that the growing power of the alien blood within him is turning his loyalties away from his Anglo-Saxon heritage toward the foreigners. I read this as an expression of Lovecraft's guilt and horror at his marriage to Sonia, and his relief that the marriage ended without issue.

Aside from the claptrap about tolerance, which is merely a product of our unenlightened times, I recommend *Lovecraft: Fear of the Unknown*. It is a useful introduction to Lovecraft which also offers many pleasures to his long-time readers.

Counter-Currents/*North American New Right*,
March 28, 2011

MACHETE

I saw *Machete* on Friday afternoon. It was gross, it was hilarious, and it communicated an important message: Mexico is a filthy, impoverished, backward, corrupt country inhabited by ugly, treacherous, cruel people. Mexicans are invading the United States, bringing Mexico with them. Mexicans corrupt every American who comes into contact with them, and their power to corrupt is so total that they even corrupt the patriots and politicians who oppose them.

In spite of their cruelty to one another, Mexicans pull together with a fierce solidarity when facing Americans, who are merely selfish individuals out to make or save a buck. People like that can always be bought off or intimidated. This solidarity gives Mexicans a vast support network in the United States—a network that includes the Catholic Church—which aids them in taking jobs from Americans, undercutting American wages, and leeching off American social services.

What do these locusts think they'll do once they strip America bare? Well, locusts don't think. But if they did, they would probably conclude (1) they would be no worse off than they were in Mexico, and (2) there's always Canada.

Machete was directed by Robert Rodriguez, a Texas-born Mexican-American (a white man by the looks of him), who is versatile and highly talented but also wildly inconsistent. (His masterpiece is 2005's *Sin City*, but he has also done some stunningly awful crap, like *Spy Kids 2*.) The character of Machete first appeared in Rodriguez's delightful *Spy Kids* movie. The movie *Machete* was based on a *faux* "trailer" in Rodriguez and Quentin Tarantino's "double feature" *Grindhouse* (2007).

Does *Machete* promote violence against whites, as claimed by some who have not seen the movie? To answer that, I must say quite a lot about the plot, so stop reading here if you don't want to know.

Machete, played by Danny Trejo (more than half Amerindian by the looks of him), is a Mexican *Federale*, a cop, whose wife and daughter have been horribly murdered by a Mexican drug lord, Torrez (Steven Seagal, who is half-Jewish, half-Irish), in cooperation with his own corrupt superiors. A few years later, Machete shows up in Texas as a day laborer. He is hired by a white American, Michael Booth (Jeff Fahey), to kill a state Senator, John McLaughlin (Robert De Niro), who is a fierce opponent of immigration. Booth explains that business in Texas depends on cheap labor. Thus the border must remain open. Thus the Senator must die. (This speech is a concise and eloquent proof that capitalism is subversive of patriotism.)

Machete takes the job, but discovers that he is being framed as a fall guy. A henchman of Booth wounds the Senator, and Machete is hunted down as the Mexican would-be assassin. It turns out that Booth actually works for the Senator, and he has cooked up the assassination attempt to revive his flagging poll numbers and stir up hatred against Mexicans. We eventually learn, however, that Booth is actually working for the drug lord Torrez, who wants the border tightened up so that the cost of his products rises in the US. He also hopes to build in back doors to the new electrified border fence proposed by McLaughlin.

McLaughlin is no sympathetic dupe, however. He is introduced hunting down illegal aliens with his friends, a posse of border vigilantes clearly supposed to be the Minutemen. The vigilante leader Von Jackson (Don Johnson) shoots a pregnant Mexican woman while making a speech about the anchor baby problem, and the Senator shoots the woman's boyfriend. He has the whole incident filmed to show it to his "big money donors."

But it is hard to say what Rodriguez's intentions are. Does he really think that immigration opponents are like this? (If only . . .) Is it an attempt to tar anti-immigration advocates by putting their messages in the mouths of ruthless killers? If so, then it fails by being too over the top. It comes off more as a parody of the paranoia and hysteria of the Left-wing critics of the anti-immigration movement.

When Jackson shoots Luz, a leader of the Mexican underground network played by Michelle Rodriguez (a Puerto Rican actress who looks about one-eighth black—hard to tell given the popularity of plastic surgery in Hollywood), the network rallies under Machete's leadership for a battle with the vigilantes.

The Mexicans attack in a fleet of chrome-plated, rainbow-tinted, bouncing and shimmying low riders and choppers. I laughed my ass off. Jackson's vigilantes look like a low rent motorcycle gang. After a brutal battle, the vigilantes are put to flight. But it is hard to have too much sympathy with them. After all, they are dupes of Jackson and Booth in league with Torrez.

So, does *Machete* promote racial war against white people? Yes and no.

Yes, since the bad guys are almost all white people.

No, because the whites are not just any white people, but corrupt traitors to their own race and dupes of said traitors.

No, because the politics of the film, insofar as it has any, is quasi-Marxist. The enemies are the rich (the Mexican Torrez, the American Booth). The good guys are "the people" — most of them Mexican, but one of them is a white American who works with Mexicans as a dishwasher. Luz's alter ego is Shé (as in Che), a revolutionary pin-up girl.

In truth, I suspect that this film's real agenda is pretty much the same as that of Rodriguez's friend and frequent collaborator Quentin Tarantino, namely: sheer nihilism.

This movie is really all about making brutal and sadistic violence funny. Machete stabs, slashes, beheads, slices, dices, and juliennes people with his machete. He also kills with guns, grenades, rockets, knives, surgical instruments, vehicles, garden tools, a meat thermometer, his bare hands, and probably his bad breath. Rodriguez follows the Chekhovian dramatic principle that if a corkscrew is left on a counter, it had better be used to gouge out someone's eye before the end of the act. In one scene, Machete rips out a man's intestines and uses them to rappel off the side of a building.

And Machete is far from the only killer in this movie. Machete's brother, a Catholic priest (Cheech Marin, who appears to be heavily Amerindian as well), dispatches a number of assassins with shotgun blasts before being crucified in his own church. Booth's slutty daughter April (played by Irish-Italian American Catholic girl Lindsay Lohan) dresses as a nun and blows the Senator away with a .45.

It is all very droll, so I guess Rodriguez can count this movie a success.

The aesthetic of *Machete* seems to be derived from biker magazines. Where else does one find hideously scarred, fat, tattooed old satyrs who are inexplicably alluring to young, scantily clad women sporting fake boobs and machine guns?

To capitalize on the controversy about the Arizona immigration enforcement law, a trailer for *Machete* was released with a warning to the state of Arizona. Having seen the movie, I have to dismiss the trailer as a cheap opportunism rather than a serious political message. For this movie has no serious political message.

Yes, *Machete* does promote Mexican solidarity against whites. Sartana, a Mexican-American immigration agent played by Mexican-American actress Jessica Alba (who cannot be more than one-eighth Amerindian) does learn the value of solidarity with her people. "There is the law," she says, "and then there's what's right." And racial solidarity is what's right.

But ask yourself: Whose mind is this message more likely to change? The mind of a Mexican, most of whom already eat, sleep, and breathe solidarity with *"La Raza"*? Or the mind of your average deracinated white American, who also gets to observe the contrast between Mexican solidarity and the corruption of his selfish, individualistic fellow whites? Mexican solidarity needs no promoting. So the result of *Machete* might be a net increase in white solidarity.

At one point in the movie, one of Booth's bodyguards remarks that it is strange that Americans allow Mexican gardeners and nannies in their homes when they don't want them in their country. Makes you think, doesn't it?

The same bodyguard speaks to Machete in Hungarian. He does not understand, of course. It points out the fact that all the other immigrant groups who came here learned English, so why don't the Mexicans learn it too? Makes you think, doesn't it?

Yes, *Machete* delivers a warning to Arizona and the rest of America, but not the one its director intended. *Machete* portrays Mexicans as profoundly alien and threatening. It shows that their racial solidarity gives them an advantage over Americans, whose selfish individualism brought them here and keeps them here even though they are destroying our society. It shows our leaders as corrupt, sociopathic race traitors.

The conclusion: If whites are going to save our country, we must first develop racial solidarity, toss out our corrupt leaders, and reign in traitorous capitalists.

I can hardly wait for the sequel.[1]

Counter-Currents/*North American New Right*,
September 4, 2010

---

[1] Greg Johnson, "Birth of a Nation: H. A. Covington's Northwest Quartet," http://www.counter-currents.com/2010/07/birth-of-a-nation/

MAN OF STEEL

I have never liked the character of Superman. He is not a man who has transcended humanity toward something higher. He is simply an alien, who looks like one of us, and who comes equipped with a whole array of superpowers. From a Nietzschean and Faustian standpoint, that translates to zero appeal. I am not interested in being rescued by a superior being. I am interested in *becoming* a superior being. Furthermore, none of the Superman movies or TV shows ever managed to make this character compelling to me (although I love the John Williams score for Richard Donner's 1978 film).

But when I went to see *Man of Steel*, I was prepared to be sold, for this movie is a team-up of two of Hollywood's leading young *goy* geniuses: director Zack Snyder (*Watchmen*) and Christopher Nolan, director of the *Dark Knight Trilogy* and *Inception*, who co-wrote the script with long-time Jewish collaborator David Goyer.

But *Man of Steel* is a deeply disappointing movie. Compared to *Watchmen* and the *Dark Knight Trilogy*, which are intellectually and emotionally deep, complex, and involving, *Man of Steel* is pretty much a brainless, soulless spectacle.

The underlying problem seems to be that Snyder and Nolan just aren't that crazy about the character of Superman either. Hence they have delivered an uninspired, by-the-numbers, would-be "Summer Blockbuster." (Aren't blockbusters also a kind of bomb?) *Man of Steel* even stoops to the last refuge of bad scripts: the movie is swarming with cameos. ("Look, it's Kevin Costner!" "Look, it's Morpheus!" "Look, it's that wog from *Battlestar Galactica!*") After this film and *Sucker Punch*, it is time to put Zack Snyder on artistic probation. *Watchmen* may have been just a fluke. This whole movie reeks of cynicism and greed.

But there is also a deeper, older stench underneath. As I have argued in my reviews of *Hellboy* and *Hellboy II: The Golden Army*,[1]

---

[1] Reprinted in *Trevor Lynch's White Nationalist Guide to the Movies*, ed. Greg Johnson, Foreword by Kevin MacDonald (San Francisco: Counter-Currents, 2012).

comic-book superheroes largely function as symbolic proxies for Jews, who virtually created the genre. Superheroes, like Jews, are always outsiders and "freaks." They are, moreover, immensely powerful outsiders who must engage in crypsis to blend in, lest they incite the fear and ire of their host populations.

The superhero genre also plays an indispensible *apologetic* role for Jewry. For in the case of superheroes, these immensely powerful and secretive aliens are benevolently disposed to their host populations, magnanimously enduring the fears and suspicions of their narrow-minded and xenophobic inferiors whose interests they serve out of a commitment to the morality of egalitarian humanism.

Jews, of course, use their superpowers and knack for crypsis to rather different ends, ceaselessly scourging the *goyim* with plagues like Bolshevism, free market capitalism, feminism, multiculturalism, pornography, psychoanalysis, non-white immigration, Zionism, endless wars, and, to top it all off, the ongoing genocide of the white race.

This, of course, is supervillain behavior, but the superhero genre inoculates us from drawing that conclusion by making supervillains into perpetual Nazis, or symbolic proxies for Nazis and other nationalistic, anti-egalitarian, xenophobic, and traditional-minded whites (but never nationalistic, anti-egalitarian, xenophobic, traditional-minded Jews).

Superman is, of course, one of the most explicitly Jewish superheroes. Superman was created in 1933 by two Ashkenazic Jews, Jerry Siegel and Joe Shuster, and from the beginning he was cast as an "American" antipode to the German "supermen" who rose to power in 1933. Like Moses, Superman was set adrift in an ark and found and adopted by an alien family. Superman's original name is Kal-El, and his father was named Jor-El, "El" being a Hebrew word for "God" and a root of such names as Israel and Elizabeth.

In *Man of Steel*, the supervillain is General Zod. We learn that Krypton is a planet that practices eugenics, has a caste system, and has engaged in colonization of the cosmos, creating giant machines that transform other planets into environments like Krypton, obliterating whatever creatures lived there before them.

After a 100,000 year Reich, however, Krypton is in deep decline. Its colonies have failed, and the planet itself is in danger of implosion due to mining its core for energy. Two men, Jor-El and General Zod, wish to save Krypton.

Jor-El is the far-sighted scientist who warned the Kryptonians of the folly of mining their planet's core (how enlightened). Jor-El and his wife Lara have created a natural child, Kal-El, a child of choice and chance (how liberal). Jor-El then somehow hides in the genetic codes of other, as yet unborn Kryptonians in the body of Kal-El (whatever that means). Then Jor-El launches the child into space in a tiny capsule. This, somehow, will save the Kryptonian race. Sounds like a plan!

General Zod, the leader of the warrior caste, attempts to restore Krypton by launching a military coup. He wishes to extinguish the bloodlines of the rulers who have brought Krypton to its sorry state. But he is captured and exiled with his followers. But when Krypton finally implodes, they are freed. They then search the universe for Jor-El's child to recover their genetic database. They track him to Earth, which they wish to seize and "terraform" into another Krypton, so they can begin their race anew. Humanity, needless to say, will be exterminated. (Inequality + eugenics + *Lebensraum* + genocide = "Nazis.")

Superman rejects Zod's proposal in the name of egalitarian humanism. A believer in diversity and open borders, he suggests that the Kryptonians share the planet. One Kryptonian tells Superman that his morality is an evolutionary disadvantage. Kryptonians have no morality and believe only in evolution. Of course Superman's egalitarianism is not the same as "morality" as such. The Kryptonians also have a moral code, namely a kind of social Darwinism, which means that they feel no obligation to any weaker species, particularly when the very survival of their race is in peril.

Well, you can't bargain with Nazis. Remember Munich, 1938? So ray guns and bullets are discharged, blows are exchanged, spaceships and airplanes and Kryptonians whoosh around, and Metropolis is pretty much reduced to rubble, all to another thundering, tuneless, dreary Hans Zimmer score. In the end, General Zod is killed and his followers are poofed into another dimension where they will be held in suspended animation until Alan Smithee's *Man of Steel II* comes out next summer.

The lesson of *Man of Steel* is the same lesson as practically any other superhero movie: white Americans must never dream of controlling our own destiny. Instead, we must trust in the benevolent hegemony of superheroes: a tiny, hidden minority of powerful aliens and freaks. Superheroes are the only thing that can save us from supervillains and all the evils for which they stand: inequality, eugenics, hierarchy, xenophobia, etc. In short, everything practiced by Jews to preserve their race, and everything which, if practiced by whites, would secure us against Jewish subversion, domination, and ultimately genocide.

Counter-Currents/*North American New Right*,
June 21, 2013

MEN IN BLACK II

My cat and I saw *Men in Black II* this past weekend, along with a cheerful bunch of white college students. My cat found the movie complex, challenging, and fully engaging. I was less impressed, but I admit that I was much amused.

The cartoonish nature of the film was underscored by the fact that it was preceded by a cartoon, just like in the good old days. The cartoon was pretty funny, and I am amazed to see what can be done these days with computer animation, along with excellent sound and projection facilities.

I was also pleased by the style of the opening credit sequence. The spaceship piloted by a she-tyrant cruising through the galaxy and disintegrating planets was right up my alley. The movie itself also has a great look and fantastic special effects.

The music was immediately identifiable as Danny Elfman's, because it sounds like everything else by Danny Elfman. Thank goodness there was relatively little contemporary "rap" noise.

MIB II is fast-paced, entertaining piffle. I can't say that I recommend this movie, but if you are dragged into seeing it, it won't be too big a waste of time. Judging from the audience, this movie will be seen by lots of bright white people. So it is worthwhile to ponder if White Nationalists can make some hay out of it. So here are some talking points.

MIB II is about the problems of policing an America infested with aliens—criminal aliens, repulsive aliens, and aliens that are just annoyingly, well, alien. These aliens are not merely invaders. The movie makes it clear that they are allowed in.

To deal with these aliens, a "secret society" of Men in Black was created. But the MIB are not really a secret society. They are a secret police force. Now, I have nothing against a secret police force *per se*. If White Nationalists are going to save our nation, that is to say, our race, then a secret police force will come in handy. Himmler's SS: The Original Men in Black.

What I object to is a secret police force designed to hide the problem of alien infestation from the host population until it is too late for them to do anything about it. And that is precisely what the Men in Black do. If a secret police force is necessary to control the aliens among us, then why not use them to solve the problem permanently?

Why is it necessary to give special attention to policing aliens? Aliens are more prone to violence. Some may be genetically predisposed to violence. But even the gentlest are foreigners, and foreigners are more likely to get into misunderstandings with the locals, and these misunderstandings can easily escalate into violence.

Aliens are more prone to criminal activity. They have trouble holding real jobs, and so end up resorting to crime. For instance, who would want to employ "Jeff," the giant worm that eats subway cars?

Aliens also have access to advanced technologies that make it easier for them to prey on the natives. (The Men in Black, however, have access to the technologies necessary to fight the aliens, but they do not share them with their fellow citizens.)

Aliens, furthermore, feel none of the bonds of social solidarity and kinship with the natives, and these bonds stand in the way of preying on others. Finally, aliens are prone to bringing their wars to our shores.

For instance, on September 11th, 2001, the war between two alien groups—Jews and Arabs—killed thousands of real Americans in lower Manhattan. On July 4th of this year, the same war flared up at the El-Al ticket counter at Los Angeles International Airport. Thank goodness nobody important was killed.

In MIB II, two alien species bring their war to Earth, and their battle threatens to blow up the entire planet, not merely a couple of buildings. Wouldn't America be better off if we were much more xenophobic and made aliens feel unwelcome?

MIB II also shows the folly of using aliens to police other aliens. Apparently the Men in Black are not immune to multicultural, egalitarian madness. Even though the survival of the planet itself depends upon their efforts, that does not deter them from hiring and promoting underqualified aliens with questionable loyalties.

For instance, the character "Jay," played by Will Smith, is clearly an alien who does not belong in our modern, technological civilization, much less in a responsible job. Aesthetically he is unappealing. His head is shaped and colored like an eggplant, with tiny, round, protruding ears. His cranium is small and his brow low, features correlated with low intelligence. His skull is so thick that it can crash into steel beams at high speeds without splitting open. His jaw is prognathous and his lips large and rubbery, clearly evolved to produce vulgar spluttering, fart-like noises to a moronic boom-chucka-lucka rhythm.

He is evidently not up to the job. It requires too much intelligence and personal responsibility. So he spends his time belittling his human partners until he is paired with a fellow non-human, a creature that looks like a small pug dog but which can talk incessantly about sex and food, which is more Jay's speed. But still Jay is unhappy, perhaps because he would be more comfortable as the wise-cracking sidekick than the senior partner.

When Jay becomes sexually infatuated with a racially similar alien, he forgets all about his responsibilities and training and breaks several important Men in Black directives.

When Jews are caught doing this sort of thing, they wring their hands and pretend to wrack their consciences over the onerous moral burden of "dual loyalties" that they have to bear. You almost feel sorry for the little traitors. But then you notice that when forced to choose between their host country and fellow Jews, there is nothing "dual" about their loyalties at all. They always choose fellow Jews, because they only have one loyalty, to the hive.

Fortunately, when the very existence of the Earth is threatened, Jay realizes that he is outmatched. So multiculturalism and affirmative action are put on hold, and Jay's human ex-partner Kay, played by Tommy Lee Jones, is hauled out of retirement to save the day. Jay is demoted to buffoonish sidekick and takes well to the role. Lesson: Never send an alien to do a man's job.

Now why, you might ask, does MIB II treat with such levity the potential destruction of the whole planet because of suicidally stupid policies like flooding the country with aliens and then hiring incompetent and questionably loyal aliens to police them? To answer this question, we must understand another kind of alien infestation that is not portrayed in MIB II. The movie is directed by Barry Sonnenfeld and produced by Steven Spielberg, who are themselves aliens, namely Jews.

Although Jews have from time to time ruled their own states, they have no genius for self-government, so these experiments have been relatively short-lived and unsuccessful. For most of their history, Jews have been aliens, living scattered amidst other peoples. Because their religion teaches them to despise and exploit non-Jews, their host populations naturally come to hate them in turn, eventually resolving to control or expel their Jewish "guests." (Or is it parasites?)

After centuries of experience, the Jews have noticed they fare best in corrupt, disorganized, multiracial, and multicultural societies that lack the social solidarity to resist them. Jews fare worst in upright, orderly, racially and culturally homogeneous societies. Therefore, Jews infesting these societies lobby to open their borders to the immigration of other even more exotic-looking aliens.

While Koreans seek monopolies on ghetto convenience stores and Pakistanis buy up cheap hotels in the South, Jews have been guided by their conviction that their destiny is to rule or destroy other peoples. Thus they seek the levers of real power: first banking, then the mass media, including Hollywood. Using their control over Hollywood, Jews produce a steady stream of propaganda to advance their subversive agenda and to conceal it from us at the same time.

MIB II is an attempt to assuage the rising anxieties of real Americans about the ongoing alien invasion. The movie attempts to convince us that an America that looks like the *Star Wars* cantina is a rich, colorful, strong, healthy, and, above all, exciting and entertaining nation.

And when the occasional problems crop up, these are no cause for alarm. They are certainly no cause for booting out the aliens and closing the borders. Oh no. Any problems will be solved by a brave and competent multiracial, multicultural secret society of Men in Black.

The purpose of MIB II is to encourage us to laugh off our ongoing extermination. The irony is that the movie contains enough of the unpleasant truth that the careful viewer can discover it "between the frames," so to speak. America really is infested with aliens. These people really do need to go back home. Our borders really do need to be sealed. The races really do need to go their separate ways. And we really do need a secret police force, our own Men in Black, not merely to contain the problem, but to solve it, forever.

VNN, July 15, 2002

MINORITY REPORT

Definition: A minority report is a statement of a dissenting viewpoint defeated by majority vote.

I saw *Minority Report* this weekend. Since I liked the last Tom Cruise movie *Vanilla Sky*, I thought I might like *Minority Report* too, even though the quality of a movie has far more to do with the director than the lead actor.

But alas, *Minority Report* is a mediocre, derivative, sometimes incoherent film, straining after metaphysical significance but falling into banality and queasy humor—straining after a brilliant vision of the future, but falling into just another D.C. political-intrigue thriller.

The premise of the film raises serious metaphysical and moral questions: If the future can be seen, then are all of our actions determined in advance? If our actions are predetermined, then how can we be held responsible and punished for them? How can a person be guilty of a crime he has not yet committed? By what right does the state prevent three clairvoyants from leading normal lives so they can be used to predict crimes?

A film that dealt squarely and plausibly with these issues would have been really significant. But they just hover in the background and are never taken seriously and addressed in a coherent way. All we get is some pretentious patter, which may impress morons but convicts Spielberg as a phony in the eyes of the intelligent.

Does the movie ever really prove that we have free choice? Or is the clairvoyant Agatha's insistence on freedom proved wrong, since things do end up happening exactly as she saw them? How does knowing the future allow us to change it? If it can be changed, then it cannot be known. If it can be known, it cannot be changed.

By not addressing these questions, the film does not establish a coherent, believable world. It lacks moral and metaphysical focus. This lack of focus is especially clear when one asks oneself if this is supposed to be a dystopia or a utopia?

The police search of the public housing building, with its little *Matrix*-derivative spiders, is pretty horrific. The eye-scanner technology is shockingly invasive. The police act like jackbooted thugs. The form of imprisonment is also shocking, especially for the claustrophobic.

But in the end it all falls flat. Spielberg never really takes a stand. Because of the void at the center of this movie, it slowly implodes under the weight of all its meaningless sci-fi trappings.

Instead of making a coherent, serious film, Spielberg tries to keep us amused with an old sub-B-movie technique: the running gag. This running gag is designed to wring nervous laughter from us. It involves eyeballs. Tom Cruise has to get a new set to evade security. So he visits a sleazy doctor with snot running out of his nose, and his sleazy assistant, who just comes out of the toilet. We cringe that these people are about to perform surgery.

The doctor turns out to be a man imprisoned by Tom Cruise's character for setting people on fire. "Will he seek revenge?" we wonder nervously. He does perform the operation, but tricks a blinded Tom into eating a rotten sandwich and drinking some green slime. We worry that Tom will go blind when the spiders peer into his new eyes, because he has not kept the bandages on long enough. We see Tom drop his old eyeballs and chase them down a hallway. They fall into the grate. Fortunately, one hangs on by some slime. He and his wife use the eyeball to open the door to his former workplace. (What, they didn't change the locks when one of their agents became a wanted criminal?)

Spielberg adds a lot more touches of the weird and the grotesque: the old woman in a greenhouse full of carnivorous plants who plants a kiss on Tom Cruise for no apparent reason, the old woman smoking a pipe in the hotel lobby (pure Lynch), the hollow eye sockets of the drug dealer, the creepy caretaker of the clairvoyants, the crippled custodian of the prisoners, the mole on the face of the nurse, etc.

All of it falls flat, though, because the grotesque also presupposes a particular metaphysics to make sense. As Flannery O'Connor tells so brilliantly, and David Lynch shows so brilliantly, the grotesque has no metaphysical weight in the modern world-picture, where all evils can be explained and ameliorated.

The grotesque is precisely that which cannot be explained by science and ameliorated by technology and liberal politics. The grotesque shows that there is moral dimension that lies beyond the capacity of science and technology to predict and control. But Spielberg never takes a coherent stand on precisely this question, so his grotesque gestures fall as flat as his science fiction futurist ones.

The character of John Anderton played by Tom Cruise is also problematic. I hate the vulgar psychoanalytic understanding of motives that is such a staple in Hollywood. Why does John Anderton join the department of pre-crime? What's his motive? Well, he was traumatized by the disappearance and presumed murder of his son six years before. He's in pain. So he tries to prevent future crimes. (The disappearance also destroyed his marriage, but for some reason he did not go into marriage counseling.) Then he goes home at the end of a long day and relives his past with his son and kills the additional pain with illegal drugs.

I frankly do not understand how rapidly he rejects the whole pre-crime concept when he finds that he is going to commit a murder. Was he not convinced of its infallibility before? If so, then why does he not even consider turning himself in? His conversion is too radical and is unsupported by anything established about his character. It certainly proves his commitment to pre-crime to be unserious, which does not make him a hero in my book. And why the hell does he shave his head at the end of the film and show off his ugly brachycephalic skull?

I just don't care about this guy. I just don't care about Tom Cruise. I have seen better-looking men walking down the street every day of my life. And he's not such a great actor. Am I missing something?

The racial politics of this movie are absurd. The very idea that all the would-be killers arrested in a six-year period in Washington, D.C., would be white is so preposterous that when the prisoners were displayed—and I saw no non-whites among them — I actually heard a couple of nervous, stifled sniggers in the sold-out showing I attended in Berkeley, P.C. capital of the universe.

And of course when you want to buy drugs in D.C., you just find a blind white man in a dark alley. In the real world, such a dealer would be killed and eaten by Negroes. And then there was the scene showing that the majority of residents of a D.C. public housing building were white. I kept thinking, "This really is science fiction."

Those problems aside, however, there was something unusual about the racial politics of this film. First of all, one of the laws of casting against type is to find attractive (i.e., white-looking) Negroes for positive roles. But the most prominent blacks in the film are really hideous and primitive-looking.

Another law of casting against type is to put really Jewish-looking Jews in positive, *Mensch* roles. But in *Minority Report*, there are a number of obvious Semites cast as sleazy characters. The would-be killer Mr. Marks is played by the obviously Semitic Arye Gross: an ugly, nasal, whiny, flabby, waddling, myopic, unmasculine nebbish. Who could blame his wife Sara Marks for having an affair with a tall, slender, handsome, blonde Aryan? This, of course, makes her husband jealous, which is the motive for his would-be double murder. Are we, perhaps, catching a glimpse of the anxieties of Spielberg, Cohen, Frank, and the other nebbishes who brought us this film? (Note to Kate Capshaw: "Don't go home. He knows.")

Then there is the Semitic-looking sicko who cares for the three clairvoyants in their isolation tank. Then there is Tim Blake Nelson as the creepy crippled custodian of the futuristic prison who plays Bach on a cheesy-sounding organ to soothe his prisoners, who are kept in some sort of suspended animation in glass pods. (How did Spielberg know my idea of hell?) Then there is the truly hideous Jason Antoon (picture Gene Simmons without the makeup), who is portrayed as sleazy, even though he helps our hero Tom Cruise. Antoon's character is named Riley, while the very handsome Irishman Colin Farrell plays a character named Danny Witwer. No comment necessary there. And finally, the man who pretends to have kidnapped and killed Tom Cruise's son is played by another Jew, Mike Binder.

There are three Swedes cast as villains: Max von Sydow as Lamar Burgess, as well as the eye surgeon and his nurse. But the lead positive roles were played by whites or by people who look white: Tom Cruise's character, his wife, the clairvoyant Agatha (played by Samantha Morton), the old woman in the greenhouse, and Colin Farrell's character Danny Witwer. The other two clairvoyants also seemed like Nordic types. One of the cops also looked like a product of the *Lebensborn* program.

If I haven't convinced you to skip this movie yet, then consider this: The ending makes no sense. The pre-crime program is shut down when it is on the verge of going national. But how did anything in the film justify shutting it down? A better question would be how they justified setting it up in the first place. And how did they manage to confine the clairvoyants' powers to the Washington, D.C., area for six years? Isn't six years a bit long for a pilot project? How did they propose to broaden the clairvoyants' powers to the entire nation? Are the clairvoyants free at the end, or just prisoners of a different sort, with lots of nice books to read?

With crap like this to work with, it is no surprise that John Williams's score is pretty undistinguished as well. And it is the best part of the film!

Don't waste your time and money on *Minority Report*.

VNN, June 25, 2002

MONEYBALL

The only thing I hate more than watching sports on TV is watching sports movies. And as for baseball, well, I would rather watch the AstroTurf grow. So when I tell you that *Moneyball* is an excellent film, that really means something. All my prejudices were against it, so the bar was set very high.

In *Moneyball*, Brad Pitt plays "Billy" Beane—the diminutive is emblematic of the arrested boyishness of sports fandom—a failed professional baseball player who is the general manager of the Oakland A's, which I learned is a baseball team here in the Bay Area. The film is supposedly based on a true story, but I have zero interest in where it mirrors or distorts history. My interest is in the drama and the psychological and even "philosophical" truths it portrays.

The film begins in 2002. The A's are facing a crisis. They have far less money than the teams against which they have to compete. (Maybe that has something to do with being located in Oakland.) The richer teams, moreover, are poaching their star players. Beane is told that he simply cannot spend more money rebuilding the team. So Beane needs to think innovatively.

But when he meets with his cabinet of scouts and trainers—a bunch of sentimental old ex-jocks—he finds them fixated on building a team of individual "star" athletes, each of whom is evaluated in terms of astonishingly superficial criteria: their looks, whether they have a "baseball body," the aesthetics of their play (the crack of the ball off their bat), the hotness of their girlfriends, and the like. Yes, of course, they also factor in athletic ability, the ideal of which is to have "tools" in as many areas as possible: hitting, running, etc.

The trouble with these star packages is that they are very expensive. Moreover, a group of prima donnas polishing their résumés and constantly searching for more lucrative contracts does not necessarily work as a winning team.

I found the "cabinet" scene astonishing. The spectacle of ostensibly straight old men making serious staffing decisions based on the looks and physiques of young men (I call it "jock-sniffing") is something I have seen again and again in the real world, but never on the movie screen.

Of course such criteria are relevant in modeling. They might be understandable in sports and acting, were these not billion dollar industries with objective standards of performance—and countless good-looking failures testifying to the enduring temptation of this particular folly.

But jock-sniffing is astonishingly common in serious endeavors, such as politics and the military, where the dire consequences of failure would seem to dictate making decisions strictly on the basis of character and objective qualifications, not looks.

I would be very interested to read a good psychological, even evolutionary psychological, investigation of jock-sniffing and "golden boys." Many elements need to be disentangled: the nostalgia of old men for their youth, romanticized self-images, vicarious gratification, latent homosexuality, etc.

Culture also surely plays a role. A German comrade once spoke disdainfully of the prevalence conscious and unconscious of "Anglo pederasty" throughout American culture, which astonished me, because I did not see it at the time. It is, however, a phenomenon that Jews see clearly and do not hesitate to exploit. Jewish philosopher Jonathan Lear once wrote about how Anglo pederasty served him well in his academic career in England and America.

Nobody involved in serious enterprises can afford to be unaware of the power of these sorts of motives, which can be profoundly destructive if allowed to work unconsciously.

Beane decides that he needs to junk the "star" system and instead focus on building a team of players who are not stars on their own but who are capable of working together as a team to outperform teams of expensive prima donnas. He is aided in this project by Peter Brand (played by Jonah Hill Feldstein, who inexplicably omits his last name from his film credit), a young Yale economics graduate. Brand obviously loves baseball. But he is not a jock. He is an obese geek with a love of sports statistics and a knack for number crunching. Together he and Beane assemble a team of undervalued players—has-beens and near-misses—

who, based on their statistics, can "in the aggregate" (e.g., as a team) outperform more expensive rosters of stars.

At first, the new team seems to be a disaster. But it is just growing pains. After Beane trades a few prima donnas for other undervalued players, and kicks a bit of middle management ass, his team hits its stride and goes on a record-breaking 20-game winning streak. Beane's new management techniques are adopted by other teams, giving the Boston Red Sox (which even I have heard of) their first World Series victory in nearly 100 years.

Beane's quantitative approach met a lot of initial resistance from old school management and fans whose approach to baseball is essentially romantic and aesthetic. They maintain that there is something mysterious and ineffable about baseball that cannot be quantified. Baseball, they say, is an art, not a science. It all smacks of 19th-century romanticism and holism. And it is true, of course, that not everything can be meaningfully reduced to numbers.

But it is also true that numerical models can have such predictive power that we can frequently act *as if* the quantifiable is the only factor that matters. For instance, we know that there is more to human intelligence than IQ, and more to the human soul than intelligence. But in terms of its predictive power for a whole array of real-world effects, it is as if IQ alone matters.

What I find objectionable about Beane is not that he subjects the hallowed traditions of baseball to empirical criticism. The ability to stand up to empirical tests (quantitative or otherwise) is what differentiates between what Edmund Burke called "blind" and "wise" prejudices.

No, the real objection to Beane is that he is using quantitative methods to subject the *game* of baseball—which is inextricably caught up with romanticism, sentimentality, and the cult of well-rounded and excellent athletic heroes—to the *business* of baseball, which rates the Oakland A's better than the New York Yankees, simply because the A's spend less money per win. To this mentality, a man who airbrushes Jesus on black velvet is superior to Michelangelo if the former produces more pictures for less money.

I admit that I am annoyed by professional sports, sports

fandom, and sports movies. I despise their ethos of self-indulgent romanticism and perpetual boyishness. I want to smack grown men for wearing baseball caps (if they are not actually playing baseball, that is). Thus I found *Moneyball*'s unsentimental, intellectual approach to baseball appealing. Part of me loved this movie *precisely because I don't love baseball.*

But that's just my prejudices speaking. If Billy Beane went to work for the San Francisco Opera (talk about self-indulgent romanticism!), rather than the Oakland A's, I would be screaming for his head too.

In the end, the romantics are right, because baseball is a *game*, after all. It *shouldn't* be serious. It belongs to the realm of play, not work; luxury and freedom, not necessity; the sacred and aristocratic (the worship of heroes), not the profane and leveling (the statistical "aggregate").

If *Moneyball* teaches us anything, it is the old lesson that the heroes of the business world are all too often the destroyers of the rest of the world: history, tradition, nature, culture, and everything that people hold sacred. *Moneyball* is another example of how the 9-to-5 world erodes and destroys the 5-to-9 world.[1]

Beane is portrayed as a character whose emotional detachment is uniquely suited to a quantitative approach. He obviously loves baseball, but it is intimated that his own professional career fizzled because he was somehow not emotionally invested in it. It is also hinted that he feels victimized by the patter of the old school scouts who convinced him to pass up a full scholarship at Stanford to go professional. Beane then went into scouting and management, which is one step removed from actual play. As a manager, he tries to remain detached. He does not attend games, and he cuts players in a cold, business-like manner. But perhaps as a sop to the romantics, the script shows that Beane has to become more of a "people person" and more emotionally invested in his new team to make it work.

I highly recommend *Moneyball*. It is a serious, intelligent film with a superb script. It is dramatically paced, beautifully photographed, and free of sports movie clichés. There really

---

[1] See Greg Johnson, "5-to-9 Conservatism," http://www.counter-currents.com/2011/10/5-to-9-conservatism/

isn't a weak link in the cast, but Brad Pitt's performance is particularly noteworthy. I would like to see him play Howard Roark in *The Fountainhead*, another story of innovation versus tradition on an even grander scale. (And unlike Billy Beane, Howard Roark's struggle is not merely a disguised form of subjecting art to commerce—although most modern architecture is precisely that.)

But best of all, *Moneyball* is not just thought-provoking and full of lessons for politics and life in general. It is also highly entertaining—which is what sports, at their best, should be.

Counter-Currents/*North American New Right*,
January 31, 2012

THE MONUMENTS MEN

When the great masterpieces of American cinema are taken back to Beijing as war booty, *The Monuments Men* will be in no danger. When I heard that it was directed by, co-authored by, and starred aging bimbo George Clooney, that was all I really needed to know.

The previews were "too much information": I learned that the film also stars Matt Damon, Bill Murray, John Goodman, Cate Blanchett, and Hugh Bonneville (better known as the Earl of Grantham), which means (1) too many cooks, (2) lack of self-confidence in the script, and (3) somewhere in this desert of screen time and top billing there must be the compensation of a tiny waterhole of prestige or numinous virtue where these pachyderm-sized egos can slake their narcissism.

And sure enough, *The Monuments Men* is about *art* and takes place during *The Holocaust* (surely it's safe now to drop the pretense of calling it World War II), which means that, in the United States, it has a natural audience of, say, ten million National Public Radio listeners, six million of them being Jews.

That's a pretty small audience for a $70 million dollar film, especially with stiff competition from real art house films and the Holocaust movie of the month. With overwhelmingly negative reviews, *The Monuments Men* is looking like a box office bomb.

The Monuments Men is about a group of Allied soldiers who were tasked with protecting monuments and preserving and recovering art treasures in Western Europe during World War II. In reality, there were about 400 such individuals, but for the sake of dramatic simplification, this movie deals only with seven Monuments Men, plus one woman, a French woman played by Cate Blanchett, who collaborated with the Nazis but who assures us that she was secretly working for the *résistance* — like 40 million other Frenchmen. Every waiter who spat in a German's food, apparently, was a member of the *résistance*.

Even this limited cast, however, proves too much for director/screenwriter Clooney. The plot of *The Monuments Men* is a confusing mess of multiple storylines and temporal leaps that will baffle most moviegoers. Quentin Tarantino can pull off such plots, but Clooney can't.

The plot would not be problematic if it were anchored in well-realized characters, which the movie lacks. Instead, *The Monuments Men* feels like an old-fashioned guy movie in which a team of cursorily characterized stereotypes comes together to pull off a caper. Such movies work, however, only if the plot is simple and straightforward, and only if the team consists of easily intelligible stereotypes: Midwest farm boy, wop, Appalachian hillbilly, streetwise urban hustler, sassy or sagacious Negro, privileged New England preppy, Southern aristocrat, cowboy, New York Jew, etc.

You can't pull it off with a team consisting of choreographers, sculptors, museum curators, architects, British aesthetes, and art historians. None of these are "types," even to NPR listeners. To most Americans, they might as well be Martians. Or they could be flaming homosexuals. I guess "He's a *choreographer* type" *does* bring certain images to mind. But no, the Monuments Men all seem to be hetero family guys. In short, characters like these need some . . . characterization.

The Monuments Men could also have been saved if it had appropriate dramatic conflict, tension, and forward drive, but it lacks those as well. World War II certainly does not lack conflict, but Clooney just coasts on the mystique of the war. He treats it as delicious nostalgia. He seems to think that all he needs to do to add gravitas is mention *The Holocaust* from time to time.

But all the elements of real dramatic conflict are present here. At the beginning of the film, Clooney's character briefs President Roosevelt on the necessity of their mission by pointing out that Allied bombs had destroyed the Abbey of Monte Cassino near Rome and nearly obliterated Leonardo's *The Last Supper* in Milan (three walls and the roof of the room were destroyed; *The Last Supper* was on the only remaining wall). This alone establishes sufficient motive for the Germans evacuating great works of art and hiding them in mineshafts, but conventional minds don't go there.

The American philistine response is that war is hell, people die and things get broken, and is it really worth spending additional lives to preserve art works and buildings? This issue comes up again and again, but nothing *dramatic* is made of it. With a few high-minded clichés, Clooney manages to turn philistine America into the protectors of European culture, and I was the only one in the theater who found this risible. (One wonders what a French director would have done with this material.)

Of course, if the Allies really cared about European culture, the British and the French would not have started World War II, and the British and the Americans would not have firebombed Dresden and countless other German cities and towns, and the Western Allies would not have saved Soviet Russia and handed over half of Europe to Stalin. Ironically, though, Communism turned out to be less destructive to European high culture than liberal democracy.

In the Second World War, it was only the Axis powers, especially Germany, that evinced any concern for the long-term survival of European culture and European man. If Germany had won the war—or, better yet, if the war could have been avoided—European civilization would not be threatened today by below-replacement birth rates, fast-breeding non-white immigrants, and creeping Islamization in the European heartland.

The Monuments Men could also have been saved if Clooney just had a clear sense of what kind of movie he was making, but even this is lacking. The tone of this movie is inappropriately light, sentimental, and comic (though seldom funny). There are numerous plot digressions that serve no real purpose: a scene in which "Have Yourself a Merry Little Christmas" plays as a young soldier dies, a scene in which two Monuments Men share cigarettes with a scared young German soldier, a scene in which Matt Damon steps on a landmine (played for laughs), etc., etc. There is also an attempted seduction (Cate Blanchett trying to tempt married family man Matt Damon) that reminded me of the romantic subplot in *The Caine Mutiny*, which is my paradigm of a morally and dramatically compromised movie. A self-confident director with a story to tell doesn't need these manipulative and pointless digressions.

Naturally, *The Monuments Men* is filled with propaganda, but it is handled in a curiously slipshod manner. At the beginning, we are told that this movie is "Based on a True Story," which means that it is false, of course. It is also based on a lot of false stories, which means that it falsifies them as well. One doesn't expect fairness to the Nazis, of course, but I did expect some piety towards the massive body of anti-Nazi propaganda and myths that have been building steadily since the 1920s. But apparently, piety towards myths does not mean preserving them unchanged, but retelling them, embroidering them, intensifying them, without any concern for plausibility or consistency.

During the Second World War, the Germans acquired a large number of works of art. These fall into four categories: (1) works they bought outright; (2) works they forced their owners to sell; (3) works that were taken as war booty; and (4) works that were taken, as it were, into protective custody to prevent their destruction from Allied bombs.

The Monuments Men repeatedly intones the high-minded principle that the great works of European art rightfully belong to mankind. But if that is the case, then (1) private collections are a violation of the rights of mankind, and (2) why does it matter where such works are displayed, as long as they are visible to the public?

Jewish collectors and art dealers, for instance, were forced to sell their art works rather than emigrate with them; many countries to this day forbid private citizens to emigrate with works of art that are considered elements of their cultural patrimony, and many countries today actively pursue the repatriation of such works as well.

Yet *The Monuments Men* deplores German forced sales of private collections as "theft," even though (1) the works were bought not stolen, and (2) the best works were reserved by Hitler for a huge museum in Linz, a museum that would be open to *the public*. Göring too intended his collections to be given to the public upon his death. Since it does not really matter *where* the great works of European art are displayed, as long as they *are* displayed and cared for properly, Hitler's "theft" of Jewish private collections has to be seen as, on balance, a good thing if we really believe that the great works of European art belong to mankind.

The same argument applies to war booty. If the great works of art belong to mankind, then what difference does it make if they become booty of war and are moved from one private collection to another, or from one public collection to another? The only *net* loss to mankind is if works are moved from public to private collections. But if Hitler and the Germans had their way, the net flow would have been overwhelmingly in the opposite direction, from private to public, which is a net boon for mankind. *The Monuments Men* obfuscates this issue, on the one hand mentioning Hitler's plans for a giant museum in Linz but on the other hand prating about how "one man" should not have too many of the world's art treasures (unless he is a Rothschild, of course).

Most of the great works of art have well-documented histories or *provenances*. These histories include many "thefts" in times of war. For instance, Van Eyck's Ghent Altarpiece, which features prominently in the movie, has been stolen in part or whole at least seven times. After the French Revolution, the altarpiece was moved to Paris where it was displayed in the Louvre. In 1815, after the fall of Napoleon, it was returned to Ghent. But the very year it was returned, two panels of the altarpiece were *pawned* by the Diocese of Ghent for a paltry sum and never redeemed. Eventually they were purchased by the King of Prussia for a vast sum of money and exhibited to the public in the Gemäldegalerie Berlin. In the meantime, in 1822, the remaining panels were damaged by fire. Two other panels were sent to Brussels. During the First World War, the remaining panels of the altarpiece were taken to Berlin. But after the war, due to an express provision in the Treaty of Versailles, the entire altarpiece (including the panels purchased by the King of Prussia) were returned to Ghent, where the whole altarpiece was exhibited, until 1934, when one panel was stolen. (It has never been recovered.) During the Second World War, Hitler ordered the altarpiece to be seized for his planned museum in Linz. Then, after the war, the American Monuments Men stole it from the Russians, since the altarpiece and thousands of other works of art were stored in a salt mine which fell within the Russian zone of occupation.

Now, if the Ghent Altarpiece is part of the cultural heritage of mankind, shouldn't the only real considerations be (1) that it be displayed to mankind, and (2) that it be properly cared for? And, given the record of the Diocese of Ghent, which pawned part of the altarpiece, allowed the bulk of it to be damaged by fire, and allowed one panel to be stolen, mankind might well have found a more caring trustee in Adolf Hitler.

Of course many art works are destroyed during war, which is also a loss to mankind. But this would happen much more often if art works were not valued. But their high value also makes them prime targets for conversion into war booty. Because Hitler, Göring, and other leaders of the Third Reich put such a high premium on art and culture—and not just German art and culture, but European art and culture as a whole—during the final months of the Third Reich they devoted many scarce and desperately needed resources to preserving works of art from Allied bombing. If only the Germans had been able to save more, and the Allies had tried to destroy less.

The Monuments Men obfuscates this fact with a vile and deliberate lie: that Hitler had ordered the destruction of great works of art to prevent them from falling into Allied hands. First, we are told of Hitler's "Nero Decree," also known as his "Scorched Earth" order: according to the movie, if Hitler died, he wanted to take Germany with him, including all of the art treasures he had stolen. As I understand it, the Nero Decree did not include cultural treasures but instead infrastructure that the Allied invaders might find useful. In the movie, though, signed copies of the decree are brandished by the Monuments Men as if the Führer himself had faxed them over. Furthermore, the day before his suicide, Hitler willed his art collections to the German nation, which hardly makes sense if he planned to destroy them.

Second, a short, ugly, sickly-looking SS officer (you know the type) is shown in one of Hitler's mineshaft repositories in Heilbronn ordering the contents reduced to ashes with flamethrowers (as if this would not kill the villains themselves from smoke inhalation). One of the incinerated paintings is Raphael's *Portrait of a Young Man*, a work which disappeared in

Silesia near the end of the war. The Polish government claims to know that the painting survived the war, but whatever its fate, it was not reduced to ashes in a mineshaft due to Hitler's Nero Decree.

When the Monuments Men search the repository, they find a carbonized frame with a metal plate engraved "Pablo Picasso." The Frenchwoman also claims that works by Picasso and Klee were burned by the Germans in Paris. This seems highly unlikely. When the Germans removed "degenerate art" from their museums, they sold it to fools abroad. And if they wanted to rid the world of Picassos, they could have gone directly to the source, since Picasso himself remained in Paris during the German Occupation, painting away.

The Monuments Men is a deeply dishonest and dumb film, but I have saved the worst for last: after the war, Clooney interrogates the weedy SS pyromaniac, who also ran "one of those camps" for lulz on the side. Clooney paints a beatific vision of his return to New York where he can buy a toasted onion bagel from Moe Dalitz or Hyman Diamond or some other stereotypically Jewish deli owner and read in the *New York Times* about this German's execution for war crimes. It is a perfect image of a WASP airhead who thinks he runs America and is magnanimously sticking up for the "poor Jews," paying them all the while to poison his body and his mind. One wonders if Clooney himself actually thinks this way, or if he is just playing dumb and sucking up to America's real rulers.

Counter-Currents/*North American New Right*,
February 11, 2014

MULHOLLAND DRIVE

David Lynch is the greatest director working today, one of the greatest of all time. *Mulholland Drive* is his latest film. It is one of his best. Those who took their grandmothers to see Lynch's last film *The Straight Story* should not take them to *Mulholland Drive*, which most closely resembles Lynch's *Lost Highway*.

Like *Lost Highway*, *Mulholland Drive* is filled with sex, violence, decadence, and dark humor. Both films have almost unintelligible plots. Both are set in Los Angeles. Both films are magnets for perforated misfits who think that Lynch is celebrating their own decadence and snickering along with them at wholesome, traditional white American values. In fact, however, *Mulholland Drive*, like all of Lynch's movies, is a categorical indictment of the decadence of modern American society by a man who truly believes in traditional white American values.

David Lynch would love to live in Twin Peaks or *Blue Velvet*'s Lumberton. He would love to live in the world of *Leave it to Beaver* and *My Three Sons*. In *Blue Velvet*, *Twin Peaks*, and above all *The Straight Story*, he celebrates the independence, resourcefulness, and Eagle Scout virtues of ordinary, sincere, straight-arrow Americans. But he knows that their world is constantly threatened by evil forces. These evil forces work through the channels of culture and politics, but they are not merely cultural and political. They are spiritual.

Lynch is a modern-day Manichean; a mystic who believes in the reality of the demonic, of evil forces that first enter and then dominate our souls through our vices, follies, and blind spots. These demonic forces are personified in different ways in different films: as The Man in the Planet in *Eraserhead*, which is the ultimate gnostic anti-sex film; as Killer Bob in *Twin Peaks*; as The Mystery Man in *Lost Highway*—and as The Cowboy in *Mulholland Drive*.

Lynch even has developed a visual code to indicate the presence of these forces: smoke; flickering electricity; movie theater drapes, especially red ones (the Veil of Maya); freakish and deformed people; time that moves backwards or in loops;

and all the machinery of Plato's Cave—the stage, the screen, the movie studio, Los Angeles itself—that stands between us and the truth, that keeps us in bondage to illusion.

So Lynch is a kind of religious conservative. But is he racially aware? I would venture to say: Yes. First, throughout his films, Lynch has cast very few Jews and non-whites. Second, most of the non-whites he has cast are criminals, lowlifes, and buffoons, e.g., Bob Ray Lemon, Reggie and the Mexican sisters Juana and Perdita in *Wild at Heart*, and the two Negroes working in the hardware store in *Blue Velvet*. The only exceptions that come to mind are in *Twin Peaks*: Deputy Hawk, an American Indian, and Albert Rosenfeld, a sneering, arrogant, urban Jew who turns out to be a good guy under it all. It should be noted, however, that Lynch was not in complete creative control of the *Twin Peaks* series.

Mulholland Drive provides the strongest evidence of Lynch's racial awareness. But first, something about the plot of the film. *Mulholland Drive* falls into two parts. The first part is a mystery story and satire of Hollywood that is engaging, suspenseful, and extremely funny. Then the story turns darker. A woman's rotting corpse is found in her apartment. Then comes a lesbian seduction. Then a journey to a mysterious club called "Silencio" where performers mime to pre-recorded tracks. We are moved by a beautiful Mexican love song sung by Rebekah Del Rio. (It is actually a translation of a Roy Orbison song.) We are encompassed by the illusion. We forget that it is an illusion. Then the illusion is shattered when the singer falls dead on the stage but the song plays on. A blue box is discovered. When it is opened, the second half of the movie commences. The second half is dark and tragic. It is told through a series of flashbacks. It culminates in madness and suicide. I am not giving anything away by saying that, as I read it, the first part of the movie is the dream of a dying madwoman, and the second part explains what drove her to madness and death.

The most remarkable feature of this movie is its entirely negative, and entirely accurate, portrayal of Hollywood Jews.

We see a beautiful blonde, blue-eyed woman, starry-eyed and grinning with joy as she arrives in Los Angeles. Her name is Betty, played by Naomi Watts. Betty has come to Hollywood to be an actress. She is a classic Lynch heroine: an earnest, wholesome, small-town girl from Deep River, Ontario. She speaks in the G-rated clichés of old Hollywood. Later we discover that she became interested in acting after winning a jitterbug contest.

Betty is next to an elderly, white-haired woman named Irene. They have met and struck up a friendship on the plane. Irene seems to be from the same wholesome mold. She and her elderly male travelling companion bid Betty goodbye and good luck. Then we see Irene and her friend in the back of a limousine, their faces insanely distorted with cynical, sniggering leers. The man has stereotypically Jewish features. (The actor's name is Dan Birnbaum.) They are apparently enjoying a good laugh at the expense of this naïve, corn-fed *shiksa*. Later they return as demonic apparitions.

Another Jew, Dan (played by Patrick Fischler), meets a well-dressed gentile, Herb, at a Winky's restaurant. The gentile is apparently a psychotherapist. The Jew is his patient. This is no surprise. Jews had to invent psychoanalysis because they practically invented neurosis, what with their "high investment" parenting strategies and the hatred and fear of non-Jews they instill practically in the womb. This Jew is certainly neurotic, but he may have a touch of divine madness.

He describes two dreams he has had, both of them set in the restaurant. In the dream, he sees through the walls. Behind them is a face that utterly terrifies him. The two men go behind the restaurant. The Jew sees the face (played by Bonnie Aarons) and faints dead away. The psychotherapist does not see it, but we will see this face again. It is the face of an embodiment of supernatural evil. It is the face of a devil, maybe the devil. It is he who is ultimately behind all the walls in this movie, pulling the strings in Hollywood, drawing people to their doom.

The central Jewish character in this movie is Adam Kesher, a hotshot young director played by Justin Theroux. We meet Kesher on a bad day. He is being pressured by two mysterious Italians, the Castiglione brothers (played by Dan Hedaya and composer Angelo Badalamenti) to cast a particular girl in his film. He refuses. The mysterious wire-puller Mr. Roque orders Kesher's movie shut down. Mr. Roque is played by Michael J. Anderson, the dancing dwarf from *Twin Peaks*. Even the drape-lined set is similar, although more luxurious, as if the Little Man from Far Away has received a promotion in the hierarchy of Hell. (Roque does not dance because he is in a wheelchair.)

Kesher then finds his blonde *shiksa* in bed with a beefy, tattooed Aryan working man played by Billy Ray Cyrus, who drives him out of his house. (The side of Cyrus's pickup truck reads "Gene Clean.") Kesher hides out in a sleazy hotel, but "they"—the wire-pullers—somehow find him. His credit cards are cancelled and his bank accounts emptied. Finally, he is told to meet with someone known only as "The Cowboy."

Kesher is filled with just the sort of cynical, sarcastic contempt for cowboys that one would expect. The Cowboy's appearance is accompanied by flickering electricity, announcing his supernatural origin. He is an enforcer in Hell's hierarchy. He looks and talks and dresses like an overgrown child in a cowboy suit that is slightly too large for him. Kesher can barely contain his arrogance. He is smug, supercilious, smirking, ironic. In The Cowboy's words, he's a "smart Alec." But this cornfed *goy* manages to scare and humble him nonetheless. He chooses the girl.

Later in the film, we see him at a party celebrating his engagement to another beautiful *shiksa*, this one a brunette. His conceit, affectedness, and irreverent frivolity are boundless. We also see from whom he gets it. His mother, played by Ann Miller, is a nasty, gnarled, snobbish old biddy with too much jewelry and too little taste.

There are other, minor Jewish characters in the film. One pair appears in a wonderfully satirical audition scene. Jimmy Katz, played by Chad Everett, looks like a dashing older WASP, while Martha Johnson (played by Kate Forster) looks stereotypically Jewish. A comment on name and nose changes, perhaps? The slightly bitchy, slightly dykey woman in Apartment 12 also looks quite Jewish, and the actress's name turns out to be Johanna Stein.

There are only two Negroes in the film, and they are there

strictly for laughs. They are backup singers in a 1950s set piece directed by Adam Kesher. Not only are the Negroes' faces comical (one looks like a drag queen), but their very presence is risible, because integrated music groups are not plausible for the period. But this is the Jew Adam Kesher's film, not David Lynch's, and in the Hollywood of today's Jews there are Negroes everywhere. I watched the film in theatres twice, and both audiences saw and laughed at the joke.

I cannot say anything more about this film without giving away the plot. Suffice it to say that *Mulholland Drive* is a beautiful, funny, shocking, mysterious film about how people like us are destroyed by the Hollywood illusion machine, a machine run by the devil but staffed by people like Adam Kesher.

Lynch strips away the Veil of Maya and tells us to be silent. Yes. Be silent. Think about what you have seen. As I pondered this deeply disturbing, uncanny film, my perplexity slowly turned to understanding, my understanding to anger, my anger to the desire to fight. Frankly, I do not know how to fight the devil. Perhaps we'll figure that out someday. But there are enough Adam Keshers to keep us busy in the meantime.

VNN, December 2001

Nebraska

Nebraska is a low-budget, black and white movie starring Bruce Dern and Will Forte (*Saturday Night Live*), as well as Bob Odenkirk (Saul Goodman in *Breaking Bad*). *Nebraska* was nominated for the Palme d'Or at the 2013 Cannes Film Festival, where Dern won the Best Actor award. Since then, *Nebraska* has been nominated for 6 Academy Awards, including Best Picture, Best Director (Alexander Payne), Best Actor (Dern), Best Supporting Actress (June Squibb, who plays Dern's wife), and Best Original Screenplay (Bob Nelson). *Nebraska* has also enjoyed generally positive reviews. Buoyed by its critical success, *Nebraska* is now showing around the country, but I urge you to skip it.

Nebraska is being sold as a heart-warming comedy/drama about rural, salt-of-the-earth white Americans in Montana and Nebraska. But it is exactly the kind of movie about such people that one would expect to find favor in Cannes and Hollywood: sneering, contemptuous, and vulgar—an insult to the very people who are being swindled into buying tickets.

But *Nebraska* is not just vicious, it is also inept. And it is not even spectacular in its ineptitude. It is just curiously flat, hollow, and dull. The acting, directing, and screenplay are utterly mediocre. I've seen better movies on the Lifetime channel.

Why, then, has such a mediocre movie been nominated for so many honors? Simply because it plays to the prejudices of the critics: urban, liberal, Jewish or spiritually Judaized, and anti-American for all the wrong reasons. (The New Right is anti-American because America is anti-white. The Left is anti-American because they are anti-white.)

Dern plays Woody Grant, a senile old drunk who lives in Billings, Montana. Woody has received a letter informing him that he might have won $1 million. It is just a gimmick for selling magazines. But Woody believes he has won, and is determined to go to Lincoln, Nebraska, to collect his winnings. No longer allowed to drive, Woody sets off on foot, only to be brought home by the police.

Finally, Woody's son David (Will Forte) agrees to drive his

father to Lincoln, using it as an opportunity to spend time with his father, who turns out to be a thoroughly unlikeable, self-absorbed individual. On the way, they have many adventures. For instance, Woody gets drunk, loses his dentures, and falls and cuts his head.

Eventually, Woody and David stop by Woody's home town of Hawthorne, Nebraska. They are then joined by Woody's wife Kate (June Squibb) and their other son Ross (Bob Odenkirk) for a family reunion. Kate is portrayed as a hateful, sex-obsessed, foul-mouthed shrew. Woody's family are portrayed as dullards, vacantly swilling beer, staring at the television, and mumbling in monosyllables.

When news of Woody's winnings gets around, family and friends start remembering old debts and trying to share in his good fortune. Other trivial events ensue. Finally, Woody gets to Lincoln, where he is informed that he is not a millionaire after all. Then David, ever the enabler, humors his father yet again, and the movie ends on a note that is supposed to be heart-warming but is really just pathetic.

As drama, *Nebraska* is flat and uninvolving. The director, screenwriter, and actors are too concerned with holding the characters at arm's length and sneering at them to actually inhabit them and turn them into interesting human beings. The comic elements of *Nebraska* are entirely at the expense of the characters, but the satire is not particularly cutting or clever. It is merely smug and self-congratulatory. This could be a really evil film, but the director and screenwriter simply lack the talent to bring something like that off.

I do not deny that there is truth in this movie's satire of working-class and rural white Americans. There are lots of obese, alcoholic, petty, greedy, vulgar, heartless, and tasteless white people in America. And I am every bit the urban SWPL as the director Payne and screenwriter Nelson. If anything, I am a far better educated and a far bigger snob. I look down on people like this too. But in the end, they are still my people, and I do not wish to see them mocked in their degraded state, particularly by denizens and profiteers of the junk culture industry that is one of the major causes of their corruption. I want to see them raised up, not put down. I want them to have better jobs, better food, better culture, and better lives. I want to destroy the system that degrades them, the system that produces crap like *Nebraska*. The creators of this movie, however, view its subjects across an abyss of alienation so vast that empathy cannot span it.

The saddest thing about this gulf, though, is that it is entirely artificial. Director Payne and screenwriter Nelson as well as the rest of the cast (aside from a couple of Mexican bit players) are all white Americans. As are most of the smug, superior urbanites who get such a good chuckle and a warm feeling of superiority from this film. The gulf, in short, is not between Jew and gentile, but between white and white: between town and country, rich and poor, big people and little people, progressive, "educated" people and "those people." It is an ancient wound in the flesh of our people, where Jews and maggots now feast. It is a wound that must be healed by an overarching sense of white kinship and solidarity if our race is to be saved.

The flaws of *Nebraska* can best be appreciated by contrasting it with a similar movie, David Lynch's *The Straight Story*, which is based on the true story of Alvin Straight, an elderly Midwesterner who, no longer able to drive a car, decided to ride his lawnmower across three states to visit his long-estranged brother who'd had a stroke. Lynch, who grew up in Missoula, Montana, tells Straight's story with affection and empathy because, ultimately, both director and subject belong to the same people, and Lynch knows and feels it. Thus we are led to admire Alvin for his strength and resourcefulness, as well as his wisdom and kindness. *The Straight Story* is a portrait of a man who deals with the debilities of age with dignity.

Nebraska is, in effect, a remake of *The Straight Story* by a mediocre director and screenwriter who feel nothing but contempt for white Americans. I suggest that you return the favor.

Counter-Currents/*North American New Right*,
February 4, 2014

PERSON OF INTEREST

Recently, while staying with a friend who had just gotten out of the hospital, I was exposed to a good deal of TV. Two shows caught my attention: *Downton Abbey* and *Person of Interest*, which runs on CBS on Thursday nights. At first, I thought *Person of Interest* might merely serve to tide me over until the next seasons of *Burn Notice* and *Breaking Bad*.

Like *Burn Notice*, the main character of *Person of Interest* is an ex-spy who uses his craft to help ordinary people in need. Like *Burn Notice*, there are also longer storylines that arch over multiple episodes.

But now, having watched the first 15 episodes of *Person of Interest*, I have to say that I like *Person of Interest* even better than *Burn Notice*, which is high praise indeed.

The premise of *Person of Interest* is that after 9/11, the US government created a computer network, "the machine," which reads all of our emails, tracks our transactions, listens to our phone calls, and analyzes all video feeds in order to predict acts of terrorism, or as they say now, in honor of George W. Bush, "terror" (pronounced with one syllable). The machine can also predict acts of violence against ordinary citizens. But the government does nothing to stop those.

The creator of the machine is a reclusive billionaire, Harold Finch, played by Michael Emerson (Ben in *Lost*, i.e., the most interesting character in the longest-running, most obnoxious cheat in television history). Finch is haunted by the fates of the random innocents the government does nothing to protect. Surely, he also feels a bit guilty for having turned Uncle Sam into Big Brother—although we learn that he tried to build in protections against that.

Finch decides he wants to try to make the world a better place by preventing the crimes the government will do nothing to stop. But he is a geek with a gimp, so he has to hire a tough guy, John Reese, a former US Army Special Forces soldier and CIA operative who is haunted by the evils he did for Uncle Sam. Reese is played by Jim Caviezel, who played Jesus in Mel Gibson's *The Passion of the Christ*. Together Finch and Reese seek to prevent crimes while being hunted as criminal vigilantes by the CIA and the New York City police (where the show is set).

Jim Caviezel is immensely impressive as John Reese. The only other role I had seen him in was Jesus in *The Passion of the Christ*, and it was not really a good gauge of his talents, given that he spent the movie speaking Aramaic and getting the bejeezus beaten out of him.

Caviezel is a tall, slim, blue-eyed man in his 40s with graying brown hair. But his most arresting features are his soft voice and astonishingly mobile face. Both are remarkably subtle and expressive. His face is handsome in repose, but when he acts, it is a play of light and shadow, in which every line, wrinkle, and crag communicates a deep and complex character. One has the impression that as age etches more lines in Caviezel's face, he will only grow more charismatic and expressive.

But Caviezel's John Reese is more than just soulful. He is also a man of action who is extremely handy with every known weapon, including his bare hands. He is definitely a man you want on your side. Reese is a classic Nordic hero: laconic, intelligent, self-aware, noble, and courageous. He does his duty without concern for the consequences to himself or others. (He leaves those for the gods to sort out.) He is deadly serious about serious things, but he also has an ironic touch when dealing with the petty and absurd.

Like Michael Westen in *Burn Notice*, John Reese exemplifies what Julius Evola calls Uranian masculinity. He is not a playboy or skirt chaser. He is focused on his mission and his ideals, which creates an aloof and emotionally self-contained quality — not unlike the Taoist sage-emperor or Aristotle's unmoved mover — that is enormously attractive to higher types of women.

If Caviezel had been born a few decades earlier, he could have given Clint Eastwood serious competition for his iconic gunslinger and detective roles — and in fair auditions, he would have beaten Eastwood every time. Imagine a Dirty Harry who actually *felt* he was dirty.

As the series unfolds, we learn that Reese came to hate himself for the things he did in the service of America. He has lost all fear of death and attachment to life. He feels that he has lost his soul. Hence his willingness to put his life on the line day after day, and his cold-blooded calm in the face of danger. But of course Reese still has his soul, or a smoldering ember of one, because he risks death only for what is right. He is really fighting for redemption. (This is a far nobler quest—and one with far greater dramatic potential—than Michael Westen's desire in *Burn Notice* to get his soul-killing job back and find out who burned him.)

Person of Interest is one of the best written shows on television. It is on par with *Breaking Bad*, one of the finest television shows of all time, in my opinion. It is written and produced by one of the best writers around: Jonathan Nolan, the brother of Christopher Nolan, director of *Memento, The Prestige, The Dark Knight, Inception*, etc. Jonathan Nolan co-authored the scripts to *The Prestige, The Dark Knight*, and its sequel *The Dark Knight Rises*, which is now in production.

Person of Interest is mercifully free of political correctness. Yes, one of the admirable characters is a black female police officer, yet she is wholly believable. But there is no egregious casting against stereotype.

The portrayal of the US government is entirely negative. The CIA agents are portrayed as treacherous and callous killers who obviously have no sense of allegiance to the United States. They sell drugs to Americans to finance the war on "terror," that is to say, the war against the enemies of Israel and Jews around the world. They refer to operations in the US as being "behind enemy lines" or "in country." (One wonders if they speak of Israel that way.) The New York City police are portrayed as riddled with corruption and cynicism.

"The machine" is Orwell's nightmare made real. (It is prefigured in *The Dark Knight*.) But the true obscenity is that it is not even used to fight crime. It is the perfect illustration of Sam Francis' concept of "anarcho-tyranny": the government violates the privacy of every decent, law-abiding citizen while allowing crime and corruption to run unchecked.

Jim Caviezel is a devout Roman Catholic. He is married with three children. His mother was Irish-American. His father is of Slovak and Swiss descent. The name Caviezel is Romansh, the language indigenous to Switzerland. Caviezel is also politically conservative. He has donated to Rick Santorum. He also made a commercial opposing embryonic stem cell research. From a white racialist point of view, these are not issues that matter, but I admire Caviezel's courage for taking politically incorrect stands.

Despite his evident talent, Caviezel has suffered career discrimination for playing Jesus in *The Passion of the Christ*, since Jews in Hollywood (and everywhere else) do not forgive or forget. Frankly, *Person of Interest* may well be his last chance before doing dinner theater. For that reason alone, I would be inclined to root for this show. But *Person of Interest* is good enough to recommend on its own merits. If you *must* watch television, then by all means, watch *Person of Interest*.

Counter-Currents/*North American New Right*,
February 18, 2012

Predators

Recently, I went to see *Predators*, a sequel to the 1987 Arnold Schwarzenegger movie *Predator*, about a group of American Special Forces commandos in the Central American jungle who find themselves being hunted by an extraterrestrial, the Predator.

Predator was not that good a movie, but the premise was interesting. It was ripped off and developed nicely in *Star Trek: Voyager* with the Hirojan race of hunters. I thought *Predators* might further develop the premise because I had heard that it was set on the Predator planet and because it was directed by the versatile and talented Robert Rodriguez.

Unfortunately, I was mistaken. Rodriguez was not the director, and the movie was a disappointing waste of time: just your standard diverse cast (two Jews, three whites, two blacks, a Mexican, and a Japanese) running around in the jungle dodging traps and rubber-headed monsters.

There is not much by way of plot or characterization, and the suspense and scares are pretty lame as well.

The cast of *Predators* is remarkably ugly, and I am not talking about the monsters. I am talking about Adrien Brody, Laurence Fishburne, and Danny Trejo. (The only head worth hunting belongs to Topher Grace.)

But the ugliest thing about this movie is its subtext of Jewish hatred for non-Jews, which is the reason I am bothering to write about it at all. Be warned: I am going to summarize the whole story. But don't worry: it is impossible to "spoil" a movie as rotten as this one.

The movie opens in free fall. Literally. A heavily armed mercenary, Adrien Brody, is plunging to the jungle. His parachute deploys at the last minute. On the ground, he finds seven others in the same situation: a female sniper from the Israel Defense Forces (one of the morally different people who wear T-shirts featuring crosshairs on a pregnant Palestinian woman and the motto "One Shot, Two Kills"), a black death squad member from Sierra Leone, a white Russian Special Forces soldier, a Mexican drug cartel enforcer, a white American psychopath on death row, a Japanese gangster, and a white American doctor. All of them are armed except the doctor, who is rather out of place.

Adrien Brody immediately recognizes the female sniper as a member of the IDF. She seems to have J-dar as well. They sync up better than the other murderers and miscreants, and they appoint themselves the leaders.

Brody is both intelligent and ruthless. By following him, the band determines that they have been spirited away from Earth and dumped on an alien planet where they are being hunted by three hideous aliens.

When the Mexican is wounded, Brody decides to leave him behind because he senses a trap. (The IDF sniper shoots him. It is all the help he can expect.)

Brody then tracks the aliens to their camp to get a look at them. He uses the rest of the party as bait. The black mercenary is killed, but Brody deems it a small price to get a look at the enemy.

Later, Brody uses the doctor as bait to hunt down an alien that is also being hunted by the Predators.

They are *goyim*, after all. They deserve to die.

The party then runs into Laurence Fishburne, a black American soldier who has been stranded and hunted for so many years that he has lost his mind. He gives them some useful information on the Predators, including the location of one of their spaceships.

The IDF sniper also has some useful information, gleaned from the no doubt Top Secret files of the US military about the 1987 incident in Central America. (What, do you think that the US government has any secrets that a humble IDF sniper can't access?)

Fishburne then tries to kill his guests, but Brody attracts the attention of the Predators, who dispatch Fishburne. Two other members of the party are also killed by the Predators: the white convict and the Russian Special Forces soldier, who kills one of the Predators as well. But they are *goyim*. Their lives aren't worth Adrien Brody's hangnail.

The two Jews, the white doctor, and the Japanese gangster flee Fishburne's lair in search of the Predator ship. They are pursued by the two remaining Predators.

For some inscrutable Oriental reason, the Japanese decides to fight one of the Predators with a samurai sword. Hey, sword fights sell popcorn! The Predator is killed, and so is the Japanese.

The two Jews and the doctor run on, pursued by the last Predator. The doctor is injured and can't walk. This makes him useless to Brody. But then an idea dawns on him. Perhaps he can be useful after all.

In the presence of the injured doctor, Brody suggests to the IDF sniper that they booby-trap him, so that when the Predator comes to collect a trophy, he gets blown up. Of course the doctor will blow up too. But he is a *goy*. His life has no value.

The doctor, of course, is horrified, and the IDF woman refuses to go along with the plan. Brody leaves them behind. They hobble along together and are snared by the Predator, who tosses them in a pit and then goes after Brody.

Brody, in the meantime, has reached the camp. When they were in the camp before, they noticed a Predator being held captive. Fishburne has explained that there are two different groups of Predators who are at odds with each other. The captive is a member of the oppressed group.

Exploiting divisions among enemies is something that comes naturally to Brody. He thinks that he can make a deal with the captive. If Brody frees him, the captive will help him get back to Earth.

It is a preposterous notion, given that he has no way of communicating and no reason to trust the prisoner. But I guess the director reasoned that anyone stupid enough to still be watching would not care.

Brody's plan seems like it is working. He races to the ship. Apparently it is on autopilot. It will just take him home. (Gee, I hope it can land itself too!) The freed Predator fights its former captor, buying Brody time, but is killed. The victor then blows up the ship by remote control.

Meanwhile, down in the pit, we discover that the cute helpless white American doctor is really a serial killer. He paralyzes the IDF sniper with a neurotoxin, telling her that it will not impair her ability to feel all the horrors she is going to suffer. She is beginning to regret her decision to save him.

I am beginning to regret the time I have wasted, the $11 for the ticket, the fare for the streetcar.

And why would the doctor decide to paralyze his only possible chance for survival?

But then Brody appears. He missed the spaceship. He saves the sniper, wounds the doctor, and booby-traps his body with grenades. When the Predator turns him over, they blow up together.

Lesson to the IDF sniper: don't get sentimental about the *goyim*. Treacherous they are. Regret it you will. Plan A (booby-trapping the wounded *goy*) was the right way to go all along.

The Predator is wounded but not killed. After a brutal fight, Brody dispatches it. The only ones left are the Jews. Talk about survivors! After exchanging names, the two *Jewbermenschen*, wounded and exhausted, fall asleep in each other's arms.

The next morning they stand in the jungle watching more parachutes falling from the sky. Brody rasps out that they are going to "find a way off this fucking rock." Roll credits.

I smell sequel.

I first sensed that this movie was not directed by Robert Rodriguez when the J-dar between Brody and the sniper went off. It is just not his style.

Then, a few minutes later, as the two Jews are discussing why they were dumped on this planet, Brody says "We were chosen." An hour later, the two Jews say "We were chosen" again. I was not the only person snickering at the obviousness of it.

When the credits started to roll, the screen went bright blue, and in a totally jarring, stupidly incongruous touch, an obnoxious R&B "oldie" started blasting out of the speakers. Was it an attempt at irony? What kind of Nimrod directed this movie anyway?

Then I saw the director's name: Nimród Antal. Now the sort of Christians who name their children Zebediah and Melchizedek would not use a name like Nimrod. But since the founding of Israel, Jews have dusted off even Old Testament names like Nimrod, which does not refer to a historical individual and was probably never even used as a name in antiquity.

According to Wikipedia, Nimród Antal is a Hungarian. A Hungarian born in Los Angeles who works in the film business. Maybe he is a Hungarian in the same way that Steven

Spielberg is an American. But if Antal is not a Jew, he is one of their faithful servants, a self-hating gentile.

I wish that *Predators* were an unusual movie, but it is not. Jewish hatred of gentiles is part of the text and subtext of practically every Hollywood film. *Predators* is just a drop in an ocean of racial hatred, just a drip of the Talmudic poison that Hollywood has been pumping into the cultural veins of Western man for nearly a century. Time to pull the tubes.

"Predators All"
The Occidental Observer, July 16, 2010

PROMETHEUS

With its stunning H. R. Giger designs and first-rate cast, Ridley Scott's classic *Alien* (1979) is imaginative, visually striking, immensely atmospheric, and sometimes just plain terrifying. Together with its worthy but very different sequel, James Cameron's *Aliens* (1986), it spawned a vast pop-culture "franchise" (which is Hollywood-speak for a mythos) including two unworthy sequels, *Alien 3* and *Alien: Resurrection*, plus two Z-grade *Alien vs. Predator* movies, plus scores of often excellent Aliens comics and novels (yes, I read a slew of them in the '90s), and now Ridley Scott's prequel *Prometheus*.

Prometheus is a visually dazzling movie (particularly in 3-D), but it is very disappointing on every other level.

On the most superficial level, it was so gross that I was reduced to dry heaves at one point—which is why I don't feel any compunction about "spoiling" the plot, such as it is. So consider yourself warned.

The deepest disappointment is that *Prometheus* severs the tap root that has nourished the vast and ramifying Alien cosmos: mystery. In *Alien*, the beacon, the crashed ship, the "space jockey," and the aliens themselves are all deeply mysterious. But it is not an unpleasant mystery, crying out for answers. Indeed, the mystery is part of the fun. It contributes to the atmosphere. This is why *Alien* is essentially a supernatural, haunted-house thriller, despite the sci-fi trappings.

Unfortunately, these trappings have invited the "there's got to be a rational explanation for this" people to chime in and try to explain the mystery away. And, to make matters worse, these vulgarians are so cynical that their rational explanation is completely incoherent. But they are apparently counting on special effects to sufficiently stupefy their audience—if they are not already stupid enough—so that nobody will ask questions.

We learn in *Prometheus* that the space jockeys are just giant humanoids under their mysterious exoskeleton-like suits and helmets.

We learn that they came to Earth, apparently billions of years ago, and seeded it with life when one of them drank a dark liquid which caused him to dismember and dissolve into a lake. Yet somehow his scattered DNA became our DNA, apparently skipping a few million generations of what we know as evolution.

Yes, a dismembered giant is part of the Norse creation myth. But don't get too excited: there are a lot of myths alluded to in this movie, but they are there merely to gild its vacuous plot, like the iridescent sheen of a soap bubble wrapped around a void.

Oddly enough, although the space jockeys' only connection to us is DNA, ancient peoples somehow had memories of them, which they expressed in their art, giving us a map to the planet from whence they came. (But wait, it turns out to be not the planet from which they came billions of years ago, but a planet where they established a bioweapons facility operating only a couple thousand years ago.)

I know, it is just a farrago of ancient astronaut lore, but it is put forward as post-religious, pseudo-scientific substitute for creation myths to explain how we got here. (But who created the space gods?)

In 2089, two archaeologists, Elizabeth Shaw (played by Noomi Rapace, the original Swedish *Girl with the Dragon Tattoo*, looking here like a young Jennifer Saunders) and Charlie Holloway (Logan Marshall-Green), find a 35,000-year-old star map in Scotland. They convince aged and ailing trillionaire Peter Weyland to fund a space mission to the planet that appears on the star map, where they claim we will find the "Engineers" of life on Earth. Weyland funds the mission, hoping that our makers will restore his health (!).

Why did Scott cast the youngish and handsome Guy Pearce as Weyland, under loads of fake-looking makeup and prosthetics, rather than just hire a genuine old man? It is not like the role, which is hardly more than a bit part, required special acting abilities, or that Pearce even has such abilities. Hell, the CGI department could have whipped up a more plausible performance.

Five years later, the spaceship *Prometheus* arrives at a small moon orbiting a larger planet. They set down near some domed cyclopean structures that resemble the weathered stumps of immense rugose cones. The scientists enter the structures and find a decapitated space jockey. Elizabeth Shaw and one of the extras take his well-preserved head back to the ship to examine it. For no apparent reason, the head oozes and explodes just like the original space jockey who seeded Earth. DNA analysis proves that he is human.

Meanwhile, David, a rather fey, blonde, and treacherous android played by Michael Fassbender (just like the treacherous android in *Alien* played by Ian Holm), has spirited away one of the many cylinders found near the dead space jockey, cylinders that for no apparent reason begin to ooze a black liquid. For no apparent reason, David puts a bit of the black ooze in a drink and offers it to Charlie Holloway, who for no apparent reason is drunk and despondent after making the greatest discovery in human history. Charlie then has sex with Elizabeth, who is sterile, so there is no need of a space condom. Post coitus, Charlie starts feeling ill.

The next day, the team returns to the domed structure to find one of the members they left behind dead and the other missing. David goes off on his own and finds the bridge of a buried spaceship. He activates the navigation program. Then he finds a living space jockey in stasis. It is the most visually stunning sequence in the film.

Charlie is now quite ill and mutating. Ice queen Meredith Vickers (Charlize Theron) refuses to let him back on the ship and then sets him on fire at Charlie's urging. (In *Prometheus*, all the really evil characters are blonde.)

Elizabeth apparently passes out. When she wakes up, David explains that she is quite pregnant with a rather unusual fetus. She wants an abortion, but David sedates her and tells her they will put her back in suspended animation. Elizabeth escapes and climbs into a surgery machine, cuts her stomach open, and extracts a kind of writhing cephalopod. A few abdominal staples later, she is on her feet and back in action, albeit in her underwear and covered with gore. (Eat light before viewing, and you can enjoy dry heaves like I did.)

We learn that Mr. Weyland is on board. He is awakened from suspended animation in order to meet the Engineer. In case you are wondering what these stupid and venal white people (and their white android) have gotten themselves into, the crusty but big-hearted black ship's captain explains it all: this is not the home world of the space jockeys. This is a facility where they developed biological weapons of mass destruction. Their weapons, however, got out of hand and destroyed them (ho hum).

Later we learn from David that the weapons were meant to destroy mankind. It seems that, for no apparent reason, our creators had a change of heart and decided to destroy us.

Elizabeth urges the captain not to allow these weapons to get off the planet, no matter what. The captain agrees.

Still feeling the staples, Elizabeth suits up and accompanies David, Weyland, and some others to the ship to awaken the space jockey. David assures them that he has deconstructed the ancient languages of the world to a root tongue that is presumably the language of the space jockeys. How this is possible, given that their only apparent contribution to Earth is DNA, is not explained.

They awaken the space jockey. David says "kalifee" or some such. But apparently that is not an acceptable greeting, so, for no apparent reason, the space jockey rips David's head off, then kills Weyland and some of the others. Elizabeth, despite some cramps and oozing about the staples, manages to escape.

As she runs back to the *Prometheus*, the space jockey activates his ship and begins to take off. Elizabeth tells the black captain to stop him, and he nobly immolates himself and his crew to save humanity by crashing the *Prometheus* into the departing alien craft. The ice queen Meredith Vickers has ejected her quarters (complete with surgical bay) from the *Prometheus*, but she is crushed by the falling alien craft. (This is probably her karmic retribution for having sex with the black captain.) David, who just keeps talking even after his head has been ripped off his shoulders, and the space jockey both survive the crash. Elizabeth takes refuge in Meredith's quarters.

David, for no apparent reason, informs her that the space jockey, for no apparent reason, is on his way to get her. How a severed head could ascertain his destination and intent is not explained. Perhaps he read it in the script. When the space jockey attacks, Elizabeth opens the door to the surgical bay, and her unwanted fetus with the tentacles, now grown horribly large, overwhelms the space jockey and sends a tube down his throat, implanting an alien embryo.

It is a rather complex reproductive cycle.

Elizabeth rescues the now nice David (both parts of him). He tells her there are other alien craft, and he can pilot them. Elizabeth sets up a warning beacon to keep people away and then leaves in search of the space jockey's home world. She wants to find out why they chose to destroy humanity, and she apparently thinks they will tell her (before they destroy her).

At this point, we expect that the space jockey with the alien inside him will trudge back to his ship, put his suit back on, climb back into his chair, and then the alien will burst from his chest, which is how he is found in the original *Alien* movie. But that would make too much sense, so it doesn't happen.

Fin.

As the credits rolled, I took off my 3-D glasses and rubbed my eyes in disbelief, trying to fathom the vulgarity of spirit behind this godawful movie. It is the same vulgarity of spirit that took the mysteries of Stanley Kubrick's *2001: A Space Odyssey* (1968) and gave us Peter Hyam's sequel *2010* (1984), where the monoliths work to prevent nuclear war. It is the same vulgarity of spirit that took "the Force" of the original *Star Wars* trilogy and explained it in terms of little measurable material widgets called "midi-chlorians" in *The Phantom Menace* (1999). It is the same vulgarity of spirit that took the mysteries of Alfred Hitchcock's *The Birds* (1963) and gave us Rick Rosenthal's made-for-TV sequel *The Birds II: Land's End* (1994), in which we are informed that the bird attacks are due to pollution.

Heidegger tells us that this vulgarization is the essence of modernity, which seeks to abolish all mystery and transcendence, replacing them with the transparent and available, which in cultural terms boils down to the vulgar and the trite.

But some of us are more modern than others, and it all fell into place when I spied the name of screenwriter Damon Lindelof, one of the principal culprits behind *Lost*, the longest, most cynical Jewish jerk-job in television history. *Lost* was masterful in sucking people in by layering mystery upon mystery, including elements of religion, myth, and science fiction. But it was ultimately arbitrary and incoherent, revealing a bottomless contempt for its audience. All of these elements were chosen merely for effect, without concern for coherence and meaning, without the slightest suggestion that they could be taken seriously, that they mean anything important, that they are anything more than boob bait. *Prometheus* is the same kind of portentous swindle: just Jews making millions peddling myths for morons.

Don't lose your money, or your lunch, at *Prometheus*.

Counter-Currents/*North American New Right*,
June 9, 2012

RED DRAGON

Red Dragon is the first chapter in the saga of Dr. Hannibal Lecter, one of my favorite movie characters. Honest to God, I love Hannibal Lecter. We have so much in common. We're both brilliant, cultivated, witty, and capable of mass murder (only of bad people, in my case, and bad musicians). And although I am a strict vegetarian, I admit that I would prefer to eat the flesh of a wicked (or merely worthless) human being than that of an innocent cow or chicken. Of course there is one major difference between us. As FBI agent Will Graham (played by Edward Norton) tells Lecter in the best line of the movie, "You have a significant disadvantage. . . . You're insane."

Red Dragon is a remake of Michael Mann's *Manhunter*, a 1986 adaptation of Thomas Harris's novel *Red Dragon*. *Red Dragon* is not a better movie than *Silence of the Lambs*, but few movies are. It is much better than *Hannibal*, which I found puke-inducingly repulsive and psychologically uninteresting. *Red Dragon* is more like *Silence*: suspenseful and creepy, but without so much gore.

Red Dragon is also a much better movie than *Manhunter*. At least I think it is. Honestly, I don't remember much about *Manhunter*. It was, in fact, so unmemorable that *Red Dragon* seemed like a completely new movie, full of surprises even though it told the same story.

The basic conceit of *Red Dragon* is similar to *Silence*. An FBI agent visits Hannibal Lecter in prison and asks him for help in tracking down a serial killer. But the situation in *Red Dragon* is more interesting because the agent, Norton's Will Graham, is the last person Lecter tried to kill and the person who sent Lecter to prison in the first place.

Edward Norton is fast becoming one of my favorite actors. I loved his performances in *American History X* and *Fight Club*, but *Red Dragon* is his finest yet. Norton is not physically impressive. He is not handsome (but he looks great in *Red Dragon* with a head of tousled blonde hair). He also has a reedy voice.

But in this movie, I was particularly impressed at how well that face and voice register his inner states and make them visible and palpable. Great actors make their audiences psychics, and Norton is well on his way to becoming the sort of mind projector that Dirk Bogarde was.

You would think Norton would be typecast as intelligent, hyper-reflexive, sensitive, ironic, prattling, neurotic weaklings. But there's no shortage of Jews for those roles. So instead, Norton excels at playing intelligent, thoughtful, sensitive, and *strong* men.

His strength is not just his ability to take decisive action when needed. It is his ability to face and overcome his fear of Lecter and his like. It is his ability to resist the wiles of madness, the succubus who shadows genius and who has seduced both Lecter and Francis Dolarhyde, alias "The Tooth Fairy," the serial killer Graham is seeking.

Ralph Fiennes plays Dolarhyde, and his performance is also most impressive. Another advantage that *Red Dragon* has over *Silence* is that "The Tooth Fairy" is a much more fully realized character than "Buffalo Bill." Even more surprising, Dolarhyde is an extremely sympathetic character as well, man and monster locked in combat.

Particularly powerful is his budding Beauty and the Beast romance with his blind colleague Reba, played by the lovely blonde-haired, blue-eyed Emily Watson. This is a complex and difficult character, and Fiennes plays him beautifully.

Fiennes has never looked more virile and handsome, even with the scar that he thinks disfigures him. (Reba is the ideal girl for him because she cannot see his face, so she does not make him self-conscious, which sets him on the path to his psychotic breaks.) Fiennes also projects great intelligence and inner turmoil.

I could have done without the typical abused-child etiology of his madness, and the character would have been just as sympathetic without plucking that particular heartstring.

In spite of his hideous crimes (chief among them destroying a painting by William Blake), I found myself hoping that Dolarhyde would be saved in the end by love. And believe me, I am not easily stirred to such sentiments!

Near the end of the movie, however, there is a plot twist

that I do not recall being in *Manhunter*, a twist that seems to undermine the coherence and appeal of Dolarhyde's character by making us question the sincerity of his inner conflict. This is not a major flaw, but it bothered me. See for yourself.

The main reason why *Red Dragon* does not quite measure up to *Silence* is the role of Hannibal Lecter. In *Silence* he was one of the major characters. In *Red Dragon* he is not. Yet after *Silence* we want him to be. The film's Jewish director Brett Ratner realizes this, and gives Lecter more screen time than he had in *Manhunter*. In the prologue, we see him as a free man, charming and witty, hunting and killing, unmasked and captured. These are very enjoyable and effective scenes.

One of the major pleasures of *Silence* was getting to know Lecter. One of the problems of *Red Dragon* (and *Hannibal*) is that we never get to know him any better. His character is complete and never undergoes development. This may, of course, be part and parcel of his madness. But it means that Hopkins simply repeats all the elements of his brilliant characterization in *Silence*: the creepy, hypnotic, Oswald Mosley eyes, the acute senses of smell and taste, the blasé voice and languid movements . . . followed by the sudden lunge.

This is frustrating, because we want to get closer to Hannibal Lecter. (But not too close.) Indeed, one healthy and sane feature of this movie is that it reminds us again and again that we can only afford to indulge our fascination and sympathy for charismatic, homicidal lunatics when they are safely locked up (without access to a telephone) or dead—or just make-believe.

There is no particularly offensive racial propaganda in *Red Dragon*. Of course, Jews were involved in the production of this movie and will profit from your ticket. There is no way of avoiding that with any movie. All the major characters, though, are Nordic whites, or at least look like them.

Of course some might object to casting Nordic whites as serial killers. It is, after all, a bit of specious "racial profiling" that serial killers are always white males. There are many Negro serial killers: Wayne Williams and the Zebra Killers chief among them.

There would be many more, but they are so stupid they get

caught after the first victim.

But white killers are just more interesting than non-whites.

I noted with pleasure that at least five of the Tooth Fairy's twelve victims were Jews, and a sixth was a member of the press. There is one skinny Oriental in the cast, typecast as a techno-geek. There are eight or ten blacks lurching around in the background or in bit parts. One is cast against type as a veterinarian. The rest are pretty much cast according to type: janitors, orderlies, and police officers in Atlanta.

One thing that struck me about *Red Dragon* is something I also noticed in *Minority Report*. We have become accustomed to seeing blacks with a lot of white blood cast in black roles. The Denzel Washington, Halle Berry types. This makes sense, because the presence of white blood makes them more attractive to us, which helps us kid ourselves that a multiracial society might work.

But in *Red Dragon* the blacks, with the single exception of the veterinarian, are all hideous blue-gums. The most frightening thing in this movie is not the blood-spattered crime scenes and photos of mutilated bodies. It is the face of the Atlanta police official. I almost screamed when I first saw him. And when I saw him the second time, too.

In one scene Will Graham is seated in a restaurant discussing the case of the Tooth Fairy. He is resistant to getting involved. But then he is reminded that human lives are at stake . . . by looking over at a family of ugly blacks stuffing their faces. (Somebody in the theater laughed at that shot, and it wasn't me.)

If Hollywood Jews think that they can sell us on these kinds of blacks, they are sorely mistaken. Perhaps they will end up undoing some of the brainwashing they have inflicted on whites. Hope springs eternal.

I enjoyed *Red Dragon* a lot. It is well-written, superbly acted, and artfully directed. The score by Danny Elfman is quite good. It is the first Danny Elfman score (after his very first) that I could not identify immediately as his. I recommend *Red Dragon*. But don't take your children (especially bedwetters) to see it.

VNN, October 6, 2002

THE ROAD

The Road makes *The Road Warrior* look like a utopia. Based on a novel by Cormac McCarthy and directed by John Hillcoat, *The Road* stars Viggo Mortensen and Kodi Smit-McPhee as a father and his little boy struggling to survive and reach "the coast" in an America devastated by some sort of ecological apocalypse.

This event apparently killed off all animals and plants, but it somehow left human beings alive to live off foraged canned goods and, when these run short, cannibalism. It is no more preposterous a premise than the average zombie film, but the art-film pretensions of the director's style make it seem silly.

Then, after two harrowing hours of wind, rain, leaden skies, depression, talk of suicide, suicide, more talk of suicide, starvation, roving cannibal gangs, ambushes, earthquakes, falling trees, mistrust, man's inhumanity to man—just one damn thing after another—a happyish ending is delivered by a *deus ex machina*.

The initial apocalyptic premise is suddenly revised. We learn that not all animals are dead, and not all people have been reduced to cannibalism. It is, in short, a happy ending, delivered at the price of turning the rest of the movie into an emotional cheat. If the movie had remained true to its original premise, the final line would be "Well kids, it looks like meat's back on the menu."

But I am not complaining. Frankly, I was glad of any ending. I just wanted out of there.

Like many people who are profoundly alienated from the system, I relish the thought of a good crash. A crash will destroy the mechanisms of social control and mental conditioning. The struggle for survival will rid us of egalitarianism, progressivism, sentimentality, mental masturbation, and pious rot. False values will be liquidated. (I watched with pleasure as the family in *The Road* walked over jewels and banknotes, searching for food.) The weak and foolish will perish, the strong and clever will survive. A spell of healthy barbarism will set the stage for the rise of a new civilization. And maybe this time we will get it right.

Post-apocalyptic movies, however, generally disappoint, since in general too much of the bad stuff survives for my taste. *The Road*, however, goes to the opposite extreme. I wouldn't have lasted five minutes in that world (not that I would have fared well in *The Road Warrior* either). But personal survival is less important to me than the survival of the white race, and, frankly, until the premise changed at the end, I saw little hope of that either.

Is there a racial meaning, message, or bias to *The Road*? Not really. The cast and extras are all white, except for two or three blacks. I like to think that in the sort of apocalypse projected in the movie, blacks would fall into cannibalism, while whites would manage to hold some semblance of civilization together in the hope of waiting out the catastrophe. Instead, we see whites reduced to cannibalism and despair.

The one black who has lines in the movie steals the white family's goods and is caught. Mortensen's character holds him at gunpoint and strips him of his clothes, leaving him naked, begging, and blubbering. The little boy prevails upon his father to leave the clothes behind, but we never learn if they are reclaimed.

I was amused to read in internet forums that this scene bothered some viewers. They were terrified of a world in which the struggle for survival cancels out white guilt and hardens the heart to Negro pleading. That, of course, is the whole pay-off for me. But these critics should be comforted, for the silly child's instincts prevailed in the end.

The Road in an unremitting downer with no redeeming dramatic or artistic value. If there is anything good in the book, it does not make it to the screen. I think this was supposed to be "art," so of course it is not entertaining. Intellectual poseurs will claim that it is thought-provoking, but it is really just perplexing.

Don't waste your time and money on *The Road*. And for God's sake don't show it to anyone who is depressed. I predict that this movie will cause more suicides than a Finnish winter.

The Occidental Quarterly Online,
November 28, 2009

Secretary

Secretary was directed by Steven Shainberg and stars James Spader and Maggie Gyllenhaal. I watched this movie for three reasons. First, because it has James Spader in it, who is one of my favorite male actors. (Although Spader is very handsome, for most of the film he has a creepy, waxen, reptilian look about him.) Second, because it was supposed to be funny. Third, because humorless, hysterical feminists hated it for being "misogynistic," thus I'd hoped there would be something true in it. Maybe it would be another *Belle du Jour* or *Mademoiselle* or *Lost Highway*.

After all, what is usually labeled "misogyny" is just "sex realism"—just as race realism is branded "race hatred." A healthy realism about women is one way for men to emancipate themselves from the tyranny of women (mothers, teachers, girlfriends) in an increasingly female-dominated society. Women claim that such alleged "misogyny" is oppressive to women. But the real reason they oppose it is that it is liberating for men.

Maggie Gyllenhaal's character has just finished a brief stay in a mental hospital. For no apparent reason, she is one of those women who cuts herself, and she accidentally cut too deep, giving her parents the impression that she was committing suicide. (The characters of the parents are, by the way, 100% cardboard; the script, acting, and directing are totally perfunctory.) Once released, she decides to get a job and is hired by lawyer James Spader to be his secretary. We are clued in to something unusual when we see that Spader has a sign outside his office reading "Secretary Wanted," which he can light up like a hotel vacancy sign. (I will use the names of the actors rather than the characters because the characters were so poorly realized that I never retained their names, and I don't care enough to spend two minutes doing a Google search to look them up.)

We soon discover the problem with Spader. He is a mean boss. And he is a mean boss because, for no apparent reason, he is a sexual sadist. Gyllenhaal, however, is not driven off, for she discovers that she is a sexual masochist. Soon she starts making intentional "mistakes" so Spader will punish her. It turns out that her cutting behavior was just a rehearsal for this. But, for no apparent reason, Spader starts feeling guilty about his desires and tries to push her away. She refuses to go. Instead, she plants herself in his office and goes on a hunger strike. After a few days, for no apparent reason, Spader relents. Like a prince in a fairy tale, he carries her off to his castle, where they live happily ever after. With whips and chains.

While she is getting spanked by her boss, Gyllenhaal is pursuing a relationship with a sweet, gentle, wimpy, emasculated, bearded, modern guy who really loves her. But he is just too nice. She wants him to spank her, and he doesn't get the hint. Finally, they have intercourse. His performance is so feeble and gentle that he might as well be 80 years old. After it is over, he says, "I hope I didn't hurt you." That was one of the three times I found this film genuinely funny. When Spader dumps her, Gyllenhaal goes back to the wimp and leads him on some more, but then dumps him cruelly when she gets Spader back. Poor chump. He believed everything that our feminized culture told him about how to be a man, and it was a complete lie.

The wimpy feminized modern man just brings out the sadist in the most passive and masochistic of women.

At first I found this movie interesting and occasionally amusing. But when I realized what it is really about, I started to hate it. You see, beneath its pretentious, arty style and feeble attempts at offbeat, dark humor, this is just a moralistic, preachy After School Special. What's the message?

Tolerance, of course. Most people find sadomasochism disturbing. But in this movie, we are shown that it can be a beautiful, loving sort of relationship that satisfies some people's deepest psychological needs. So who are we to let our outdated prejudices to stand in the way of something so lovely? Yadda, yadda, yadda.

Director Shainberg is, frankly, pathetic. Unable to recognize a good script, develop three-dimensional characters, or coax convincing performances from talented actors, he simply falls back on the same tired clichés of transgression and emancipation, hoping that conventional people will overlook his incompetence because his heart is in the right place.

The feminist reaction to *Secretary* is ironic, since both they and Shainberg really have the same agenda: the destruction of normal, healthy sexual relationships by exalting pathological ones. But Shainberg could not calculate the infinite perversity of feminists. You see, normal people find sadomasochism disturbing because it seems exaggerated and extreme and therefore unhealthy. That is why Shainberg is pimping for it.

Feminists, however, oppose sadomasochism because it is just an exaggeration of normal heterosexual intercourse, in which men are active and women passive, men dominant and women submissive, men sadists and women masochists. In short, Shainberg's celebration of perversion brought down the wrath of feminists because it still smacks too much of healthy heterosexuality.

Poor chump. Let's hope he fares better with his next movie. Perhaps he should keep "pushing the envelope." How about a dark, quirky comedy with a serious heartfelt message about a young lad who fights and eventually wins out against archaic social prejudices after he discovers that a dog really is *Man's Best Friend*?

The fuss over *Secretary* illustrates an important truth about the culture destroyers: Looked at in isolation, the culture destroyers sometimes seem to be moving in different directions and working at cross purposes. But the same can be said of a tornado. If you isolate different parts, some will be moving in different directions, some north and some south, some east and some west. But when you step back and look at the whole, you see that it is a single, unified destructive force. And it is headed straight for us.

VNN, 2003

"I AIM TO MISBEHAVE."
SERENITY

Joss Whedon's 2005 film *Serenity* is the sequel to his short-lived 2002 science fiction series *Firefly*. Even though only 14 episodes of *Firefly* were shot, and their quality is somewhat uneven, it is one of the best science fiction series ever and showed enormous promise. Whedon, who also created *Buffy the Vampire Slayer*, *Angel*, and *Dollhouse*, is one of tvland's most versatile and compelling storytellers, effortlessly combining comedy, satire, and farce with extremely moving drama.

Although *Firefly* has a multiracial cast, the show is quite politically incorrect in other ways, chief among them the fact that the villains are liberal humanists. The back story of this archeofuturistic "Space Western" is based on the Confederates who went west after the American Civil War, some of them becoming outlaws. The heroes are Captain Malcolm Reynolds and the crew of his spaceship *Serenity*. Reynolds is a former Independent or "browncoat" who fought to secede from the centralizing Alliance, which defeated the Independents and drove its survivors into the less civilized, less settled "final frontier" of space. Although the crew of *Serenity* are smugglers and thieves, their individualistic and chivalrous values are treated as natural and noble, as opposed to the meddlesome liberal paternalist technocrats of the Alliance. *Firefly* is also strongly paleomasculine and gives a serious and dignified treatment to traditional manners and morals and even religion. (I discuss all these matters in greater detail in my review of *Firefly* above.)

Firefly developed a large and passionate following during its brief lifespan, and when Fox canceled it, the fans, who dubbed themselves browncoats, lobbied furiously to have the series relaunched, and their efforts paid off with *Serenity*, which solves two of the series' chief mysteries and gives the story a sense of closure. *Serenity* does not equal *Firefly* at its best, but at times it comes close.

There are a few jarring discontinuities between series and film. In order to make the film relatively self-contained, a large cast of characters we had come to know over 14 episodes had to be re-established quite quickly so they did not baffle viewers who had never seen the series. But especially in the case of Mal Reynolds, the effect is almost parody. Also, although only a couple of years passed between the series and the film, the glossy medium of the film dramatically ages some of the characters, particularly Mal Reynolds and Simon Tam. But Wash (Alan Tudyk) looks a bit less like a Muppet, with those flat cheekbones and lifeless goggle eyes.

In *Firefly*, the most mysterious members of the crew are River and Simon Tam, a brother and sister who are fugitives from the Alliance. Simon is a talented doctor, and River appears to be some sort of autistic savant. It turns out that she has an unusually high IQ, psychic abilities, and extraordinary physical reactions as well. The Alliance had been doing unethical experiments on River, hoping to harness her powers as a weapon. So Simon broke her out of their clutches and went on the lam.

The opening of *Serenity* shows Simon spiriting River away. (*Firefly* gives a rather different impression of River's escape.) The opening also makes clear that the Alliance wants River back not just because she is a valued asset, but also because they fear that her psychic powers tapped into the darkest secrets of the high political leaders to whom she had been exhibited by her overly proud trainer.

One of these secrets concerns the origin of the "Reavers," a group of savages who roam the margins of Alliance space. Reavers attack ships and settlements, raping, torturing, and eating their victims, then festooning their ships with the remains. Not only are Reavers extremely aggressive, they also seem unconcerned with self-preservation. They mutilate their own bodies, peeling off their skins and piercing their flesh with metal. They fly their ships without nuclear core containment, contaminating their living spaces with radiation. They also ram other ships without hesitation. According to Whedon, the Reavers were modeled on the Apaches as savage, terrifying nomadic bogeymen.

Naturally, the Reavers are feared more than any other force in the cosmos. They appeared only ten years before the story begins, and there are many theories about their origins. The minister on *Serenity*, Shepherd Book, believed that the Reavers had simply gone mad in the vastness of space. They had stared too long into the void.

But hidden in River Tam's fractured psyche is the truth: the Reavers were somehow connected to a planet called Miranda, whose populace supposedly perished in a terraforming accident. As River and the *Serenity* are pursued by an Alliance black ops specialist (the "Operative"), who methodically kills everyone associated with *Serenity*, Mal Reynolds is increasingly determined to solve the mystery. So he disguises *Serenity* as a Reaver vessel and (in an imaginative and surreal sequence) flies through Reaver space to Miranda.

When *Serenity* arrives at Miranda, the crew sees no signs of catastrophic environmental failure. The planet and all its facilities are intact. But its 30 million inhabitants are dead, with no sign of violence. They simply seem to have lain down and died. Then the crew discovers a rescue vessel and finds a recording which reveals the truth. The Alliance tried a mass social engineering experiment on Miranda. In order to make a better world, they tried to suppress human aggression by introducing a drug, G-23 Paxilon Hydrochlorate, "Pax" for short. "Pax" is Latin for "peace." (It is ironic that the movie sets up an opposition between *Serenity* and Pax.)

The attempt to induce pacifism through chemicals backfired, however. Without aggression, the vast majority of the population simply gave up on life. But the Pax had a very different effect on a tiny minority, intensifying aggression to the point of madness, which gave rise to the Reavers.

I won't give away any more details of the plot. Suffice it to say that Mal Reynolds and his crew are determined to broadcast the truth far and wide. Mal states his reasons clearly. Unless the secret of Miranda is exposed, the Alliance will someday try "to make people better." But he rejects that philosophy, saying simply, "I aim to misbehave."

To me, the most valuable message of *Serenity* is the idea that aggressive impulses are integral to human health, thus a completely pacified world would also be a dehumanized one. Since all forms of liberalism aim at creating a world free of conflict, the idea that aggression and conflict are ineluctable human traits is a fundamental rejection of liberalism, even the radical libertarian individualism that the movie seems to promote.

Libertarian individualism is, of course, completely incompatible with White Nationalism, which is a form of racial communitarianism. White Nationalists grant that freedom, individualism, and private property are values. But we believe that racial preservation and progress are higher values, which trump libertarian values whenever conflicts arise.

I also think it is unfortunate that *Serenity* appeals to reactionary anti-psychiatric, specifically anti-psychopharmacological, attitudes which prevent many people with chemically-based mental illnesses from getting better. (The name "Paxilon" is, of course, meant to remind us of Paxil, a widely prescribed drug that has helped thousands of depressed people get their lives back.)

The purpose of every decent government should be to "make people better." Every decent government should also be paternalistic. When people act like children—as we all do from time to time—of course they need someone who is empowered to play the role of parent. Forcible medication also makes sense for people with mental problems that prevent them from taking care of themselves, including taking the medicines necessary to get better.

The problem with liberalism is not that it tries to make people better, or that it paternalistically meddles in people's lives when they act childish, or even that it makes crazy people take their meds. The problem with liberalism is that it does all these things in the service of false values and a false vision of human nature, torturing and mutilating mankind in the process.

Counter-Currents/North American New Right,
February 18, 2014

A Serious Man

I don't have much use for light comedies, but I love dark ones. Thus I have been a fan of the Coen brothers ever since their first movie *Blood Simple*, which I regard as a masterpiece.

But not all of their movies succeed. The Coens are at their best when they are working with tight and ingenious plots. *Blood Simple*, *Miller's Crossing*, *Fargo*, *The Hudsucker Proxy*, and *No Country for Old Men* (no comedy that) come immediately to mind. However, when they stray from tight plotting, their movies tend to fail. But one still has to grant that films like *Barton Fink*, *The Big Lebowski*, and *O Brother, Where Art Thou?* are at least *interesting* failures.

At first viewing, I thought *A Serious Man* was just another interesting failure. But my mind kept coming back to it, like a tongue seeking a sore tooth, until I broke down and watched it again. This time, I think I got it. And I like it. I am going to summarize pretty much the whole story, so if you have not watched it, bail out here.

A Serious Man consists of two apparently unrelated stories. The first is only a few minutes long. It is set in a 19th-century Polish *shtetl*. The dialogue is entirely in Yiddish. One snowy night, Velvel (Allen Lewis Rickman) returns home from selling some geese and tells his wife Dora (Yelena Shmulenson) that on his way home, he met the Reb Groshkover. Dora says that this is impossible, for Groshkover is dead. Velvel must have met a *dybbuk*, a demon that possessed the body of the dead rabbi. Just then, there is a knock at the door. Dora is horrified. Velvel has invited Reb Groshkover in.

Dora does not waste time with pleasantries. She accuses Groshkover (Fyvush Finkel) of being a *dybbuk*. He denies it with good-natured irony, and they begin arguing the point back and forth. Dora ends the argument by plunging an ice pick into Groshkover's chest. He just stares wide-eyed, then continues his ironic *spiel*. But there is no blood. Dora takes this as proof that he really is a *dybbuk*. Then blood appears around the wound. But there is no anger, no sign of pain. Groshkover just says he is not feeling well, gets up, and totters off into the snowy night *kvetching* to himself. Velvel cries out that they are ruined. Dora just praises God and slams the door. The end.

It is bizarre and enigmatic. But one thing is clear: Reb Groshkover really is a *dybbuk*. Or he is something far more terrifying: a man so alienated from reality and from his own life that he can be stabbed with an ice pick and apparently feel no pain, a man whose life is ebbing away yet shows no anger or fear, a man whose relationship with reality is so mediated by words that he never stops talking long enough to confront concrete existence (like the ice pick in his chest), a man whose relationship to values is so distanced by irony that he cannot even take his own death seriously. In short, he is not a serious man. And as a rabbi, he is the embodiment of Jewish tradition.

As I see it, *A Serious Man* is a movie written and directed by two secular Jews in which they explore their own awakening to the fundamental inadequacy of Judaism to deal with the serious questions of serious men. And the most serious question is the problem of evil: if God is good, all-powerful, and all-knowing, then why is there evil in the world? God wants good; he can foresee evil; he can quash evil. So why is there evil? Why do bad things happen to good people? The second part of *A Serious Man* is a retelling of the biblical book of Job, which raises the problem of evil but gives no serious answer to it.

This movie portrays Judaism as offering no meat, no marrow, no spiritual sustenance. It is just a dry bone that gets stuck in the throat, a bone that one can neither swallow nor spit out. (See also Kevin MacDonald's review in *The Occidental Observer*.[1])

The main story of *A Serious Man* takes place in 1967 somewhere in the upper Midwest, pretty much the time and place that Joel and Ethan Coen came of age. Their equivalent in the movie is Danny Gopnik (Aaron Wolff), a 14-year-old about to have his bar mitzvah. Danny is introduced in Hebrew school, bored out of his mind, listening to Jefferson Airplane's "Somebody to Love" on a radio with an earpiece. (Or is it a cassette player? The fact that somebody else later in the film listens to

---

[1] http://www.theoccidentalobserver.net/2010/05/kevin-macdonald-the-coen-brothers-a-serious-man/

the same song on it leads one to think it is a tape player. But did they even exist in 1967? Is this an anachronism?)

Danny is caught by his teacher, and his device is confiscated. Unfortunately, he has hidden $20 in it to pay a fellow classmate, the bully Flagel, for marijuana. So he is in for a tense bus ride home. At home, he will listen to a Hebrew cantor on LP to prepare for his bar mitzvah and suffer through yet another fuzzy broadcast of *F Troop* because dad needs to climb up on the roof and adjust the aerial.

These petty concerns are introduced to contrast to the bigger problems faced by Danny's father Larry Gopnik (Michael Stuhlbarg), who is the Job character.

Where to begin?

Larry is a physics professor at a university. He is going up for tenure. He is informed by his department chair that somebody has been writing anonymous letters to the committee accusing him of moral turpitude. But not to worry, they won't affect the decision. When a Korean student, Clive Park, fails his midterm, he comes to Larry demanding a passing grade. He leaves behind an envelope of cash. Later in the movie, Park's father confronts Larry and threatens to sue him for taking bribes if he does not raise his son's grade. And he threatens to sue him for defamation if Larry tries to return the bribe. (Did we even have Koreans in 1967?) Oh, and Dick Dutton from the Columbia Record Club keeps calling Larry's office demanding payment for his selection of the month (Santana's *Abraxas* — not released until 1970, by the way).

After just such a typical day at work, Larry returns home to his harpy wife Judith (Sari Lennick), who tells him that she is leaving him. She wants a divorce and a *gett*, a Jewish ritual divorce so she can marry Sy Ableman. (The incredulous question "Sy Ableman? *Sy Ableman?*" is a constant refrain in this movie. The unspoken thought is: "Why would any woman want *Sy Ableman?*") Sy Ableman (Fred Melamed) is a hugger and a toucher, a lumbering, soft-spoken, "sensitive" guy who uses his New Age persona as a passive-aggressive wedge to invade people's space. Oh, and we later find out that he is the creep writing letters to Larry's tenure committee.

Sy and Judith think it is reasonable for Larry to move out of his house into a hotel before the divorce. It is, of course, out of the question that Judith move in with Sy. Judith later empties the couple's bank account to hire an aggressive divorce attorney. The divorce seems to be called off, however, when Sy is killed in a car accident. Judith, however, thinks it is reasonable for Larry to pay for Sy's funeral.

Then there is Larry's brother Arthur (Richard Kind), a brilliant but troubled loser who is staying with the family. Arthur is in constant rows with Larry's homely daughter Sarah over the use of the bathroom. (Remember when houses had just one bathroom?) Sarah needs the bathroom to wash her hair. Arthur needs the bathroom to drain his facial cyst. Arthur spends his time scribbling in a notebook. He is working on "the mentaculus," a mathematical theory to tie together all of reality and help him make money at cards. When Larry sneaks a peek, the pages are filled with gibberish. Arthur is just insane. He is picked up by the police for gambling. Later, he is arrested for soliciting sodomy, adding to Larry's mounting legal bills.

And finally there are the *goys* next door: buzz-cut, blonde, blue-eyed *goys*, tossing baseballs around and shooting deer. The *goys* are encroaching on the Gopniks' property, mowing over onto their lawn and building a boat shed (but of course) too close to the line. Larry has to shell out money to yet another lawyer to look into it. He is told that his money has been well-spent, that the lawyer stumbled across something that everybody else would have overlooked. But before he can tell Larry, he drops dead of a heart attack right in front of him. Later Larry has a nightmare that he and Arthur are being hunted by the *goys* like deer. Always innocent. Always persecuted. Such is the burden of being a Jew.

It is all too much. Larry needs help. A woman he knows tells him that he doesn't have to go through it alone. He's a Jew. Jews have this great well of tradition to draw upon. He should talk to the rabbi. The fact that she is a cripple in leg braces gives her suggestion some credibility. Surely she has suffered and found solace.

The first rabbi he sees, Scott Ginzler, is a freshly minted junior rabbi who goes by Rabbi Scott. What he lacks in life experience he makes up for with enthusiastic blather. How should Larry deal with his problems? By trying to look at them in a new perspective. He should try to see the hand of God in his troubles. God is everywhere, says Rabbi Scott, even in the parking lot. Of course, Larry's problem is not that he doesn't see God's hand. He wonders why God is giving him the finger.

Rabbi Scott was no help, so Larry goes up the hierarchy to Rabbi Nachtner (George Wyner), who fobs Larry off with God's answer to Job: "I'm the boss around here. Who are you to complain? Where were you when I created the world? I have no obligations to you. No, you can't know why." Nothing that a serious man can take seriously.

Then Rabbi Nachtner launches into a well-rehearsed *spiel* about another congregant, a dentist, who finds Hebrew letters on a *goy*'s teeth. The letters spell out "Help me." He is thunderstruck. Is it a message from God? He begins looking in other mouths, but nothing. He translates the letters into numbers. It looks like a phone number. He calls it. It is a grocery store. No answer there. Eventually, he comes to the Rabbi Nachtner to ask him what it means. Does it mean he should help people? The rabbi has no answer for the dentist either. But helping people? Can't hurt. Eventually, the dentist just stops thinking about the issue. Rabbi Nachtner suggests that Larry will eventually stop thinking about his problems too.

The Rabbi Nachtner working a suicide hotline? Probably not a good idea.

Larry, stunned by the unhelpfulness of it all, at least wants to know "What happened to the *goy*?"

"Who cares?" says the rabbi.

Rabbi Nachtner's message at Sy Ableman's funeral is similarly unhelpful. He speaks of *"olam ha-ba"* — the promised world to come, surely a topic of interest at a funeral. What is *olam ha-ba*? It is not a place, like Canada, says the rabbi. It is not the land of milk and honey. It is not the heaven of the gentiles. It is the bosom of Abraham. Yes, well, but what does that mean? Does it mean the Jewish community? Well, Sy has died and left that.

Nachtner's handling of Danny Gopnik's bar mitzvah is similarly inept. He reels off his speech as if he has a cab waiting.

Larry does not get to see the senior rabbi, Rabbi Marshak, who is reputed to be a very learned man. But the rabbi won't see him. He is busy. He's thinking.

Young Danny Gopnik does, however, get to see Rabbi Marshak. The old *tzadik* always speaks a few words of wisdom to the bar mitzvah boy. Danny enters the rabbi's vast office, passing from room to room past paintings, books, and artifacts that exhale an air of wisdom, arcane knowledge, and secret traditions. As the old bearded face comes into view, I was half-expecting to see the *dybbuk* Groshkover. But no.

Rabbi Marshak pulls out Danny's confiscated music device and intones: "When the truth is found to be lies. And all the hope within you dies . . ." It is the Jefferson Airplane song Danny was listening to when the device was confiscated, although the rabbi has changed the word "joy" to "hope." The words, and the fact that Rabbi Marshak chooses to utter them, perfectly sums up the disillusionment with Judaism that is the theme of the whole movie.

The rabbi then reels off the names of four members of Jefferson Airplane: Marty Balin, Grace Slick, Paul Kantner, and Jorma Kaukonen. (Aside from Slick, who is descended from *Mayflower* settlers, they are all Jews.)

Finally, to underscore the emptiness of it all, the rabbi returns Danny's device and says "Be a good boy." That's it.

Jews cannot swallow their tradition or spit it out, so they enact it in "scare quotes," with irony. But why does any serious man remain a Jew? Well, many Jews who are serious about intellectual or spiritual matters *don't*.

And as for the ones who do, their motives are hinted at in *A Serious Man*. As the movie rolls on, it becomes clear that virtually everyone Larry Gopnik knows is a fellow Jew, even the people one does not initially think are Jews, for example, the first lawyer he sees, who has an office full of fishing trophies and who seems never to have heard of a *gett*; Larry's department chair, who gives him tenure despite the fact he has never published (as Kevin MacDonald points out, Elena Kagan is not at all unusual[2]); even the pot-smoking, two-timing painted Jezebel next door.

When it comes to the spiritual problems of serious men, there are better religions than Judaism. (Not that much better, really, since some questions just can't be answered.) But when it comes to delivering the goods of community, no religion can compare. And it is the Jewish disdain for the *goys* so evident in this movie, as well as the Jewish dual ethical code—one standard for the Jews, another standard for the rest of us—that has sustained their community down through the millennia. That's why the Jews are still with us and the Hittites aren't.

There are lessons here for serious men: white men serious about our own people's survival.

The Occidental Observer, February 18, 2011

---

[2] http://www.theoccidentalobserver.net/2010/06/kevin-macdonald-our-new-unprincipled-elite/

Signs

I loved M. Night Shyamalan's *The Sixth Sense* and *Unbreakable*. And I love his new movie *Signs*. *Signs* does not have the amazing twist ending of *The Sixth Sense*, but it has a twist of its own. Ostensibly a suspenseful, scary sci-fi thriller with many wonderful comic scenes, *Signs* turns into something far more serious and profound. It is a meditation on the nature of manliness and its connection to religious faith.

Signs stars Mel Gibson as Graham Hess, an ex-Episcopalian priest, Joaquin Phoenix as his brother Merrill, Rory Culkin as his son Morgan, Abigail Breslin as his adorable daughter Bo, and Shyamalan himself as a local veterinarian named Ray Reddy.

On the surface, the plot of *Signs* is very simple. I promise I won't give away any of the good stuff. Crop circles start appearing all over the world, including on the Hess farm in Bucks County, Pennsylvania. Then lights start appearing in the sky. Then aliens are sighted. The world sits glued to television sets trying to interpret the meaning of it all. Then the aliens land, and they are clearly hostile. The Hess family barricades the house and keeps the aliens at bay. When they wake up the next day, they hear the news that the aliens were defeated and have fled, leaving behind some of their wounded.

The key scene is when Graham Hess and his brother sit in front of the television. Merrill is worried and turns to his brother for comfort, as do his children, as do his fellow townsmen, who have not gotten used to the fact that he left the priesthood six months before.

Graham says there are two kinds of people. One kind sees an event as a sign of divine providence. They feel that all events are meaningful. They believe that even the worst events produce a higher good. They believe that they are not alone in the universe. So they are filled with hope. The other kind of person looks at the same event and sees only an accident. There is no divine providence, just contingency. The world has no meaning beneath its surface. Evils are just evil. They are not means to a higher good. Mankind is alone in the universe. So when we face the mysterious, we are filled with fear. (In terms of Quentin Tarantino's *Pulp Fiction*, the first kind of person is Jules Winnfield and the second is Vincent Vega. Where Jules sees a miracle, Vincent sees only a freak accident.)

When Graham Hess was a priest, he was the first kind of person. But when his wife died in an apparently meaningless accident, he became the second kind. He lost his faith. He interprets her dying words as just meaningless babble generated by misfiring synapses at the moment of her death. Shyamalan's script and Gibson's acting are masterful in showing, throughout the film, that this loss of faith has unmanned Graham. To all appearances, he is a big, strong, masculine, competent man. But in key scenes, his nerve and his paternal authority fail. He lacks faith, so he is filled with fear, which means that he cannot stand his ground or inspire confidence in others.

One scene is especially telling. After barricading the house, Graham tries to distract and comfort his family by preparing everyone's favorite foods for dinner. He tries to be lighthearted, but of course the idea sounds like a condemned man's last meal. But the children cannot find comfort merely in food. They want their father to pray over it. And he refuses. But he too recognizes that a purely material meal contains no comfort. By refusing to pray, Graham does not communicate optimism to his children, but fear. They begin to cry and he succumbs to crying too. Crying, of course, is always a sign of self-pity. Instead of making the best of a bad situation with a relaxed and pleasant meal, the family collapses into a huddled, sobbing mass, certain of their impending doom.

The deeper plot of *Signs* has nothing to do with aliens and crop circles. A thousand other circumstances could have been invented to tell the same story. Instead, it is about the recovery of faith and manliness and paternal authority. This takes place in two stages. First, Graham's son Morgan has a serious attack of asthma, and his medicine is on the other side of the door with the aliens, so Graham has to talk Morgan through it. He sits his son on his lap and tells him to pay attention to his father's own breathing. He tells him to believe in his father and in himself. He inspires confidence through his own example, and it works. Graham has seen how his son has been strengthened by his faith in him. Graham himself, however, did not reach out to God for strength, but instead curses God. It is a complex, powerful, moving, brilliantly constructed scene. The next step of Graham's transformation is when he himself reaches out to God for strength. Then he begins to see signs. Signs that are far less obvious and far more important than mere crop circles.

In the end, we realize that Shyamalan has created yet another movie in which each and every detail is integrated into the plot, in which there are no freak accidents, in which everything makes sense, in which all the bad things contribute to a higher good—and yet nothing was merely predictable. Shyamalan is the directorial equivalent of a provident God, creating a universe in which hope and courage can flourish. This is a director of genius.

And what of the racial politics of the film? It seems ironic that Shyamalan, a Hindu Indian, has created the most sympathetic portrayal of white, Christian, rural Americans since David Lynch's magnificent *The Straight Story*. *Signs* has one of the whitest casts of recent films. The only non-white in the cast is Shyamalan himself. The Hess family are portrayed as intelligent, resourceful, morally earnest people. The kind of people who built America.

Christians should love this film even though the religious message is not specifically Christian. The plot is, if you will, a pragmatic argument for faith in divine providence, and the idea of providence is not specifically Christian. In one scene, it is mentioned that the people of the world are flocking to "temples, synagogues, and churches" to make sense of the appearance of the aliens, which indicates the ecumenical tone of the religious message.

The mention of synagogues is the only whiff of Jewry in this film. The average Hollywood Jew would portray the Hess family as hypocritical, intolerant, superstitious, stupid rednecks. Their fear of the aliens would be portrayed as paranoid, ignorant, racist xenophobia. Jews would never portray a white family united in solidarity against an alien invader. Instead, they would divide the parents from the children. The parents would be strait-laced, sexually repressed disciplinarians. The kids would be the epitome of "cool": promiscuous, perforated, tattooed, hip-hop rebels. The foolish parents would wish to resist the aliens, but their wise children would see that their parents are merely "scapegoating" the aliens because they cannot face up to their own psychosexual inadequacies. Thus the courageous children would take the risk of extending a welcoming hand. They might even hide the aliens from their parents' wrath, concealing them in the attic. Just like poor little Anne Frank. In any confrontation between whites and aliens, Jews automatically identify with the aliens. Shyamalan may be an alien, but he seems to identify with and appreciate white Americans.

There is one scene in the film that seems, at first glance, to be drawn from the Jewish playbook. The Hess family is having pizza together two days after the first strange happenings. They clearly have aliens on the mind. Suddenly, they see an alien: Shyamalan. He has dark skin. He clearly isn't from around there. They all stare at him. He drives off, clearly uncomfortable and unnerved. In any other movie, this would be a scene showing how intolerant and xenophobic the Hess family is. But in this movie, we learn that it has a different significance. Shyamalan plays Ray Reddy, the man who fell asleep at the wheel of his truck and killed Graham's wife, Morgan and Bo's mother. That is why they are staring at him. Shyamalan is a meticulous director. He knew that this scene would be interpreted exactly as I interpreted it. But then he subverts the interpretation. What is that a sign of?

In a White Nationalist America, M. Night Shyamalan would not be a citizen of this country. His movies would be "foreign" films, even if he chose to make them in America. But I would rush to see every one of them. If, however, the American film industry is going to be dominated by aliens, then I am rooting for Bollywood to buy out Hollywood! Believe me, we would have a much healthier popular culture.

It is laughable that one of the newsmagazines has proclaimed Shyamalan the "next Spielberg" when Shyamalan's weakest film, *Unbreakable*, is already better than Spielberg's best. Try the next Kubrick, the next Lynch, the next Hitchcock.

From a technical point of view, everything about this film is superb, but I must single out James Newton Howard's score for special mention. In places, it is worthy of Bernard Herrmann's best work for Hitchcock.

Signs is the best movie I have seen since *The Lord of the Rings*. I urge every White Nationalist to see it.

VNN, August 3, 2002

SPY KIDS 2:
THE ISLAND OF LOST DREAMS

I liked the first *Spy Kids* movie a lot. It was a simple, enjoyable adventure story, told with humor and style and livened up with imaginative sets and great gadgets. I liked the premise: Gregorio and Ingrid Cortez are spies, a job they have to keep secret from their kids. The kids are smart, though, so they find out. This is good, because the parents get into trouble, and their kids have to rescue them by using the full range of spy techniques and technologies. The message of the movie is a healthy one. The children and the parents are brave, intelligent, and resourceful, but the real key to their success is when they put aside the things that divide them and work together as a united family. The importance of family solidarity is hardly the usual message promoted by Hollywood.

A friend of mine was bothered because Robert Rodriguez, the director, set the movie in an advanced Western society that just so happened to be Spanish-speaking and "Hispanic." My friend thought this was not only pandering to America's Mexican invaders, but an attempt to convince the American public that nothing important would be lost if they were Mexicanized. He might very well be right about what appealed to the Jews who control the film industry, but I do not think that it is the message of the movie or the intent of the director.

I do not use the concept of "Hispanic" because it is a cultural-linguistic category, not a racial one. It embraces Nordic, Celtic, and Mediterranean whites, American Indians, Negroes, and even Asians like Peruvian President Alberto Fujimori—plus every conceivable form of racial mongrel. But I am all for white people from Spain and Portugal and Latin America.

A lot of Nordic White Nationalists have strong prejudices against Mediterranean whites. Personally, I love Mediterranean cuisines, cultures, and climates, from Iberia across the South of France to Italy and Greece. I also find Mediterranean physical types very attractive as well. But I admit that I am annoyed by the corruption, chaos, and inefficiency that plague all these countries, especially their former New World colonies.

Nevertheless, galling though it may be to Nordicists, the whitest countries in the Western Hemisphere are now Argentina and Uruguay, and those Latin American countries with multiracial populations are ruled by white elites that are far more racially conscious than those of more Nordic countries.

So I did not object to the "Hispanic" cast of *Spy Kids* because it was virtually all white. I admit that one character, Uncle Machete, looked like a mestizo. He was cast as a brilliant inventor but looked like he would be challenged to operate a leaf blower.

Spy Kids 2 is a terrible movie. It is proof positive that Robert Rodriguez just lucked out with the first film. He has no idea of how to make a good movie, so he could not repeat his success. The main problem with *Spy Kids 2* is that its plot literally does not make sense. I am pretty smart, and I could not figure it out. The kids in the theater were even more perplexed, and quite a few of them were bored and fidgeting. Like every movie without a plot, *Spy Kids 2* is just one damn thing after another. To conceal the lack of a good story, director Rodriguez falls back on spectacular sets and special effects as well as lame gags and gadgets. A lot of the gadgets seem to have been stuck in the movie merely to sell toys and Happy Meals. Rodriguez tries to redeem this crass commercialism by pausing to stick wholesome little messages in the film, but the messages are not integrated into the overall story, so they come off as just . . . messages.

Another annoying feature of this film is its self-conscious postmodernist allusions to other films. Yes, even in a kids' movie! In one scene, the kids find the golden idol from the opening sequence of *Raiders of the Lost Ark*. Then there is an allusion to *The Lord of the Rings*. Then there is a tribute to the sword-fighting skeletons and battling monsters created by the great Ray Harryhausen. It's all very amusing. But it is no substitute for a plot.

If you wish to subject yourself and your kids to this plotless, boring, pathetic excuse for a movie, you can at least take solace in the fact that, like the first *Spy Kids* movie, there is nothing racially offensive here. The cast is virtually all white. This movie is set in the United States, whereas I do not recall any indication of where the first movie was set. There are more Nordics in this movie. One of the main plot elements is the rivalry between the Latin Cortez family, who have red or brown hair and green or brown eyes, and the Nordic Giggles family, who have blonde hair and blue or green eyes. But it would require more paranoia than I can muster to make much of this. Besides, the conflict just does not map out neatly along an opposition between Nordics and Mediterraneans. Papa Giggles and his son Gary turn out to be bad guys, but little blue-eyed blonde Gerti Giggles turns out to be OK. (She betrays her family to do the right thing.) The Cortez girl is attracted to blonde bad boy Gary, and the Cortez boy is attracted to the hyper-Nordic daughter of the US president. Papa Cortez is played by Antonio Banderas, but his wife Ingrid is a green-eyed redhead, her mother is a blonde, blue-eyed Nordic, and her father is played by Ricardo Montalbán.

Skip *Spy Kids 2* and spend the time reading to your children. Take them to an art or science museum. Teach them a useful skill. Tell them stories about your family and its history. Take them to the woods or the seashore and teach them about nature. Point out the constellations under a starry sky. Give them a perspective on things that allows them to see movies like *Spy Kids 2* and the gadgets and fads they spawn as the trivial waste of time they really are.

VNN, August 12, 2002

STAR WARS: EPISODE II
ATTACK OF THE CLONES

I regard *Star Wars* movies as entertaining but juvenile spectacles. I know that some people take them much more seriously. But that is just a sad indicator of the poverty of the culture that is supposed to cultivate our spiritual longings. That said, I have seen the new *Star Wars* movie *Attack of the Clones* twice now, first in Marin County, then in Berkeley (which resembles the *Star Wars* cantina more and more every day).

The last *Star Wars* installment, *The Phantom Menace*, was a wretched movie, and virtually anything would be an improvement, but *Attack of the Clones* is not merely relatively better, it is absolutely good.

I rank *Attack of the Clones* close to my favorite *Star Wars* film, *The Empire Strikes Back*. Both films are the centerpieces of a trilogy. Both have a darker quality and a harder edge. There are other parallels too: a chase through an asteroid field, a mysterious floating city, a bounty hunter surnamed Fett, flying fixtures as weapons, a hero who loses a hand in a lightsaber duel, etc., etc. These parallels are not, however, mere derivativeness, but the magical "correspondences" that knit together a mythical universe.

I must confess that I have always sided with the Empire. Given the cynicism of Lucas's portrayal of the corrupt democracy of the Galactic Republic in the last two films, I wonder about his sympathies as well. I was seduced by the Dark Side of the Force long before the first *Star Wars* movie, so Darth Vader has always been my favorite character. I like his tragic grandeur. I like his ruthlessness. I even like his clothes.

Am I the only person who would like to sweep into a room wearing a black cape to the sinister strains of John Williams's brilliant "Imperial March," telekinetically strangle some bumbling henchman, then blow up an entire planet because it obstructs my view of the next planet over? I think not.

Am I the only person who would eagerly trade our sordid democracy for a populist dictatorship of wise but ruthless men with sexy uniforms and a knack for political pageantry? I think not.

Since *Attack of the Clones* deals with the rise of the Empire and the maturation of Darth Vader, it holds many charms for authoritarian personalities like me.

I was surprised at how much I liked Hayden Christensen, the handsome ephebe with red-brown hair and blue eyes who plays Anakin Skywalker, the young Darth Vader. One of the great flaws of *The Phantom Menace* was that a prepubescent Anakin was too young for the role. The film would have been much improved if the character had been played by a sexy, edgy teenager rather than a homely, toad-faced little moppet. A teenaged Anakin would have made the daredevil racing more plausible. He would have made the individuation struggle with his mother more plausible as well. And he would have allowed for some sexual chemistry with Queen Amidala. This, in effect, is the Anakin played by Christensen.

Christensen has a difficult role. Not only must he play a psychologically complicated and evolving character on the cusp of manhood, he has to utter the film's worst lines and play opposite Natalie Portman, who plays Amidala, Anakin's love interest. Portman is pretty, particularly for a Jewess, but she is such a wooden actress that the only explanation for her career is Jewish networking. The great irony of the film is that little rubber Yoda gives a far more human performance. Despite these handicaps and a number of scenes that simply do not work, Christensen makes Anakin a compelling character. Although he is tall and thin, his physical presence communicates strength and flexibility, like a slender blade of tempered steel. His movements in the action scenes are graceful and completely convincing. Even some of the awkward love confessions come off as the kind of thing one might expect from a brilliant, messed-up kid a long time ago in a galaxy far, far away. Particularly thrilling is the scene where he tells of single-handedly slaughtering an entire enemy tribe, his blue eyes wild and flashing, homicidal and vulnerable at the same time, an exterminating angel.

There are other good performances: Christopher Lee (who played Saruman in *The Lord of the Rings*), with his resonant voice and imposing presence is superb as the villainous Count Dooku. Ewan McGregor has gotten much more comfortable in the role of Obi-Wan Kenobi. But it is Yoda who steals the show in the end, first as field marshal of a hijacked clone army, then hilariously dropping his crotchety old persona and leaping like a deranged Chucky doll into a lightsaber duel.

Visually, *Attack of the Clones* is stunning. It is the first major movie to be recorded entirely digitally, which accounts for its amazing detail, depth, clarity, and color. The special effects are remarkable, particularly the three computer-generated monsters that appear in the arena scene. The action sequences are breathtaking, however implausible they may be. The sets and landscapes are always fantastic, beautiful, even sublime. The lightsaber duels are beautifully choreographed and genuinely thrilling. (These were the most successful sequences in *The Phantom Menace*.) Another remarkable feature of this film is how well it communicates palpable, gritty physical presence through details like the reflections of the lightsabers in the eyes of the combatants or the clouds of dust covering the battlefield in the climactic scene.

Like the movie as a whole, John Williams's score is far superior to his work for *The Phantom Menace*. The single CD of selections does not do it justice, but eventually the complete score will appear on two CDs. The "Love Theme" is truly beautiful, and Williams masterfully uses themes from his earlier scores, such as "The Force," "The Duel of the Fates," and the "Imperial March," to give us insight into Anakin's psychological transformation.

Of all the *Star Wars* films, this one is almost free of embarrassingly juvenile moments. There are no lines about scruffy-looking nerf herders, no Wookies, no Ewoks, and mercifully little of Jar Jar Binks. In *The Phantom Menace* Jar Jar looked and acted like Roger Rabbit seen on a bad acid trip. Thankfully, in this movie he seems to have been sedated for his few brief scenes. In one scene Senator Amidala gently cuts Jar Jar off when he threatens to go on too long. This is Lucas signaling that he feels our pain. R2-D2 burbles and chirps amiably, and C-3PO utters a couple of groaners, but in some scenes they are genuinely funny. Perhaps the stupidest thing about the movie is the title.

It seems silly to complain of the presence of non-whites and Jews in a cast consisting mostly of people in rubber masks representing even more disgusting races. In such a context, racial casting decisions are far less loaded with offensive messages than in films set in the present day, which cast non-whites as implausible heroes and whites as villains. I have already complained about the dreadful Natalie Portman. The only prominent Negro in the cast is Samuel L. Jackson as Jedi Master Windu. Perhaps a Negro would be plausible as a man of nobility and sagacity a long time ago in a galaxy far, far away. But not on this planet. Queen Jamillia of Naboo may have her face painted blue, but she is obviously being played by an Indian, Ayesha Dharker, who is very attractive without the greasepaint. The bounty hunter Jango Fett is played by a handsome, swarthy actor with a fine stage presence. At first glance, I could not determine his race. "Dago Fett?" I wondered. But as soon as I heard his New Zealand accent, I knew he was a Maori—a descendant of the tattooed, stone-age Polynesian warriors who fought the British Empire to a draw. The actor's name is Temuera Morrison. His son—actually his clone—Boba Fett is also played by a Maori actor, Daniel Logan. Their father-son relationship is one of the minor pleasures of the film.

One of the more interesting aspects of the reception of *The Phantom Menace* were the debates about the sexual and ethnic identities of the non-human characters. At first some homosexuals argued that Jar Jar is really gay, and that makes him a good character. Then the Negroes piped up and complained that Jar Jar is really black, and he casts them in a bad light. Then the Orientals objected that the evil fish-faces of the Trade Guild talk like Chinese waiters and dress like Fu Manchu. Finally, Jews complained that the ugly, greedy, dishonest, hook-nosed Watto is an anti-Semitic stereotype.

Perhaps we have Negro whining to thank for Jar Jar's diminished role in *Attack of the Clones*. Lucas may have reasoned that if Jar Jar does not crowd his way into every scene acting like an infantile, appetitive idiot, Negroes will not think that he is supposed to be one of them. But the evil capitalist fish-faces still talk like and dress like movie gooks from the '30s and '40s. And, as if to intentionally goad the Jews, the loathsome Watto appears this time with a wide black hat above the huge hooked proboscis, making him look not just Jewish, but Hasidic! You heard it here first!

Many people are hesitant to run out and see *Attack of the Clones*. This is logical, given how awful *The Phantom Menace* was. The trailers and advertisements for *Attack of the Clones* are also poorly conceived. They demonstrate that the movie is a spectacle, but nothing else, which leads naturally to the suspicion that it is nothing else. Finally, the title sounds like a parody. If you have been waiting for the reviews, then wait no longer. *Attack of the Clones* is a thoroughly entertaining spectacle. It is one of the best of the *Star Wars* series. See it, and maybe you too will start dreaming of an earthly Imperium.

VNN, May 2002

Sucker Punch

I saw Zack Snyder's *Sucker Punch* a few days ago, but I wanted to wait until my ears stopped ringing before I wrote a review. Frankly, I needed the time to come up with something to say. *Sucker Punch* is often a great music video. It is frequently a great video game. But it never adds up to being a good movie. Indeed, *Sucker Punch* is a repugnant, pointless, and depressing movie, in spite of the fact that it is visually stunning and brilliantly directed.

This is a shame, because Zack Snyder is a very talented director. I would argue that his *Watchmen* is the greatest superhero movie of all time. But *Watchmen* had a great script, a 19th-century Romantic novel disguised as a comic book, whereas *Sucker Punch* has a train wreck of a script, a mash-up of *Brazil*, *Suddenly Last Summer*, *The Lovely Bones*, *Moulin Rouge*, *The Lord of the Rings*, *Inception*, and I am sure a host of video games I am too hopelessly unhip to know anything about.

I have no idea why it is called *Sucker Punch*, unless it is a cynical reference to how well the movie delivers on its marketing.

Since you are unlikely to want to see *Sucker Punch* anyway, I am going to summarize the plot as I understand it. If you don't want to know, then stop reading here.

Sucker Punch is supposedly set in 1955, but there is no attempt to make the music, technology, or racial composition of the cast realistic for that time. A wealthy young woman, known only as "Babydoll" (played by Australian actress Emily Browning), is committed to an insane asylum by her stepfather, a monstrous figure who may have murdered his wife to gain control of her money only to discover that the money went to her two daughters. Enraged, he attacks the daughters, and Babydoll, in self-defense, accidentally kills her baby sister. (All this is related, by the way, during the pre-title sequence entirely without dialogue. As with the opening credits of *Watchmen*, this shows that Zack Snyder is truly a great silent movie director.)

The wicked stepfather commits Babydoll to an insane asylum and bribes a sleazy Semitic orderly "Blue" (Oscar Isaac) who has a racially mixed set of henchmen, to have Babydoll lobotomized by faking the signature of Dr. Gorski (the ravishing Carla Gugino), the psychiatrist in charge. When a doctor comes to perform the lobotomy, Babydoll slips into a fantasy world, which is pretty much the whole rest of the film.

In her fantasy, Babydoll and four other girls (two of them white, one Chinese, and one mystery meat) are in a brothel run by Blue, who is a gangster/pimp. Instead of being scheduled for a lobotomy, Babydoll's virginity will be sold to a man known as "The High Roller" who will arrive five days hence. Determined to escape, Babydoll enlists the help of four other girls to steal the things they will need to escape: a map, a lighter, a knife, a key, and a mysterious fifth item.

Within Babydoll's main fantasy, there are four other fantasies, which are basically video games: in one Babydoll fights three giant samurai *à la Brazil*; in another the five girls fight steampunk German zombies in the trenches of the First World War while majestic zeppelins soar overhead; in the third, the girls fight orcs and a dragon in a castle; in the fourth, they try to save a futuristic city on another planet from destruction by a nuclear device on a speeding train guarded by robots.

In the brothel fantasy, one of the girls is killed by a cook while trying to steal his knife. Two others are brutally murdered by Blue. And one of them, Sweet Pea (Australian actress Abbie Cornish), escapes because Babydoll chooses to remain behind, sacrificing herself, a gesture that is sanctified with some pretentious voice-over rubbish about guardian angels. In the real world, however, Babydoll is simply lobotomized and nobody escapes. Blue, however, is caught and rats out Babydoll's stepfather. The end.

Oh, and if you stay through the credits, you can see the repulsive Blue in his pimp getup performing Roxy Music's "Love is the Drug" *à la Moulin Rouge* with Dr. Gorski in a red wig.

The biggest question is: Who is the natural audience of this film? I think it is pretty much evenly split between teenage girls attracted by the girl power fantasies and child molesters attracted by the powerless girl realities: the hot, wholesome, helpless Mark Rydenesque waifs being locked up, strapped down, beaten, lobotomized, raped, and murdered. That left me, and pretty much the rest of the human race, feeling rather out in the cold, and frankly a little sick.

(The sad truth, of course, is that these girl power fantasies lead young women to take foolish risks that make them more likely to become victims of rapists and murderers.)

It is a mystery to me how this movie got anything less than an R rating, even from the Semitic Legion of Indecency. Parents of young girls should consider vacationing in Iran until this movie is gone from the theaters and the flocks of pimps, perverts, and fedora-in-lap types who are surely buzzing around it like latrine flies have dispersed.

Counter-Currents/*North American New Right*,
March 30, 2011

THE TOURIST

The Tourist, starring Johnny Depp and Angelina Jolie, was released in December of 2010 and has come and gone in theaters, but it is now available on DVD. I recommend it highly. It is not a "great" or "serious" movie, nor does it try to be. It is, instead, something far rarer: an unabashedly entertaining movie that is entirely free of vulgarity, stupidity, and political correctness (or propaganda of any kind, for that matter). It is directed by Florian Henckel von Donnersmarck, the 6'8" German aristocrat who also directed the superb 2006 German film *The Lives of Others*.

The Tourist reminds me of the romantic-comic thrillers of the 1950s such as *To Catch a Thief*. Only the technology—which, mercifully, remains mostly in the background—gives one a clue that this is not a lost film from another, better time. The cast is entirely white, even the extras. The plot is cleverly constructed with a twist ending that I did not see coming—and I can usually spot them a mile away. The dialogue is intelligent, witty, and free of slang and vulgarity. This is a suspenseful and romantic movie, but it is also extremely funny without ever resorting to crudeness. The movie was filmed on location in Paris and Venice, and the settings are absolutely gorgeous. Yet the director does not let the locations do all the work, instead seeking out new and breathtaking panoramas. The score, by James Newton Howard, is also quite good. At 1 hour, 43 minutes, *The Tourist* is masterfully concise and fast moving without resorting to flashy and jarring editing.

Angelina Jolie is perfect in this movie. I have never been much of a fan before, but I am converted now. She is also absolutely ravishing. Her clothes and bearing bring to mind the glamor queens of the 1950s, Sophia Loren and Grace Kelly to be precise. There is absolutely nothing masculine or feminist about her character. She even gives her opposite number Johnny Depp some lessons in "game." She is a real woman, impatient with the modern world's shortage of real men. Depp is also brilliant as a shy, somewhat bumbling American tourist who bumps into a seductive stranger on a train (Jolie) and is drawn into a web of intrigue and danger. There is not a weak link in the rest of the cast, either, which includes Timothy Dalton and Steven Berkoff.

The Tourist is a monument to the beauty, sophistication, and glamor of the European race and civilization at their finest. This is a movie that racially conscious whites can enjoy without guilt or qualifications. Why then, was I surprised to learn that this movie was widely panned by mainstream critics, who were obviously reaching for the lamest excuses to keep you from seeing it? Consciously or subconsciously, they did not want white people seeing this movie because everything about it is a celebration of white virtue and achievement (even the villains are interesting), rather than the studies of white depravity and non-white greatness that the establishment deems salutary. Fortunately, *The Tourist* did well at the box office in spite of the critics. See it, and see why.

Counter-Currents/*North American New Right*,
April 27, 2011

Vanilla Sky

Cameron Crowe's *Vanilla Sky* should be called *Vanilla Movie*—and I *like* vanilla. It achieves a near impossible feat. Although it is a product of Hollywood and is set in New York City, the only non-whites in the movie are extras! I think that one Negro utters a line. He is a doorman. In virtually every other film, the character of the psychologist would have been cast as a Negro. After all, the character is an educated, intelligent, sensitive man. These are all the qualities that we must be convinced are present in Negroes—because they are so rarely present in Negroes. Instead, Kurt Russell plays the part.

What's more, the film is utterly devoid of anti-white, anti-Western propaganda. Aside from one Jewish-looking character, there is nothing identifiably Jewish about this film, either, which is based upon a Spanish film, *Abre Los Ojos* (*Open Your Eyes*) written by Alejandro Amenábar and Mateo Gil. Even the psychologist is not a Freudian, but a follower of the Aryan Jung, judging from one of the props, a copy of Jung's *Memories, Dreams, Reflections*.

And to top it all off, it is a *good* movie—a serious, thoughtful movie—beautifully directed, well-written, well-cast, and well-acted.

Plain vanilla for me!

Vanilla Sky is not without its flaws. The major flaw is a sudden change of genre in the last fifteen minutes, not unlike the psychological turn for the worse near the end of *Fight Club*. This change, of course, is combined with a *deus ex machina* almost as blatant as at the end of *The Abyss*.

Vanilla Sky begins as a very suspenseful, very enjoyable psychological thriller. Tom Cruise starts out playing himself: rich, phony, vain, and self-absorbed. This Tom, however, is a magazine publisher and a casual seducer of women. He is named David Aames. Within five minutes, I found myself thinking: "I hope something very bad happens to this guy."

Something very bad does indeed happen. Something worse than I expected. Frankly, I was stunned. But it gets worse and worse. Treachery looms at every turn. Who has been murdered? Is David guilty or was he framed? Was it his company plotting against him? Was it his friend Brian Shelby, played by Jason Lee, a Jewish-looking writer who resents David's wealth and the fact that he stole his girlfriend? Is it the ex-girlfriend, Julie Gianni, played by Cameron Diaz? Is he awake or dreaming? Is he sane or insane? The suspense became unbearable.

Just when I found myself wondering, "How are they going to wrap this plot up in a satisfactory way?" they wrapped it up in a less than satisfactory way. The last few minutes of the movie are science fiction. There is way too much narration. Instead of *showing* the story, it *tells* the story. What story? *The Matrix* is the story: The hero is offered the choice of real life or fantasy. He is reminded that each passing moment is potentially a moment of decision, an opportunity to turn one's life around. He chooses, and the movie ends. With a very good thriller well in hand, they reach for science fiction with a serious existential-moral theme — and drop the whole thing.

Oddly enough, though, I was not terribly disappointed. Serious movies are so rare these days that a near-miss is still welcome. Furthermore, *Vanilla Sky* has so many other good elements that it is pleasurable trying to figure out how the ending could have been improved.

The NC-17 rating is based on some dirty talk and the fact that Tom Cruise simulates intercourse with two exquisitely beautiful women, Penélope Cruz and Cameron Diaz.

I usually find Tom Cruise very annoying, but I think this is his best movie. Cameron Diaz is spectacular. She deserves a Best Supporting Actress nomination. The rest of the cast is also quite good. Tom Cruise's contract must specify that no men better looking than himself be cast, but there are some very beautiful women in minor roles and decorating the very beautiful sets. I love the whole "look" of this movie.

The bottom line: After you see *The Lord of the Rings* three or four times, try *Vanilla Sky*.

VNN, December 2001

YOUTH WITHOUT YOUTH

Youth Without Youth (2007) is Francis Ford Coppola's stunning film adaptation of a novella of the same name by Mircea Eliade (1907–1986), the Romanian scholar of comparative religion and former member of the Iron Guard. I highly recommend this beautiful, mysterious, endlessly captivating movie. In style, it is classic; in substance, it is eternal.

Filmed on location in Romania, Switzerland, India, and Malta, *Youth Without Youth* looks, feels, and sounds like a European movie from the 1950s. The color is sumptuous and the cinematography astonishingly detailed, almost tactile. The pacing and editing are generally languid and sinuous, although they are often intercut with annoying, herky-jerky interludes, to farcical effect. The special effects date from the silent age and are entirely effective. The score by Osvaldo Golijov (who describes himself as an East European Jew born in Argentina) is in the lush, late Romantic idiom, although it avails itself of Oriental and "modernist" styles when the film requires it.

Since this movie is long gone from the theaters, I have no compunction about summarizing the whole story. *Youth Without Youth* strikes me as a retelling of the Faust myth, particularly Goethe's *Faust*. As in *Faust*, the main character is a scholar who late in life despairs that his life's work is a failure but who is given miraculous gifts, including restored youth, by which he might continue his quest for knowledge.

Youth Without Youth begins in Piatra Neamt, Romania, in 1938. Dominic Matei (played by Tim Roth), a former teacher in a provincial college or *lycée*, has just turned 70. He is experiencing the onset of senility and despairs of finishing his life's work, an investigation into the origins of language and consciousness that has stalled before the dark abysses of prehistory. He decides to kill himself and chooses a particularly horrible death: strychnine.

He travels to Bucharest on Easter weekend to take the poison far from home, where nobody will know him. But as he approaches his final destination, he is caught in a sudden downpour and struck by lightning, which incinerates his clothes and burns every inch of his body.

Astonishingly, he is not killed. He is taken to a hospital, where he is bandaged from head to toe and watched over by doctors who fully expect him to die. But to everyone's surprise, he slowly recovers, and when the bandages are removed, they find a man in his 30s. Dominic Matei has been miraculously regenerated. He also discovers that his memory and other mental faculties have not just been regenerated but enormously enhanced, eventually developing into powers of telepathy and telekinesis. He can learn other languages telepathically and "read" books simply by holding them for a few seconds and concentrating on them.

Furthermore, he encounters a "double": an entity that looks exactly like him but who is wiser and more powerful and who can thus offer him guidance and protection. (The double first appears in mirrors and dreams before being seen in the real world. We learn that he is not an illusion when another character sees him as well.) The double functions as a guardian angel, a *daimon*, a spiritual guide. Perhaps he can do this because he *is* Dominic, but a Dominic whose powers are fully actualized. As an interlocutor, however, the double has a Mephistophelean quality, for he clearly rejects Dominic's Western ethical humanism in favor of a Hindu-like non-dualism and transhumanism, and the double urges Dominic to do and accept things he finds abhorrent.

As with Faust, Dominic's new form of existence can, apparently, be prolonged indefinitely under the right conditions. But as with Faust, it can also end. When Faust feels satisfaction, he dies, and his soul is forfeit. Dominic's double tells him he is free to accept or reject his gift and free to use it for good or for evil.

Word of Dominic's astonishing transformation spreads around the world. He is placed under constant surveillance by the Romanian Secret Police, who are in a heightened state of alert because they are doing battle with the Iron Guard. (Corneliu Codreanu had been arrested in April 1938 and was murdered that November.) They even suspect that Dominic may be an Iron Guard leader hiding in the hospital under a false identity. (There is, of course, something autobiographical about the character of Dominic Matei, for Eliade too was a scholar of language and myth who was suspected, rightly, of Iron Guard connections. Eliade also wrote the novella in old age, when time is short and the mind is given to nostalgia and fantasies of regeneration.)

The Gestapo also take an interest in Dominic because he seems to confirm the theories of a German scientist, Dr. Josef Rudolf, who hypothesizes that high voltage electrocution might spark the evolution of a higher form of humanity. Matei's doctor and host, Professor Stanciulescu (Bruno Ganz), realizes Dominic's powers when he sees two roses from his garden materialize in Dominic's room with the help of the double. Thus the professor refuses to allow the Germans to take Matei, citing medical grounds. They threaten to return with a German doctor who will do their bidding. Thus Stanciulescu arranges false papers so that Matei can leave Romania for Switzerland.

Coppola's treatment of the Germans is one of the few places the movie rings false and silly. He seems to think that Romania was under German occupation in 1938 or '39, which never happened. The Germans, of course, are portrayed as fanatics and martinets, and their leader even gives the Hitler salute to Professor Stanciulescu. I have not read the novella, but it is impossible to believe that such farcical inaccuracies are found in the original.

Dominic Matei spends the Second World War in neutral Switzerland, where he leads a life that is part Mircea Eliade, part James Bond. He continues his research into the origins of language and consciousness. He also develops new powers, including abilities to create false identities and beat the house in casinos, which is how he supports himself.

One night, Dominic is confronted in an alleyway by the Nazi scientist Dr. Rudolf. Rudolf explains to Dominic that he must return with him to Germany, because only with his help can Rudolf construct a bridge from man to superman, which is the only way that mankind can survive the coming nuclear apocalypse. Rudolf wishes to preserve the high culture of the West: music, art, philosophy, and science. He claims that Dominic was sent by some sort of providence to help save mankind. He promises to admit him to the godlike presence of Adolf Hitler. But Dominic refuses to cooperate with the Nazis. Rudolf pulls a gun and tries to abduct Dominic. When a female Romanian agent of the Gestapo tries to defend Dominic, Rudolf shoots her. The double, who evidently wants Dominic to go with Rudolf, tells him that he has no choice in the matter. But Dominic does have a choice: he telekinetically forces Rudolf to shoot himself, then he escapes.

Dominic is also convinced that the Second World War will not be the last. He anticipates that mankind will be almost annihilated by nuclear warfare, and he fears that "post-historical man" will succumb to despair. Thus he begins to tape a record of his transformation, depositing the tapes in a bank vault. He hopes that they will somehow survive the end of history and be deciphered by men in the future, giving them hope that humanity might evolve. Of course he has no assurance that the tapes will survive, but believes it anyway, because without this belief, his life would have no meaning.

The second half of the movie begins in 1955, when Dominic encounters a young German woman on vacation in Switzerland (Alexandra Maria Lara). Her name is Veronica, but she is the very image of Laura, Dominic's former fiancée, who a lifetime ago had broken off their engagement because he was too involved in his work. She then married another man and died in childbirth a year later. The double confirms that Veronica is the reincarnation of Laura. (She is roughly analogous to Gretchen in Goethe's *Faust*.)

Veronica's car is struck by lightning, and her companion is killed. When Dominic finds Veronica, she is speaking in an ancient Indian dialect and claims that her name is Rupini, a woman of the Kshatriya caste, a descendant of one of the first families to convert to Buddhism, who had left the world behind to meditate in a cave.

Veronica/Rupini becomes an international sensation, because she seemingly provides proof of reincarnation. (Veronica herself later suggests spirit possession as an alternative hypothesis.) Veronica/Rupini demonstrates knowledge that Veronica did not and could not have learned during her lifetime. Dominic becomes her caretaker. He summons leading orientalists to study her case, and eventually she is flown to India, where she finds Rupini's cave, complete with her mortal remains. Then Rupini's personality disappears and Veronica's re-emerges. She and Dominic fall in love. Veronica tires quickly of being a world celebrity, so she and Dominic flee India to a secluded villa on Malta.

On Malta, Dominic discovers he has to power to induce trances in which Veronica regresses to past lives, speaking ancient Egyptian, then Akkadian and Sumerian, then unknown protolanguages which Dominic eagerly records and transcribes. He recognizes that Veronica might be the vehicle he needs to pierce the veil of prehistory and reach the origins of language and consciousness. The double confirms this.

But with each trance, Veronica becomes increasingly drained and begins to age rapidly. Dominic realizes that if he continues to induce regressions, she will wither and die, so he has to choose between Veronica and the completion of his life's work. He tells Veronica that they must part. If they stay together, she will die. If they part, her youth and beauty will be restored.

In 1969, when he is 101 years old, Dominic sees Veronica and her two children get down from a train. Heartbroken, he surreptitiously photographs her. He returns to his home town in Romania. In the mirror of his hotel room, he has a conversation with his double. The double reveals that he is indeed the harbinger of a new race, which will arise from the electromagnetic pulse released by an approaching nuclear holocaust. Most of mankind will perish in the process, but a superhumanity will emerge. Disgusted at the sacrifice of man to create the superman, Dominic smashes the mirror, rejecting his gift. The double, gibbering some unknown language, disappears.

Dominic then goes to his old haunt, the Café Select, where he hallucinates an encounter with friends from the 1930s. During the conversation, he rapidly ages, then stumbles out into the night. The next morning, he is found frozen to death in the snow.

But the end is ambiguous, for at the very end of the film, we hear Veronica's voice ask Dominic, "Where do you want me to put the third rose?" which then appears in his hand. So is Dominic Matei really dead? He has been all but dead before, remember. So is this just another start? Will he keep coming back until he learns his lesson and his mission is fulfilled? Or is he really dead, but under the protection of Veronica, like Faust whose soul is saved in the end by the intercession of the Eternal Feminine?

Youth Without Youth is a movie about transcending the human condition: backwards, toward the pre-human origins of language and consciousness, and forwards, toward the advent of the superhuman. Dominic Matei is given the power to do both.

He could have arrived at the origin of human language and consciousness through Veronica's trances, but he was unwilling to sacrifice her to his quest for knowledge.

He is already superhuman, but he could choose to help prepare the way for superhumanity. He had a chance to assist Dr. Rudolf, but he rejected it because he thought that Hitler was the devil himself. In the end, he rejected his own superhumanity simply because he was repelled by the idea that superhumanity would emerge from the destruction of humanity.

In both cases, the path to transcendence of the human realm was blocked by Dominic's humanistic ethics, the idea that every human being has a dignity or worth that forbids its sacrifice for higher values. Thus *Youth Without Youth* explores the same fundamental conflict that animates Christopher Nolan's *Dark Knight Trilogy*: the ethic of egalitarian humanism versus the ethic of superhumanism, of the individuals who raise themselves above humanity either through a Nietzschean rejection of slave morality and a Heideggerian encounter with mortality and contingency (the Joker) or through the initiatory knowledge of the League of Shadows. (As I argue in my review of *The Dark Knight Rises*, the two forms of superhumanism are compatible, but Nietzsche, Heidegger, and the Joker only grasp a small part of a much greater truth.[1])

---

[1] My review is reprinted in *Trevor Lynch's White Nationalist Guide to the Movies*.

Youth Without Youth is, in short, a deeply serious film: a feast for the intellect as well as the senses. A commercial and critical flop when it was released in 2007, *Youth Without Youth* is, in truth, one of Francis Ford Coppola's finest films.

Counter-Currents/*North American New Right*,
March 12, 2013

Appendix

Ten Favorite Movies

The following text is a scrap rescued from obscurity and buffed up a bit. In 2002, a reader of *Vanguard News Network* suggested that the site's movie reviewers post their "Ten Best" lists. I found it impossible to settle on just ten best films. So I decided to produce a "Favorites" list instead. I came up with more than 30 movies. These are films I like to re-watch and show to my friends. I think the list includes some of the best films ever made, but it also contains some that are pretty far from the best. So here are ten movies that are near the top of my favorites list.

1. *Network* (directed by Sidney Lumet, starring William Holden, Peter Finch, and Faye Dunaway).

This is the best movie ever made. The story is wonderful, the script brilliant, the acting stunning, the satire cutting and hilarious, and the message serious and profound. *Network* shows how capitalism works in the realm of culture, how the culture industry works to debase public standards and corrupt public morals.

The only real flaw of the movie is that it hides the role of Jews in the television industry and the general corruption of culture. The big villain is a blonde from the Midwest named Diana Christensen (Faye Dunaway) who somehow manages to corrupt, manipulate, and exploit the old-timers from the New York media (none of whom are portrayed as explicitly Jewish). The other villain, Mr. Jensen (Ned Beatty), also has a Scandinavian name. A former salesman from Oklahoma, Mr. Jensen has built a vast business conglomerate which has purchased the TV network of the title and wishes it to spread the Kojèvian gospel of the universal homogeneous consumer society.

But it turns out that the network is not solely controlled by sinister Scandinavians. Some Semitic foreigners also want to buy in, so Howard Beale, the mad prophet of the airwaves, alerts America to the danger of the world's most powerful tool of propaganda and brainwashing falling into the hands of . . . Saudi Arabians.

These mounting absurdities should come as no surprise, though, given that the script was written by the Marxist Jew Paddy Chayefsky.

But greed alone—and therefore Marxism alone—is not enough to explain the behavior of the media. One can be a gentleman and a patriot and still make money. No, one must also add such elements as alienation from and hostility toward the dominant culture, boundless cynicism, and crazed, hate-filled ethnocentrism to the mix to explain the modern media. In short, one has to add Jews (and their spiritual kinsmen and collaborators).

Favorite scenes: Howard Beale's "I'm as mad as hell and I'm not going to take it anymore!" speech; Mr. Jensen's chilling "End of History"/"New World Order" speech; Mrs. Schumacher's tirade to her cheating husband (four minutes of screen time that won her an Oscar for Best Supporting Actress); and any scene featuring the Afro-headed, fried chicken-slurping, gun-firing, money-grubbing, bad-ass Commie Negroes Lorraine Hobbes and The Great Ahmed Khan.

When is white America going to say, "I'm as mad as hell and I'm not going to take it anymore!"?

2. *Vertigo* (directed by Alfred Hitchcock, starring James Stewart and Kim Novak).

This is the other best movie ever made, and in terms of sheer beauty, it is far superior to *Network*. The story of *Vertigo* is a tragedy worthy of Euripides. The film is visually stunning, emotionally wrenching, and beautifully acted, with magnificent music by Bernard Herrmann. *Vertigo* is so effective that I have to let a couple of years pass between viewings. One minor pleasure is that *Vertigo* is set in my favorite American city, San Francisco, and environs, and gives a glimpse of what a paradise urban life was in America before racial integration and non-white immigration.

3. *Pulp Fiction* (directed by Quentin Tarantino, starring John

Travolta, Bruce Willis, and Samuel L. Jackson).

Yes, I like *Pulp Fiction*. Why? Because the postmodern, consumerist world is a sewer. *Pulp Fiction* is a cool, funny tour of that sewer. But it has a serious side. It shows us the qualities of character that either raise us out of the sewer or drag us further down into it. The movie is filled with situations demanding moral decisions. The characters who are ruled by their appetites (John Travolta's Vincent Vega and Uma Thurman's Mia Wallace) make very different decisions and have very different fates than the characters who are willing to risk comfort, security, money, and even life itself in order to do what they think is right (Bruce Willis's Butch and Samuel L. Jackson's Jules Winnfield).

Don't be put off by the Negro characters and the race-mixing. No portrait of the sewer would be complete without them. My favorite scene is when the black gangster Marsellus Wallace offers Butch the same deal that modern bourgeois society offers us all: abandon your pride, abandon your principles, and you can have money, comfort, security. Your soul is a small price to pay for all that, isn't it America? Most Americans seem to agree.[1]

4. *Blue Velvet* (directed by David Lynch, starring Kyle MacLachlan, Isabella Rossellini, Dennis Hopper, and Laura Dern).

This is more than a movie, it is a myth: It is a coming of age tale, an initiation tale, a descent into the underworld and resurrection tale. Jeffrey Beaumont (Kyle MacLachlan) discovers evil in society and the potential for evil in his own soul. He also discovers the artifices that we create to keep evil in check. And finds the strength in himself to do battle against it.

Lynch is not arguing that the idyllic white America of Lumberton is somehow a fraud because it has an evil underbelly. That is the common Leftist misunderstanding of the movie. Lynch thinks that evil is not a product of a particular social system that can be abolished by social reform. Evil is metaphysical and will always be with us, and social conventions and artifices like those of Lumberton are justified by keeping evil in check.

---

[1] See my extensive review essay on *Pulp Fiction* in *Trevor Lynch's White Nationalist Guide to the Movies*.

I have seen this movie 25 times, and I still find Dennis Hopper's Frank Booth absolutely terrifying. His performance is so compelling that he has been playing Frank Booth characters ever since!

5. *Ran* (directed by Akira Kurosawa).

King Lear set in feudal Japan, *Ran* is pure poetry, one of the most beautiful movies ever made with exquisite music by Toru Takemitsu. A lesson in Hobbesian political realism: authority without the ability to enforce it by violence is worthless; sovereignty is one and cannot be divided without lapsing into civil war.

6. *The Birds* (directed by Alfred Hitchcock, starting Tippi Hedren and Rod Taylor).

Another Hitchcock masterpiece set in San Francisco and points nearby, I read this movie as an anti-feminist allegory by the most extreme misogynist in film history. Melanie Daniels (played by the exquisite Tippi Hedren) uses her wealth and social status to violate the laws of nature. She is independent, mischievous, and sexually aggressive in pursuing lawyer Mitch Brenner (played by the extremely masculine Rod Taylor). The forces of nature, in the form of the birds, punish her for her independence, and every attempt at self-assertion is struck down, until by the end of the movie she is reduced to a state of battered, shocked, almost comatose dependence on Mitch.

7. *Sunset Boulevard* (directed by Billy Wilder, starring Gloria Swanson, William Holden, and Erich von Stroheim).

Dark comedy or tragic satire about Hollywood and the corrupting power of fame and money, this movie features an extraordinary performance by washed-up silent movie star Gloria Swanson as washed-up silent movie star Norma Desmond.

8. *The Bridge on the River Kwai* (directed by David Lean, starting Alec Guinness and William Holden).

This is a tragedy that Sophocles could have written. It is David Lean's best film: the directing, script, acting, and music are all superb. Fans of Julius Evola's *The Metaphysics of Sex* will appreciate seeing his contrast between the higher (Uranian) and lower (Tellurian) types of masculinity exemplified by Alec Guinness and William Holden respectively. There is also a splendid score by Malcolm Arnold.

9. *The Talented Mr. Ripley* (directed by Anthony Minghella, starring Matt Damon, Jude Law, Gwyneth Paltrow, and Cate Blanchett).

I love this movie, and not just because I love its Italian settings. In spite of his being "a gay serial killer," I found Matt Damon's Tom Ripley a deeply believable, sympathetic, and moving character. Not only does Ripley have education and taste, he actually has a conscience, which is more than can be said for his first two victims. It is only because Ripley has genuinely good qualities that the movie turns tragic in the end as his powers of deception fail him, he thinks he is trapped, and he lacks the courage to come clean.

10. *The Lord of the Rings: The Fellowship of the Ring* (directed by Peter Jackson, starring Viggo Mortensen, Elijah Wood, Ian Holm, and Ian McKellen).

See my review, and my reviews of the rest of the trilogy, in *Trevor Lynch's White Nationalist Guide to the Movies*. The second movie in the trilogy, *The Two Towers*, turned out to be my favorite of the three.

VNN, June 20, 2002

INDEX

Note: Numbers in **bold** indicate an entire chapter or section devoted to the indexed term.

2001: A Space Odyssey, 140
2010, 140
8 Mile, **47–52**
9/11, 127

A
Aarons, Bonnie, 121
abortion, 14, 24, 138
Abraham, 159
Abraxas, 157
Abre los Ojos (Open Your Eyes), 3, 180
The Abyss, 180
Afghanistan, 9, 12
Agora, **1–5**
Akkadian, 186
Alabama, 85
Alba, Jessica, 91
Alexander, **6–15**
Alexander the Great, 6–14, 41
Alexandria, 1–7
Alien, 136
Alien 3, 136
Alien: Resurrection, 136
Alien vs. Predator, 136
Aliens, 136
aliens, 87, 89, 94–101, 132–36, 162–65
Allies (World War II), 114, 117
altruism, 20–21
Amarcord, 40
Amenábar, Alejandro, 3–5, 180
America: A Prophecy, 26–27
American Civil War, 48, 53, 151
American History X, 142

American Indians, 120, 167
Americans, 12, 54, 88, 91, 96, 100, 113–14, 119, 124–29, 164–65, 191
Ammianus Marcellinus, 1
Ammonius, 2, 5
Andersen, Hans Christian, 40
Anderson, Michael J., 122
Angel, 55, 151
Anglo-pederasty, 108
animal rights, 84
Antal, Nimród, 134–35
anti-white agenda, ideology, propaganda, 6, 10, 47, 63, 81, 124, 180
Antoon, Jason, 105
Anwar, Gabrielle, 32
Any Given Sunday, 10
Apaches, 152
Apocalyptic events, 146–47
Aramaic, 128
Archeofuturism, 36, 54
Argentina, 168, 182
aristocracy, 14, 19, 37, 59, 69–70, 110; German, 178; Persian, 9; Southern, 113
Aristotle, 6,
Aristotle's unmoved mover, 128
Arizona, 91
Arlington Road, **16–18**
Armitage, Richard, 62
Arnold, David, 47
Arnold, Malcolm, 193
Art Deco, 22, 23
Aryans, 9, 12–15, 46, 54, 70, 73, 105, 122, 180
Asia, 25
Asians, 11, 25, 67, 167
At the Mountains of Madness, 87

atheism, 28, 42, 55
Atlanta, 19, 145
Atlas Shrugged: Part I, **19–24**
Axis powers, 114

B
Babylon, 7, 27
Baccarin, Morena, 54
Bachchan, Amitabh, 70
Bachchan, Jaya, 70, 71
Balin, Marty, 160
Ballets Russes, 35
Banderas, Antonio, 169
bar mitzvah, 156–57, 160
Barhom, Ashraf, 5
Barton Fink, 155
baseball, 107–10, 158
Basinger, Kim, 51
Battlestar Galactica, 53, 93
Beale, Howard, 189–90
Beatty, Ned, 189
Beaux, Ernest, 35
Bell, Coby, 33
Belle du Jour, 148
Bengali, 69
Benton, Thomas Hart, 22
Berkeley, California, 105, 170
Berkoff, Stephen, 179
Berry, Halle, 45–46, 145
Big Brother, 127
The Big Lebowski, 155
Billings, Montana, 124
Binder, Mike, 106
Binks, Jar Jar, 172
The Birds, 140, **192**
The Birds II: Land's End, 140
Birnbaum, Dan, 121
blacks, 5, 48–51, 67, 77–81, 105, 131, 145–47; see also Negroes
Blade Runner, **25–31**
Blake, William, 27, 143
Blanchett, Cate, 112, 114, 193
blondes, 8, 46, 51, 78, 83–85, 105, 120, 122, 138, 142–43, 158, 169, 189
Blood Simple, 155
Blue Velvet, 119–20, **191–92**
Bogarde, Dirk, 143
Bollywood, **68–73**, 165
Bolshevik Revolution, 35
Bolshevism, 87, 94
Bond, James, 44–47, 184
Bonneville, Hugh, 112
Bored of the Rings, 64
Born on the Fourth of July, 10
Bowler, Grant, 21
Brazil, **22**, 175–76
Breaking Bad, 124, 127, 129
Breker, Arno, 22
Breslin, Abigail, 162
The Bridge on the River Kwai, **192–93**
Bridges, Jeff, 16
Brody, Adrien, 131–34
Brooks Brothers, 22
Brosnan, Pierce, 45–46
Browning, Emily, 175
Bucephalus, 41
Bucharest, 182
Buddhism, 55, 185
Buffy the Vampire Slayer, 55, 151
Bureau of Land Management, 17
Burke, Edmund, 109
Burn Notice, **32–34**, 127–29
Byrd, James, 81

C
The Caine Mutiny, 114
calligraphy, 59
Campbell, Bruce, 32–33
Campbell, Ramsey, 86
Canada, 88, 159
Cannes Film Festival, 124
cannibalism, 146–47
Capel, Arthur, 35
capitalism, 19–20, 48, 89, 91, 94, 189
Capitolium, 2

Capshaw, Kate, 105
Carpenter, John, 86
Carr, Jonathan, 80–81
Carr, Reginald, 80–81
Casino Royale, 45
caste, 68–69, 94–95, 185
"The Cat Lady," iii
Catholic Church, 88
Caucasians, 11, 73
Caviezel, Jim, 127–30
CBS, 127
Celts, 63, 167
cephalopods, 138
Chanel, Gabrielle Bonheur "Coco," **35–38**
Chanel No. 5, 35
Chattopadhyaya, Saratchanda, 69
Chayefsky, Paddy, 190
Chekhovian dramatic principle, 90
Cheung, Maggie, 59
Chicago, 69
China, 57–60, 74, 76
Christensen, Hayden, 171
Christianity, 1, 3
Christians, 1–5, 29, 134, 164
Churchill, Winston, 37
CIA, 127–29
Clinton, Bill, 48
Clooney, George, 112–18
Coco Chanel & Igor Stravinsky, **35–38**
Coen Brothers, 155
colonialism, 25, 77
Columbia Record Club, 157
Communism, 39–43, 114
Communist Party, 41
Communists, 39–41
Confederates, 151
Congress (US), 83–85
Connery, Sean, 44
Constantinople, 1, 3
Cooper, Gary, 22

Coppola, Francis Ford, 182, 184 188
Cornish, Abby, 176
Costner, Kevin, 93
Counter-Currents/*North American New Right*, iii
Covington, Harold, 17, 92n1
Coyote, Wile E., 61
crop circles, 162–64
Crow, Sheryl, 47
Crowe, Cameron, 180
Cruise, Tom, 102–106, 180–81
Cruz, Penelope, 181
crypsis, 42, 94
Culkin, Rory, 162
The Culture of Critique, 20
Curb Your Enthusiasm, 39
Cusack, Joan, 16
cutting behavior, 149
Cyril, Bishop of Alexandria, 2–5
Cyrus, Billy Ray, 122

D
Dalton, Timothy, 45, 179
Damon, Matt, 112, 114, 193,
The Dance of Reality, **39–43**
The Dance of Reality: A Psychomagical Autobiography, 39
Daoming, Chen, 59
Darius III, 7–12
The Dark Knight Trilogy, 93, 129, 187
Dark Side of the Force, 170
Dawson, Rosario, 9, 13
de Lempicka, Tamara, 22
De Niro, Robert, 89
death, 1–4, 8–9, 27–30, 40, 66, 76, 81, 87, 115, 120, 129, 131–32, 156, 163, 182, 186; see also mortality
Deep River, Ontario, 121
Del Campo, Carlos Ibáñez, 41
Del Rio, Rebekah, 120
del Toro, Guillermo, 86

democracy, 19, 114
Dench, Judi, 45
Depp, Johnny, 178–79
Dern, Bruce, 124
Dern, Laura, 191
Detroit, 50–51, 77
deus ex machina, 146, 180
Devdas, **68–73**
Devil, 121, 123, 187; see also Satan
Dharker, Ayesha, 173
Diaghilev, Serge, 35
Diamonds Are Forever, 45
Diaz, Cameron, 181
Dick, Philip K., 26
Die Another Day, **44–47**
Dionysus, 1
disco, 50
diversity, 12, 65, 95
Dixit, Madhuri, 70
Do Androids Dream of Electric Sheep?, 26
Dollhouse, 55, 151
The Doors, 10
Donner, Richard, 93
Donnersmarck, Florian Henckel von, 178
Donovan, Jeffrey, 32–33
double, 183–86
Downton Abbey, 127
Dresden, 66, 114
"The Duel of the Fates" (John Williams), 172
Dun, Tan, 60
Dunaway, Faye, 189
Dune (book), 39
Dune (movie), 39, 42
dybbuk, 155–56, 160
Dzielska, Maria, 3

E
Easter, 182
Eastwood, Clint, 128
The Education of Cyrus, 59

egalitarianism, 19, 95, 146
Egypt, 8, 11, 12
Egyptian, 1, 4, 27 186
El Topo, 39
Elfman, Danny, 97, 145
Eliade, Mircea, 182, 184
Emerson, Michael, 127
Eminem, 50, 52
Empire (*Star Wars*), 170–71
The Empire Strikes Back, 170
empirical tests, 109
equality, see inequality
Eraserhead, 119
Euripides, 190
Europe, 6, 112, 114, 182
European art, 115–17
European man, 114
European race, 179
Evans, Rupert, 3
Everett, Chad, 122
evil, 7, 13, 25, 34, 84, 119, 121, 125, 138, 156, 162, 173, 183, 191
Evola, Baron Julius, 33, 128
evolution, 95, 137, 184
Ewoks, 172

F
F Troop, 157
Fahey, Jeff, 89
Fando y Lis, 39
Far East, 11
Fargo, 155
Farrell, Colin, 8, 13, 106
fascism, 20–22
Fassbender, Michael, 138
Faust, 182–83, 185
Faustian man, 53, 93
Faye, Guillaume, 36
FBI, 16–17, 142
Feldstein, Jonah Hill, 108
Fellini, Federico, 39
feminism, 14, 67, 83, 94
feminists, 148,

Fields, Sally, 85
Fiennes, Ralph, 143
Fight Club, 142, 180
film industry, 60, 68, 165, 167
Finch, Peter, 189
Finkel, Fyvush, 155
Finnish winter, 147
Firefly, **53–56**, 151–52
The First Emperor, 60
Fischler, Patrick, 121
Fishburne, Laurence, 131, 132, 133
"The Force" (John Williams), 172
Forster, Kate, 122
Fort Knox, 44
Forte, Will, 124
The Fountainhead, 19–24, 111
Fox Network, 53
Frank, Anne, 165
Frankfurt School, 20
Freeman, Martin, 62
Freemasons, 41
Frenchmen, 112
Freudianism, 180
Fu Manchu, 173
Fujimori, Alberto, 167
Futurism, 36

G
Gaiman, Neil, 86
Galactic Republic, 170
Garcia, Jsu, 21
Gathegi, Edi, 21
genes, 13, 31, 43, 73
German Occupation, 37, 118, 184–85
Gestapo, 37, 184, 185
gett, 157, 160
Ghent Altarpiece, 116–17
Gibbon, Sir Edward, 4
Gibson, Mel, 4, 162, 163
Giger, H. R., 136
Gil, Mateo, 180
Girl with the Dragon Tattoo, 137

Glass, Ron, 55
Gless, Sharon, 32
God, 25–29, 34, 42–43, 71, 83, 94, 142, 147, 156–59, 164
Goethe, 182, 185
Goldeneye, 45
"Golden Boys," 108
Goldfinger, 44
Golijov, Osvaldo, 182
Goodman, John, 112
Göring, Hermann, 115, 117
Goyer, Daniel, 93
goyim, 40, 56, 94, 132, 134, 158, 159, 161
Grace, Topher, 131
Great Wall of China, 59
Greece, 6, 8, 11, 167
Greeks, 6, 8–11
Greenberg, Drew Z., 56
Greene, Sonia Haft, 86, 87
Grindhouse, 88
Gross, Arye, 105
Gugino, Carla, 176
Guinness, Alec, 192–93
Gyllenhaal, Maggie, 148–49

H
Hannibal, 142
Happy Meals, 168
Harris, George, 77
Harris, Thomas, 142
Harryhausen, Ray, 168
Hasids, 174
Hauer, Rutger, 25
Hawthorne, Nebraska, 125
Heaven and Earth, 10
Hedren, Tippi, 192
Heidegger, Martin, 140, 187
Heilbronn, Germany, 117
heliocentric hypothesis, 3
Hellboy, 93
Hellboy II: The Golden Army, 93
Hercules, 7, 10
Hermeticism, 4

Hero, **57–60**, 74–75
Herrmann, Bernard, 166, 190
hierarchy, 60, 96, 122, 159
Hierax, 2
high investment parenting, 121
Hillcoat, John, 146
Hindi, 68, 69
Hinduism, 42–43, 69, 72
Hirojans, 131
Hispanics, 167–68
Hitchcock, Alfred, 166, 190, 192
Hitler, Adolf, 115–18, 184–87
Hittites, 161
Hobbesianism, 192
The Hobbit: An Unexpected Journey, **61–63**
The Hobbit: The Battle of Five Armies, **66–67**
The Hobbit: The Desolation of Smaug, **64–65**
Holden, William, 189, 192–93
Hollywood films, movies, or product, 8, 16, 49, 51, 60, 72–73, 78, 83, 104, 123, 135, 167, 180; see also film industry
Hollywood Jews, 83, 100, 120, 145, 164
Holm, Ian, 62, 138, 193
holocaust, Jewish, 112–13
holocaust, nuclear, 186
The Holy Mountain, 39
homosexuality, 13–14, 85, 108
homosexuals, 13–14, 41, 85, 113
Hopkins, Sir Anthony, 8, 144
Hopper, Dennis, 191
Hopper, Edward, 22
Hôtel Ritz Paris, 37
House of Flying Daggers, **74–76**
Howard, James Newton, 178
The Hudsucker Proxy, 155
Hungarian, 91, 134
Hyam, Peter, 140
Hypatia of Alexandria, **1–5**
Hypatia of Alexandria, 3

I

immigrants, 73, 87
immigration, 12, 89, 91, 100, 190
immortality, 30–31
"Imperial March" (John Williams), 170, 172
The Incal, 40
Inception, 93, 129, 175
India, 7, 70–73, 182, 186
individualism, 19–20, 54, , 91, 154
inequality, 95–96
The Interpreter, **77–79**
intolerance, 164–65
IQ, 49, 50, 109, 152
Iraq, 12
Iron Guard, 182–84
Isaac, Oscar, 3, 175
ISIS, 5
Islamization, 114
Israel, 12, 14, 94, 129, 131, 134
Israel Defense Forces, 131–34

J

Jackson, Michael, 46
Jackson, Peter, 22, 24, 61, 63–67, 193
Jackson, Samuel L., 173, 191
Jason, 7, 10
Jasper, Texas, 81
J-dar, 132, 134
Jefferson Airplane, 156, 160
Jesus, 4, 21, 29, 109, 127–30
Jewbermenschen, 134
Jews, 1–2, 10, 12–15, 20, 41, 43–46, 73, 81–82, 83, 94–100, 105–12, 118–41, 143–45, 156–61, 164–67, 173–74, 189, 190; Jewish agenda, 12, 81; Jewish networking, 171; Jewish subversion, 20, 87; Jewry, 20, 94, 164
JFK, 10
Jhelum River, 10
Job, 156–59

jock-sniffing, 107–108
Jodorowsky, Alejandro, 39–43
Jodorowsky, Brontis, 39
Johnson, Don, 89
Joker, 187
Jolie, Angelina, 8, 178–79
Jones, Grace, 46
Jones, Tommy Lee, 99
Joshi, S. T., 86
Judaism, 156–61
Julian "the Apostate," 1
Jung, C. G., 180

K
Kabhi Kushi Kabhie Gham, **68–73**
Kagan, Elena, 160–61
Kajol, 71
Kantner, Paul, 160
Kapoor, Kareena, 71
karmic retribution, 139
Kaukonen, Jorma, 160
Khan, Shahrukh, 70–72
Kidman, Nicole, 3, 77–78
Kilmer, Val, 8
Kind, Richard, 158
King Kong, 63, 64, 66
Kirkpatrick, James, 23
Klee, Paul, 118
Koreans, 44, 46, 100, 157
Krypton, 94–95
kshatriya, 185
Kubrick, Stanley, 140, 166
Kurosawa, Akira, 58, 192
Kutschmann, Walter, 37

L
La Raza, 91
Lang, K. D., 47
The Last Supper, 113
Latin America, 167–68
Law & Order: Special Victims Unit, **80–82**
Law, Jude, 193
Lazenby, George, 45

LBJ, 48
League of Shadows, 187
Lean, David, 192
Lear, Jonathan, 108
Leave it to Beaver, 119
Lebensborn, 106
Lebensraum, 95
Lecter, Dr. Hannibal, 142–44
Lee, Christopher, 171
Lee, Jason, 181
Leftists, 9–10, 36, 191
Legally Blonde 2: Red, White & Blonde, **83–85**
Leonardo da Vinci, 113
Lerner, Michael, 21
Leto, Jared, 8
Leung, Tony, 59
Li, Jet, 59
libertarianism, 54, 154
Library of Alexandria, 1, 5
License to Kill, 45
Lifetime Channel, 124
Limbaugh, Rush, 48
Lincoln, Nebraska, 124
Lindelof, Damon, 140
Live and Let Die, 46
The Lives of Others, 178
The Living Daylights, 45
Lloyd Wright, Frank, 22
Logan, Daniel, 173
Lombardi, Vera Bate, 37
London, 71
Lonsdale, Michael, 3
The Lord of the Rings, 22, 61–67, 166, 168, 171, 175, 181, 193
The Lord of the Rings: The Fellowship of the Ring, 66, **193**
The Lord of the Rings: The Two Towers, 47, 67, 193
Los Angeles (LA), 25–27, 98, 119–20, 134
Lost, 127, 140–41
Lost Highway, 119, 148
"Love is the Drug," 176

"Love Theme" (John Williams), 172
Lovecraft, H. P., **86–87**
Lovecraft: Fear of the Unknown, **86–87**
The Lovely Bones, 63, 175
Lucas, George, 170–73
Lumet, Sidney, 189
Lynch, David, iii, 103, 119–26, 164, 166, 191
Lynch, T. C. (a.k.a. "The Cat Lady"), iii.

M
MacDonald, Kevin, 33, 67, 93n1, 156, 160, 161n2
Macedonia, 1, 8–12, 14
Machete, **88–91**
MacLachlan, Kyle, 191
Mademoiselle, 148
Malta, 182, 186
Man of Steel, **93–96**
Man of Steel II, 96
Mandarin, 55
Manhunter, 142, 144
Mann, Michael, 142
Maoris, 173
Marin, Cheech, 90
Marin County, 170
Marquess of Cambridge, 37
Marsden, Matthew, 21
Marshall-Green, Logan, 137
martial arts, 57, 74
Marxism, 190; Marxism-Leninism, 41
masculinity 32, 33, 49, 54, 128, 151, 163, 193
masculinity, Uranian vs. Tellurian, 33, 128, 193
masochism, 24, 148–50
mass man, and mass society, 19
Massachusetts, 85
master race, 83
masturbation, mental, 146

The Matrix, 103, 181
McCarthy, Cormac, 146
McGregor, Ewan, 172
McKellen, Ian, 62, 193
McQueen, Butterfly, 48
Mediterranean whites, 8, 167, 169
Medusa, 10
Melchizedek, 134
Mememto, 129
Memories, Dreams, Reflections, 180
Men in Black II, **97–101**
Mesopotamia, 10, 11
mestizos, 21, 25, 40, 168
The Metabarons, 39
metaphysics, 103
The Metaphysics of Sex, 193
Mexicans, 88–91
Mexico, 88
Miami, 32, 33
Michelangelo, 109
Middle Earth, 65, 67
Mikkelsen, Mads, 35
Milan, 113
military-industrial complex, 10
Miller, Ann, 122
Miller's Crossing, 21, 155
Minghella, Anthony, 193
Minghella, Max, 4
Minority Report, **102–106**, 145
Minutemen, 89
miscegenation, 9–14, 79, 87
misogyny, 148, 192
Missoula, Montana, 126
MLK, 10
modernism, 182
Moneyball, **107–11**
Mongoloids, 11
Montalbán, Ricardo, 169
Montana, 124, 126
Monte Cassino, 113
The Monuments Men, **112–18**
Moore, Roger, 45
morality, 7, 20, 21, 28, 29–30, 55, 59, 83–84, 94–95, 187, 189, 191

Mormons, 50
Morricone, Ennio, 60
Morrison, Temuera, 173
Mortensen, Viggo, 146–47, 193
Morton, Samantha, 106
Moses, 94
Mosley, Oswald, 144
Mouglalis, Anna, 35
Moulin Rouge, 69, 175, 176
MTV, 49, 68
Mulholland Drive, **119–23**
Mumbai (Bombay), 68
Munich, 95
Murray, Bill, 112
Mussolini, Benito, 20
My Three Sons, 119
mysteries, ancient, 1, 4, 87
mysteries, cinematic, 140, 151

N
narcissism, 112
National Public Radio (NPR), 112, 113
National Socialism ("Nazism"), 22, 37, 41–42, 94–95, 112, 115, 185
National Vanguard, iii–iv, 79
NBC, 80–81
Near East, 6, 11, 12, 14
Nebraska, 124
Nebraska, **124–26**
necessity, 110, 113
Negroes, 10, 48, 54, 65, 83, 105, 113, 120, 122–23, 144, 147, 167, 173, 180, 190–91
Negroid, 8
Nelson, Bob, 124
Nelson, Tim Blake, 105
Nero Decree, 117–18
Network, **189–90**
neurosis, 121
Never Say Never Again, 45
New Deal, 22
New Delhi, 70, 71

New Right, 54, 124
New York City, 51, 180
New York City police, 128, 129
New York Times, 118
New York Yankees, 109
New Zealand, 173
Nietzsche, Friedrich, 29, 187
Nietzscheans, 4, 19–20, 187
niggers, 48–50
nihilism, 21, 90
Nijinsky, Vaslav, 35
No Country for Old Men, 155
Nolan, Christopher, 93, 129, 187
Nolan, Jonathan, 129
Nordic, 8–9, 21, 44, 46, 63, 78, 106, 128, 144, 167–69
Norse creation myth, 137
Norse sagas, 31
Norton, Edward, 142–43
Notre Dame de Paris, 5
Novak, Kim, 190

O
O Brother, Where Art Thou?, 155
O'Connor, Flannery, 103
Oakland A's, 107, 109, 110
Objectivism, 19, 20
Objectivists, 19–22
The Occidental Observer, iii, iv, 67n1, 135, 156n1, 161
Octopussy, 45
Odenkirk, Bob, 124
Oedipus, 7, 10
Old Testament, 134
On Her Majesty's Secret Service, 45
open borders, 95
Operation Modellhut, 37
Orbison, Roy, 120
Orestes, 2–3
Orphism, 4
Osiris, 1–2
The Others, 3
Oxyartes, 9

P
pagans, 1–2, 4, 5
Pakistanis, 100
Palestine, 11
Palme d'Or, 124
Paltrow, Gwyneth, 193
Papuans, 65, 67
Paris, 35–38, 116–18, 178
The Passion of the Christ, 4, 128, 130
Payne, Alexander, 124–26
Pearce, Guy, 137
Pellington, Mark, 16
Penn, Sean, 77–78, 79
Persia, 11
Person of Interest, iv, **127–30**
PETA, 84
Peterson, Seth, 32
The Phantom Menace, 63, 64, 140, 170–74
Philip II of Macedon, 6, 8
Phoenix, Joaquin, 162
Piatra Neamt, Romania, 182
Picasso, Pablo, 118
Pike, Rosamund, 46
Pinocchio, 41
Pitt, Brad, 107, 111
plantation system, 25
Plato, 30
Plato's Cave, 120
Platoon, 9–10
play vs. work, 110
Polito, Jon, 21
Pollack, Sydney, 77–78
Portman, Natalie, 171, 173
Portrait of a Young Man, 117
Porus (Indian king), 7, 10
post-modernism, 168
Powell and Pressburger, 40
Predator, 131
Predators, **131–35**
Predators (aliens), 131–35
The Prestige, 129
Price, Robert M., 86–87
prima donnas, 107–109
progress, 25, 154
proletariat, 40
Prometheus, 10, **136–41**
psychoanalysis, 94, 104, 121
Psychomagic: The Transformative Power of Shamanic Psychotherapy, 39
Ptolemy I of Egypt, 7, 8
Ptolemy II of Egypt, 7
Ptolemy III of Egypt, 1
Pulp Fiction, 163, **190–91**
pyramids, 25–27

Q
Qin Shi Huang, 57–60

R
race realism, 148
race traitors, 48, 92
racial nationalism, 19
Rai, Aishwarya, 70
Raiders of the Lost Ark, 168
The Rainbow Thief, 39
Ran, **192**
Rand, Ayn, 19–23
rap, 48–51, 97
Rapace, Noomi, 137
Raphael, 117
Rashomon, 58
Ratner, Brett, 144
Reavers, 152–53
Red Dragon, **142–45**
"The Red Shoes" (story), 40
The Red Shoes (film), 40
rednecks, 54, 56, 164
religion, 14, 42, 55, 72, 100, 141, 151, 161
replicants, 25–27
Res Gestae, 2
Résistance, French, 112
Rickman, Allan Lewis, 155
Riefenstahl, Leni, 22
The Rite of Spring: Pictures from Pagan Russia, 35–36

The Road, **146-47**
The Road Warrior, 146-47
Robbins, Tim, 16
Rodriguez, Michelle, 89
Rodriguez, Robert, 88-90, 131, 167-68
Roerich, Nicholas, 35
Roger Rabbit, 172
Romania, 182-86
Romansh, 130
Romanticism, 109-10
Rome, 1, 37, 84, 113
Roosevelt, Franklin, 48, 113
Roshan, Hrithik. 71
Rossellini, Isabella, 191
Roxane (Wife of Alexander the Great), 7, 9, 13
Roxy Music, 176
Ruby Ridge, 16
running gag, 103
Russell, Kurt, 180
Russia, 35-36, 114
Russian Special Forces, 131-32
Ryden, Mark, 176

S
sadism, 40, 42, 78, 81, 90, 148-50
sado-masochism, 72, 149-50
Salafists, 5
Samir, Sami, 5
San Francisco, 13, 110, 190, 192
San Francisco Opera, 110
Santa Sangre, 39
Santana, 157
Santiago, 41
Santorum, Rick, 130
Satan, 25-29; see also the Devil
Saturday Night Fever, 50
Saturday Night Live, 124
Saudi Arabians, 190
Saunders, Jennifer, 137
Savitri Devi, iii, 9n1
Schellenberg, Walter, 37-38
Schilling, Taylor, 21

Schwarzenegger, Arnold, 131
science fiction, 25, 28, 39, 53, 104-105, 141, 151, 181
Scotland, 137
Scott, Ridley, 25, 136-37
Seagal, Stephen, 89
SEALs (Navy), 32
Secretary, **148-50**
Senate (Alexandrian), 5
Serapeum, 1-5
Serapis, 1
Serenity, 54-56, **151-54**
A Serious Man, **155-61**
Serra, Eric, 47
sexual realism, 148
The Shadow Out of Time, 87
The Shadow Over Innsmouth, 87
Shainberg, Steven, 148-50
Shakespeare, William, 22, 73
Shiksas, 121-22
Shmulenson, Yelena, 155
shoggoths, 87
Shore, Howard, 63
Shuster, Joe, 94
Shyamalan, M. Night, 162-65
Siegel, Jerry, 94
Signs, **162-66**
Silence of the Lambs, 142-44
Simmons, Gene, 105
Sin City, 88
The Sixth Sense, 162
Slick, Grace, 160
Smith, Will, 98
Smithee, Alan, 96
Smit-McPhee, Kodi, 146
Snyder, Zack, 24, 93, 175
Social Darwinism, 95
Socialist Realism, 21-22
solidarity, racial, 68, 88-92, 100, 126, 164, 167
"Somebody to Love," 156
Sonnenfeld, Barry, 100
Sophocles, 73, 192
Spader, James, 148-49

Spielberg, Stephen, 102–103, 104–105, 134–5, 165
The Spiritual Journey of Alejandro Jodorowsky, 39
sports, 107–11
Spy Kids, 88, 167–68
Spy Kids 2: The Island of Lost Dreams, 88, **167–69**
Squibb, June, 124–25
Srikanta, 69
SS, 37, 97, 117, 118
Stalin, 40–41, 114
Stanford University, 110
Star Trek, 53, 55, 131
Star Wars, 100, 140, 170, 172, 174
Star Wars: Episode II — Attack of the Clones, **170–74**
statistics, 108–10
Stein, Johanna, 122
Stephens, Toby, 46
stereotypes, 83, 113, 121–22, 129, 173
Stewart, Jimmy, 190
Stone Age, 54, 173
Stone, Oliver, 6, 9–14, 24
Stott, Ken, 62
Straight, Alvin, 126
The Straight Story, 119, 126, 164
Stravinsky, Catherine, 35
Stravinsky, Igor, **35–38**
Stroheim, Erich von, 192
strychnine, 10, 182
Stuhlbarg, Michael, 157
Sucker Punch, 93, **175–77**
Suddenly Last Summer, 175
suicide, 17, 42, 67, 117, 120, 146, 147, 159
Sumerians, 186
Sunset Boulevard, **192**
superheroes, 93–96
superhumanity, 186–87
Superman, 93–95
"Surrender," 47
Swanson, Gloria, 192
"Sweet Home Alabama," 50
Switzerland, 36, 38, 130, 182, 184–85
swordsmanship, 59
SWPLs, 125
Sydow, Max von, 106
Symposium, 30
synagogues, 164
Synesius, Bishop of Cyrene, 3
Syria, 11, 12

T

Takemitsu, Toru, 192
Taliban, 1, 5
The Talented Mr. Ripley, **193**
Taoist sage-emperor, 128
Tarantino, Quentin, 88, 90, 113, 163, 190
Taylor, Rod, 192
Tea Party, 19, 23
technology, 21, 103, 104, 175, 178
telekinesis, 183
telepathy, 183
terraforming, 95, 153
Texas, 81, 85, 88–89
Theodosius "the Great," 1–2
theology, 28
Theon of Alexandria, 3–4
Theosophists, 42
Theron, Charlize, 138
Theroux, Justin, 121
Third Reich, 117
Thurman, Uma, 191
To Catch a Thief, 178
Tocopilla, Chile, 39, 40
Toland, John, 4
tolerance, 87, 149
Tolkien, J. R. R., 22, 61–67
Tomorrow Never Dies, 45, 47
TOQ Online, iii, iv
Torres, Gina, 55
The Tourist, **178–79**
transvestites, 41
Travolta, John, 191

Trejo, Danny, 87, 131
Trevor Lynch's White Nationalist Guide to the Movies, iii, 191n1, 193
Triumph of the Will, 60
Tudyk, Alan, 55, 152
Turner, Aiden, 62
Tusk, 39
Twilight, 21
Twin Peaks, 119–20, 122
tzadik, 160

U
Unbreakable, 165
Uncle Sam, 127
Ur, 8
Uruguay, 168
USA Network, 32, 33

V
values, 20–21, 30–31, 49, 54–55, 73, 83, 119, 146–56, 187
Vanguard News Network (VNN), iii, iv, 80, 189
Vanilla Sky, 3, 102, **180–81**
Vatican, 1, 5
veil of maya, 119, 123
Vertigo, **190**
Vidor, King, 22, 24
Vietnam War, 10–11
A View to a Kill, 46
vigilantes, 89–90, 128
Voltaire, 4

W
Wall Street, 10
Washington, D.C., 16, 83–84, 104, 106
Washington, Denzel, 49, 145
WASPs, 118, 122
Watchmen, 93, 175
Watson, Emily, 143
Watts, Naomi, 121
The Way of Tarot: The Spiritual Teacher in the Cards, 39

We the Living, 20
Weisz, Rachel, 3
Whedon, Joss, 53–56, 151–52
whiggers, 48–52
white guilt, 147
White Nationalism, iii, 5, 17, 84, 97, 154, 165–66, 167
whores, 41, 54
Wild at Heart, 120
Williams, John, 93, 106, 170, 172
Williams, Wayne, 144
Winky's Restaurant, 121
Wisocky, Rebecca, 21
Wichita, Kansas, 81
Wichita Massacre, 80–81
Witherspoon, Reece, 83
Wood, Elijah, 193
Woodward, Frank H., 86
Wookies, 172
Woolley, Sir Leonard, 8
The World Is Not Enough, 45
World War II, 112–14
wuxia cinema, 57

X
xenophobia, 12, 86, 96, 164
Xenophon, 59
Xi'an, China, 59

Y
Yale University, 108
Yen, Donnie, 59
Yiddish, 155
Yimou, Zhang, 57, 73
Yin and Yang, 42
Youth Without Youth, **182–88**

Z
Zappa, Frank, iii
zamindars, 69
Zebediah, 134
Zebra killers, 144
Zhao, 58
Zimmer, Hans, 95
Zionism, 19, 94

ABOUT THE AUTHOR

Trevor Lynch is a pen name of Greg Johnson, Ph.D., Editor-in-Chief of Counter-Currents Publishing Ltd. and Editor of *North American New Right*, its webzine (http://www.counter-currents.com/) and occasional print journal.

He is the author of *Confessions of a Reluctant Hater* (San Francisco: Counter-Currents, 2010), *Trevor Lynch's White Nationalist Guide to the Movies* (San Francisco: Counter-Currents, 2012), and *New Right vs. Old Right* (San Francisco: Counter-Currents, 2013).

He is editor of Alain de Benoist, *On Being a Pagan*, trans. Jon Graham (Atlanta: Ultra, 2004); Michael O'Meara, *Toward the White Republic* (San Francisco: Counter-Currents, 2010); Michael J. Polignano, *Taking Our Own Side* (San Francisco: Counter-Currents, 2010); Collin Cleary, *Summoning the Gods: Essays on Paganism in a God-Forsaken World* (San Francisco: Counter-Currents, 2011); Irmin Vinson, *Some Thoughts on Hitler & Other Essays* (San Francisco: Counter-Currents, 2011); *North American New Right*, volume 1 (San Francisco: Counter-Currents, 2012); Kerry Bolton, *Artists of the Right: Resisting Decadence* (San Francisco: Counter-Currents, 2012); James J. O'Meara, *The Homo & the Negro: Masculinist Meditations on Politics & Popular Culture* (San Francisco: Counter-Currents, 2012); Jonathan Bowden, *Pulp Fascism: Reactionary Themes in Comics, Graphic Novels, & Popular Literature* (San Francisco: Counter-Currents, 2013); Jonathan Bowden, *Western Civilization Bites Back* (San Francisco: Counter-Currents, 2014); James J. O'Meara, *The Eldritch Evola . . . & Others* (San Francisco: Counter-Currents, 2014); and Collin Cleary, *What is a Rune? & Other Essays* (San Francisco: Counter-Currents, 2015).

www.ingramcontent.com/pod-product-compliance
Lightning Source LLC
Chambersburg PA
CBHW031600170426
43196CB00031B/310